SUBSAHARAN AFRICA
IN THE 1990s

SUBSAHARAN AFRICA IN THE 1990s

Challenges to Democracy and Development

Edited by
Rukhsana A. Siddiqui

PRAEGER

Westport, Connecticut
London

Library of Congress Cataloging-in-Publication Data

Subsaharan Africa in the 1990s : challenges to democracy and
    development / edited by Rukhsana A. Siddiqui.
        p.   cm.
    Includes bibliographical references and index.
    ISBN 0–275–95142–1 (alk. paper)
    1. Africa, Sub-Saharan—Economic conditions—1960– . 2. Africa, Sub-
Saharan—Social conditions. 3. Africa, Sub-Saharan—Politics and
government—1960– . 4. Sustainable development—Africa, Sub-Saharan.
I. Siddiqui, Rukhsana A.
HC800.S8253   1997
338.967—dc20   96–44681

British Library Cataloguing in Publication Data is available.

Library of Congress Catalog Card Number: 96–44681
ISBN: 0–275–95142–1

First published in 1997

Praeger Publishers, 88 Post Road West, Westport, CT 06881
An imprint of Greenwood Publishing Group, Inc.

Printed in the United States of America

The paper used in this book complies with the
Permanent Paper Standard issued by the National
Information Standards Organization (Z39.48–1984).

10 9 8 7 6 5 4 3 2 1

To little Alina and Zoya
and our nonhuman animal companion
Moshi

Contents

III
The Problems of Development Management

IV
Women and Empowerment in Africa in the 1990s

V
Toward the Sustainable Development of
African Ecology and Environment

Acknowledgments

The idea for this volume was conceived during my sabbatical year as a Fulbright senior scholar at Yale University, from where I reached out to many colleagues in North America, Africa, and the United Kingdom. The enthusiasm of those who submitted their pieces in response to my first invitation was truly encouraging. My last volume had taught me the hardships of soliciting a publishing contract from Pakistan; hindsight made me determined to move back with one this time. Praeger's serious interest in this project was my reward.

The work then moved with me to Islamabad. This led to a long and difficult gestation, during which I have incurred many debts of gratitude both to individuals and to institutions.

The chapters that comprise this volume are more than just a collection of individual writings solicited and put together by the editor; they also are a result of a cross-continent dialogue, a protracted discussion among us for more than a year. It not only has enriched us with each others' current research but also has led to a wider interdisciplinary collaboration, which I cherish. I am, thus, deeply grateful to all the contributors who, despite their demanding work and travel schedules, took time to revise and update their manuscripts. The introduction of electronic mail to my tiny city made it more challenging to track them down, sometimes from Johannesburg to Lagos to New York, for revisions.

Yale provided the great advantage of a stimulating academic environment. I also was made associate fellow at the Southern African Research Program. Its weekly seminars were of immense benefit to me. Space limitations make it impossible to thank everyone individually, but a few who made a difference, both academically and morally, are Professor Leonard Doob, Professor Bill Foltz, Professor Leonard Thompson, Adriana Copeman, Nancy Phillips, Usman Rabbani, Seth Messinger, Peta Katz, Brooks Prouty, and Ben Carton.

I am most grateful for having access not only to the African Collection of the Sterling Memorial Library but also to its legendary and wonderful curator, J.M.D. Crossey, who always provided new information and insight with his encyclopedic knowledge of things African.

I would like to thank the Center for the International Exchange of Scholars and the United States Educational Foundation for Pakistan for the Fulbright Award, which made this effort possible, and Quaid-i-Azam University and the University Grants Commission, Islamabad, for their assistance in the final stages of the manuscript.

My family as always has been there with its unconditional and untiring support, especially little Alina, playing with whom during editing breaks made going back to work more fun.

Words are insufficient to thank Tony Zwicker, my "zweite Mutter" in New York, who had all the ingredients ready for my home in New Haven even before my arrival, including her blue Ford Escort, in which I happily shunted between New Haven and Gramercy Park all year. It was sometimes very hard to go back to Yale after spending an exhilarating weekend in her fabulous art world.

A special note of thanks to James Dunton, Catherine Lyons, and Ellen Dorosh for electronically navigating me from all that distance and taking time to respond with minute details.

I am grateful to the Library of Congress, Islamabad, and its field director, Jim Armstrong, an Africanist historian himself, for his comments on parts of the manuscript.

For their invaluable assistance as computer gurus par excellence who brought e-mail to Pakistan, making my work infinitely easier, I would like to thank the SDN team for coming to the rescue whenever a file got lost and during many a communication snafu.

Last but not least, I am indebted to Moshi, my loyal friend, who spent much time in my study, wide awake in late hours as I strained on the text, giving moral support in silence when his time could have been better spent chasing cats in the neighboring forest.

Introduction

The economic performance of African countries south of the Sahara — particularly in east and southern Africa, with the exception of South Africa — during the last two decades has been generally poor. Per capita food production has declined. The growth rate of agricultural output has not kept pace with the growth rate of the population, and the decline in food production has not been accompanied by an increase in export production. External factors such as high oil prices, deteriorating terms of trade, wars, and aggression all have contributed to this poor performance. Moreover, formidable internal factors, like violence, corruption, chauvinism, and authoritarianism, have plagued the region over the years.

The 1980s in the subsahara was a decade overwhelmed by debt burden, deregulation, and drought; the 1990s is groping with the paradox of civil strife and a complex transition to democracy. Many countries in the region are pulled toward multiparty democracy on the one hand and economic disintegration on the other, the contrast, for example, between Zambia and Tanzania with Somalia and Rwanda. To ameliorate these conditions, new prescriptions were offered in the form of "structural adjustment" by the International Monetary Fund and the World Bank, the response to which has been mixed. The dictates of the bank and fund have had a profound impact on Africa's fragile and vulnerable political economies, an impact that is likely to be extended and exponential rather than short and specific. It is argued that the advocates of adjustment lacked any sense of the historical and structural characteristics of these political economies, which rendered their initial policy responses both superficial and controversial. Neither debt repayments nor policy reformulations could overlook the extroverted dualism of Africa in class, sector, space, gender, and generation.

Any contemporary debate on Africa must put into context the post–Cold War realities, the so-called new world order, and the renewed international division of labor and power. The continent no longer is preoccupied with apartheid as such, and nonalignment has waned. African studies for the 1990s and beyond require a new set of approaches that take into account the new challenges posed by privatization, pluralism, the shrinking of the formal sector, and diminishing state structures, which are being replaced by the ever expanding nongovernmental organizations (NGOs). The distinctive features of the continent in an era of national adjustments and global transformations need to be recognized and incorporated into both examination and prescription.

Although both civil society and political economy are in transition, it would be erroneous to impose extra-African perceptions, prescriptions, and expectations on the region. Orthodox analysis of security in Africa was based on statist assumptions that emphasized great powers and the Cold War on the one hand and national resources and capabilities on the other. Such an approach is already being revised by incorporating perspectives on gender, ecology, and food. Conflict in Africa can no longer be treated only as a function of "strategic" issues but also must include and prioritize a range of new forces of gender and population, ecology and environment, food and nutrition, and NGOs.

Population and reproduction are controversial issues in Africa, as elsewhere, especially for women and regimes. Patriarchal prejudices still claim that there is excess land on the continent, but land alienation and hunger are increasingly apparent (for example, in Kenya, Senegal, Nigeria, Burundi, and Zimbabwe). The combination of economic and ecological crises in the 1980s has led to a new policy and political context: many governments have moved toward acceptance and advocacy of child spacing, if not family planning.

Despite orthodox customs and religions, African women are insisting on their rights, whether over socioeconomic status or reproduction, in part because they suffer the highest rates of maternal death in the world — officially 700 per 100,000 live births. Unsanitary illegal abortions and child abandonment continue to increase in the absence of effective, pro-choice legal rights, and fertility rates remain higher in Africa than in any other region. Gabon, Kenya, and the Ivory Coast lead the list of international population growth rates, at 4 percent per annum.

Some of the ecological crises in Africa are desertification; soil erosion; depletion of forests, water resources, and biodiversity; pollution; and chronic food insecurity. The environmental degradation in Africa, as elsewhere, is inextricably linked with political and economic policies. A balanced use of resources is a prerequisite for the sustainable development of a continent that is known for its wealth in minerals, biomass, forests, water, and wildlife.

This book surveys the major political, economic, social, ecological, and gender-related aspects of Africa's struggle toward democracy in the 1990s. The following chapters, then, fundamentally pose two sets of ideas: first, the internal equilibrium can be restored only through institutional changes within these countries; second, the subjects of women and environment and how the polity and economy of these societies has played havoc with, and are causes of, the problems related to these issues.

There are five thematic sections in this collection. The first theme is entitled "Civil Society and Democratic Transition." It begins with a chapter by Larry Diamond, who argues that the long-term consolidation of democracy in the subsaharan region in general and South Africa in particular requires participation, moderation, restraint, tolerance, and successful economic performance. In the next chapter, Edward R. MacMahon shows how the inability of single-party states in Africa to provide adequate services, such as health and education, has led to the proliferation of NGOs, which have the potential of becoming agents for democratic consolidation. Citing the example of Angola, William Minter looks at how the recent elections can be used as a lesson in conflict resolution and transition to democracy in one African country and how it can be compared with elsewhere.

The second thematic section, entitled "The Politics of Economic Reforms," begins with a chapter by Alfred B. Zack-Williams, who situates the African crisis in terms of the failure of the postcolonial mode of accumulation, in particular, the import substitution strategy. He argues that the economic failure also is closely linked to the decline of participatory democracy. Taking Kenya as a case study, Rukhsana A. Siddiqui analyzes the role of privatization in the economic performance of the country and its sociopolitical implications. Using a Latin American model in the Kenyan context, she argues that the recent trend of privatizing transitional economies in Africa needs to be understood in the context of policy substitution, ideological consideration, and pragmatism. Larry A. Swatuk explores Botswana's fast-growing economy as both a success story and a destabilizing factor for the society. He demonstrates that economic pragmatism brings contradictions with potentially negative consequences that can be far-reaching for the country.

The third theme is entitled "The Problems of Development Management." It begins with a chapter by Peter Koehn and Olatunde Ojo, who explore the performance of NGOs and government-organized NGOs (GONGOs) as agents of development in Africa and critically review the Development Fund Model for dispensing donor aid, as advocated by Goran Hyden. Sandra Maclean's chapter argues that the process of "managing" development is a composite of various issues and actors and examines questions like who is setting the development agenda that is being "managed" and who benefits from it.

The fourth section, called "Women and Empowerment in Africa in the 1990s," begins with Lynn Berat supporting the need to redefine the nature of international human rights for women and how such rights can be employed by African women to secure economic and social gains. Mary J. Osirim's chapter explores the goals and potentials of NGOs on women. Focusing on women who work as "microentrepreneurs" in southern Nigeria, she argues that poor and low-status women have benefited most from their own efforts to create associations that directly address their class needs. Governmental and some non-governmental organizations may have voiced the same concerns of the poor but have served mainly the interests of elite women.

The last section is entitled "Toward the Sustainable Development of African Ecology and Environment." Moses K. Tesi explores the neglect over the years by African governments of ecological issues in the region. He argues that the relationship between ecology and development is crucial and the rise of this issue to the top of the agenda during the 1990s has very much changed the dynamics of policy making. The last chapter, by E. Ike Udogu, is an attempt to ascertain the progress, or lack of it, in the course of African ecological preservation and development.

I

CIVIL SOCIETY AND DEMOCRATIC TRANSITION

1

Civil Society and Democratic Consolidation: Building a Culture of Democracy in a New South Africa

Larry Diamond

On April 26–28, 1994, South Africa scaled an extraordinary hurdle on its road toward democracy. To conduct the first nonracial, democratic elections in its history, it had to overcome daunting political and logistical challenges: a legacy of brutal and pervasive racial exclusion, traumatic preelection violence and terror, widespread ignorance of the electoral process among an electorate of whom 80 percent had never voted before — and all without a voters' register or any real road map for an administrative task of this scale. Yet, the election came off without violence, terror, or serious disruption or controversy. More than 80 percent of the eligible population turned out to vote. Even when the inevitable logistical problems arose, people waited patiently, many for hours in the blazing sun, to cast their precious votes. That South Africa reached and crossed this threshold is an eloquent tribute to the skill, dedication, and pragmatism of its political party leaders, particularly in the African National Congress and the former ruling National Party. However, perhaps no less important was the extraordinary mobilization of civil society, not only in resisting and bringing down the apartheid state but also in beginning to develop the participatory knowledge, skills, values, and structures of democratic citizenship and in organizing the more than 30,000 domestic monitors who did so much to instill confidence in the integrity of the electoral process.

Although a permanent constitution remains to be written during the five-year term of the new National Assembly, it can be argued that the transition to democracy is now complete and that South Africa has entered upon what will no doubt be a rather prolonged attempt to consolidate its new democratic institutions. Consolidation is the process by which democracy becomes so broadly and profoundly legitimate among its citizens that it is very unlikely to break down. It involves behavioral and institutional changes that normalize democratic politics and narrow their uncertainty, transforming "the accidental arrangements, prudential norms, and contingent solutions that have emerged during the transition into relations of cooperation and competition that are reliably known, regularly practiced, and voluntarily accepted by . . . politicians and citizens."[1] This normalization or regularization of politics requires, most of all, political institutionalization — building up stable, efficacious, and enduring political parties and state structures. It is, therefore, vital that intellectuals and civil society activists not disparage parties or the state — or the whole messy process of politics, per se — in a way that would discourage such political development. However, democratic consolidation also requires the expansion of citizen access, development of democratic citizenship and culture, broadening of leadership recruitment and training, and other functions that clearly benefit from (if they do not absolutely require) a vigorous and autonomous civil society.

CIVIL SOCIETY AND THE CONSOLIDATION OF DEMOCRACY: CONCEPTUALIZING CIVIL SOCIETY

Civil society is the realm of organized social life that is voluntary, self-generating, (largely) self-supporting, autonomous from the state, and bound by a legal order or set of shared rules. It is distinct from "society" in general in that it involves citizens acting collectively in a public sphere to express their interests and ideas, achieve mutual goals, make demands on the state, and hold state officials accountable. Voluntary collective action within the public sphere takes place in competitive ideological markets; civil society, thus, implies notions of partialness, pluralism, and competition. Organizations that seek to monopolize a sphere of collective life (in the sense of denying the legitimacy of competing groups) or to envelop totally the lives of their members are, thus, not part of civil society. Civil society also excludes the private dimensions of individual and family life, the inward-looking activities of parochial groups, the profit-making enterprise of individual business firms, and political efforts to take control of the state. Actors in civil society recognize the principles of state authority and the rule of law, and need the protection of these in reality to prosper and be secure. Thus, civil society not only contains state power but also legitimates state authority when that authority is based on the rule of law.[2]

Organizations in civil society may be formal and enduring or informal and temporary (such as social networks and movements). The principal types of organizations in civil society are: economic (productive and commercial associations and networks); cultural (religious, ethnic, communal, and other institutions and associations devoted to the preservation and practice of values, faiths, beliefs, and symbols); informational and educational, devoted to the production and dissemination (whether for profit or not) of knowledge, ideas, news, and information; interest-based (designed to advance or defend the common functional or material interests of their members, as with trade unions, producer associations, and professional associations); developmental (organizations that combine individual resources to improve the infrastructure, institutions, and quality of life of the community); issue-oriented (movements for environmental protection, women's rights, land reform, consumer protection, and so on); and civic (seeking in nonpartisan fashion to improve the functioning of the polity and make it more democratic, such as human rights groups, voter education and mobilization, poll-watching groups, and anticorruption movements).[3]

From the above, it should be clear that civil society is not some mere residual category, synonymous with "society" or with everything that is not the state or the formal political system. Beyond being voluntary, self-generating, autonomous, and rule abiding, civil society organizations are distinct from other groups in society — or what might be termed "parochial society" — in several respects. First, as emphasized above, civil society is concerned with public rather than private ends; it mediates between the state and society. Second, civil society relates to the state in some way but does not seek to win formal control over or position within the state. Rather, civil society organizations pursue from the state concessions, benefits, policy changes, relief, redress, or accountability to their scrutiny. Civic organizations and social movements that seek to change the nature of the state and displace the existing regime still may qualify as part of civil society if their effort stems from a concern about the public good and not from a group goal to capture state power for the group per se. Thus, peaceful movements for democratic transition typically spring from civil society. Third, civil society encompasses pluralism and diversity. To the extent that an organization — such as a religious fundamentalist, ethnic chauvinist, revolutionary, or millenarian movement — seeks to monopolize a functional or political space in society, crowding out all competitors while claiming that it represents the only legitimate path, it would contradict the pluralistic and market-oriented nature of civil society. Related to this is a fourth distinction, partialness, signifying that no group in civil society seeks to represent the whole of a person's or a community's interests; rather, different groups represent different aspects of interest.[4]

Civil society must be distinct and autonomous not only from the state and parochial society but also from a fourth arena of social action, political society. Political society encompasses those organizations and networks that compete for placement in or control over the state, within the established institutional parameters of that state. In a democracy, political society mainly consists of political parties; affiliated networks, organizations, and campaigns; plus the campaign organizations of individual candidates. Organizations and networks in civil society may form alliances with parties, but if they become captured by political parties — or hegemonic within them — they thereby move their primary locus of activity to political society and lose much of their ability to perform a number of unique mediating and democracy-building functions.

HOW CIVIL SOCIETY CONTRIBUTES TO DEMOCRACY

In recent years, there has been an unprecedented flourishing of studies about civil society. An important reason is the manifest and strategic role that civil societies have played in the democratic transitions of this recent "third wave" of democracy.[5] Guillermo O'Donnell and Philippe Schmitter recognized, in their "tentative conclusions" about Latin American and Southern European transitions from authoritarianism, how important to the process was the "resurrection of civil society," the restructuring of public space, and the mobilization of all manner of independent groups and grass-roots movements.[6] Even a most casual observer could not miss the central place of "people power" in toppling the regime of Ferdinand Marcos in 1986. In many other countries subsequently, including South Korea, Taiwan, Chile, Poland, and Czechoslovakia, extensive mobilization by civil society (taking different shapes in different countries) was a crucial source of pressure for democratic change.

In the wreckage left by predatory and weak, incompetent states, the mobilization of civil society for democracy has been most striking perhaps in Africa. In a wide range of countries in subsaharan Africa — including Benin, Cameroon, Nigeria, Niger, Ghana, Kenya, South Africa, Zambia, Zimbabwe, and even such relentlessly unyielding dictatorships as Mobutu's in Zaire and Banda's in Malawi — the pressure for democratic change has been generated or advanced by autonomous organizations, media, and networks in civil society. Since the early 1980s, it has become increasingly apparent that the impetus for political renewal and resistance to authoritarian domination in Africa has come from students, the churches, professional associations, women's groups, trade unions, human rights organizations, producer groups, intellectuals, journalists, and informal networks that are either autonomous from the state or struggling to break free from its control.[7]

First, then, vigorous, independent associations and media are important to democracy because they provide "the basis for the limitation of state power, hence for the control of the state by society, and hence for democratic political institutions as the most effective means of exercising that control."[8] Mobilization from civil society is in theory and has been in practice a major means for containing the abuses and undermining the legitimacy and authority of undemocratic regimes. It is also an important means for containing the power of democratic governments, checking their potential abuses and violations of the law and holding them accountable to public scrutiny. Pluralism and openness in the flow of information — possible only with a vigorous civil society — are indispensable to achieving real accountability in governance. "If the state controls the mass media, there is no way of exposing its abuses and corruption."[9]

Second, a rich associational life supplements the role of political parties in stimulating political participation, increasing the political efficacy and skill of democratic citizens, and promoting an appreciation of the obligations as well as rights of democratic citizenship. These represent important respects in which civil society generates a more democratic political culture. Alexis de Tocqueville was among the first to observe and demonstrate this linkage empirically in his observations on democracy in the United States in the early nineteenth century.[10] The voluntary participation of citizens in all manner of associations outside the state struck him as a bedrock of democratic practice and culture, and of independent economic vitality, in the young nation. Voluntary "associations may therefore be considered as large free schools, where all the members of the community go to learn the general theory of association."[11]

Third, civil society can be a crucial arena for the development of other dimensions of a democratic political culture, such as tolerance, moderation, a willingness to compromise, and a respect for opposing viewpoints. These values and norms become most stable when they emerge through intense practice, and organizational participation in civil society provides an important form of practice in political advocacy and contestation. A culture of compromise and bargaining will emerge only gradually in South Africa, and only in the context of genuine empowerment of the long disenfranchised nonwhite communities, because, as studies of negotiation show, effective bargaining demands a context of mutual confidence in which contending parties believe themselves to be equal. Civil society in South Africa (through the trade union movement and the civic associations) has been and will continue to be important in helping to produce this empowerment.[12]

A fourth way in which civil society may serve democracy is by structuring multiple channels, beyond the political party, for the articulation and representation of interests. This is related to the participatory function but involves a higher level of aggregation that is more likely to provide access to the policy-making process. This function is important particularly for providing traditionally excluded groups — such as women and racial or ethnic minorities — access to power that has been denied them in the "upper institutional echelons" of formal politics. Although women have played a major role in the struggle for liberation in South Africa, they face a powerful legacy of gender as well as racial domination, which they are determined to overcome. Only with sustained, organized pressure from below, in civil society, can political and social equality be advanced and the quality, responsiveness, and legitimacy of democracy, thus, deepened.[13]

Fifth, a rich and pluralistic civil society, particularly in a relatively developed economy, will tend to generate a wide range of interests that may crosscut, and, so, mitigate, the principal polarities of political conflict. As new class-based organizations and issue-oriented movements arise, they draw together new constituencies that cut across long-standing regional, religious, ethnic, or partisan cleavages. These new formations may generate a modern type of citizenship that transcends historic ethnic, racial, and nationality divisions and, so, diminishes potential future conflict along these lines. To the extent that individuals have multiple interests and join a wide variety of organizations to pursue and advance those interests, they will be more likely to associate with different types of people who have divergent political interests and opinions. These attitudinal cross-pressures will tend to soften the militancy of their own views, generate a more expansive and sophisticated political outlook, and encourage tolerance for differences and a greater readiness to compromise.[14]

A sixth function of a democratic civil society is recruiting and training new political leaders. Civil society leaders and activists acquire, through rising in the internal politics of their organization and through articulating and representing the interests of their members in public policy arenas, a range of leadership and advocacy skills (and self-confidence) that qualifies them well for service in government and party politics. They learn how to organize and motivate people, debate issues, raise money, publicize programs, administer staffs, canvass for support, negotiate compromises, and build coalitions. At the same time, their work on behalf of their constituency, or of what they see to be the public interest, and their articulation of clear and compelling policy alternatives may develop for them a wider political following. Interest groups, social movements, and community efforts of various kinds may, therefore, train, toughen, and thrust into public view a richer (and more representative) array of potential new political leaders than might otherwise be recruited by political parties. Because of the traditional dominance by men of the corridors of power, civil society is a particularly important base for the training and recruitment of women (as well as racial and ethnic minorities) into the political process. Where the recruitment of new political leaders within the established political parties has become narrow or stagnant, this function of civil society can be critical for enhancing the vitality, inclusiveness, and legitimacy of democracy.

Seventh, many civic organizations, institutes, and foundations have explicit democracy-building purposes beyond leadership training. Nonpartisan election-monitoring efforts have been critical to deterring fraud, enhancing confidence in the electoral process, affirming the legitimacy of the result, or, in some cases (as in the Philippines in 1986 and Panama in 1989), demonstrating an opposition victory despite government fraud. This function is particularly crucial in founding elections like those which initiated democracy in Chile, Nicaragua, Bulgaria, Zambia, and, most recently, South Africa.[15] Democracy institutes and think tanks are working in a number of countries to reform the electoral system, democratize political parties, decentralize and open up government, strengthen the legislature, and enhance government accountability.[16]

Eighth, a vigorous civil society widely disseminates information and, so, empowers citizens in the collective pursuit and defense of their interests and values. An autonomous and pluralistic press is only one way of ensuring that a variety of perspectives and informative reports reach a wider audience. Independent organizations also may provide citizens with information about government activities that does not depend on what government *says* it is doing and that may have been gathered only through exhaustive and enterprising investigation. Interest groups also can make it their business to find out what the government is planning that will affect their members, and spread that information more widely than the government would. This is one of the primary resistance techniques of human rights organizations. By contradicting the official story, they make it more difficult to cover up repression and abuses of power.

The mobilization of new information and understanding is essential to the achievement of economic reform in a democracy, and this is a ninth function that civil society can play. Although economic stabilization policies typically must be implemented quickly and forcefully by elected executives in crisis situations, without widespread consultation, more structural economic reforms — privatization, trade and financial liberalization — appear to be more sustainable and far-reaching (or, in many post-Communist countries, feasible only) when they are pursued through the democratic process.[17] In Asia, Latin America, and Eastern Europe, new actors in civil society — such as economic policy think tanks, chambers of commerce, and economically literate journalists, commentators, and television producers — are beginning to overcome the barriers to information and organization, mobilizing support for (and neutralizing resistance to) reform policies.[18]

Finally, there is a tenth function of civil society that derives in part from the success of the above nine. "Freedom of association," Tocqueville mused, may, "after having agitated society for some time, . . . strengthen the state in the end."[19] By enhancing the accountability, responsiveness, inclusiveness, effectiveness, and, hence, legitimacy of the political system, a vigorous civil society gives citizens respect for the state and positive engagement with it. In the end, this improves the ability of the state to govern and to command voluntary obedience from its citizens. In addition, "By bringing people together in endless combinations for a great diversity of purposes, a rich associational life may not only multiply demands on the state, it may also multiply the capacities of groups to improve their own welfare, independently of the state, especially at the local level."[20] Effective grass-roots development efforts may, thus, help to relieve the burden of expectations fixed on the state and, so, relieve the intensity of politics.

At the same time, societal autonomy can go too far. However, a strong civil society (or a powerful constellation of rent-seeking forces in society) completely free from state influence and control can overwhelm democracy with the diversity and magnitude of its competing demands. The state itself must have sufficient autonomy, legitimacy, capacity, and support to mediate among the various interest groups and to implement policies and allocate resources in ways that synthesize the claims of competing groups. Many states in the developing world have been unable to implement policy effectively because of the relative "strength" of powerful but fragmented societal forces.[21]

THE INTERNAL ORGANIZATION OF CIVIL SOCIETY

In addition to autonomy from the state, several internal characteristics of civil society mediate and enhance the contribution it can make to the consolidation and maintenance of democracy. These factors are particularly important in determining the degree to which civil society will contribute to the development of a democratic culture.

First, the goals and methods of groups in civil society, especially organized associations, must be compatible with the practice of democratic politics. The chances for stable democracy significantly improve if civil society does not contain maximalist, uncompromising interest groups or groups with antidemocratic goals and methods. To the extent that these groups seek to displace the state or other competitors, they may not qualify as constituent elements of civil society at all, but their presence in society can do much damage to the aspirations of democratic forces in civil society. Maximalist interest groups are more likely to bring down repression from the state that may have a broad and indiscriminate character, affecting the core of civil society.

A second important feature of civil society is its level of organizational institutionalization. Like institutionalized political parties, institutionalized interest groups contribute to the stability, predictability, and governability of a democratic regime. Where cleavages are organized in a structured, stable manner, bargaining and the growth of cooperative networks are facilitated. Social forces do not face the continual cost of setting up new interest organizations, and if the organization expects to continue to operate in the society over a sustained period, its leaders will have more reason to be accountable and responsive to the constituency and may take a longer-range view of the group's interests and policy goals, rather than seeking to maximize short-term benefits in an uncompromising manner.

Third, the democraticness of civil society itself affects the degree to which it can socialize participants into democratic — or undemocratic — forms of behavior. If civil society organizations are to function as "large free schools for democracy," they must function democratically in their internal processes of decision making and leadership selection. Constitutionalism, representation, transparency, accountability, and rotation of elected leaders within autonomous associations will greatly enhance the ability of these associations to inculcate such democratic values and practices in their members. Many (but by no means all) of the new popular organizations that have been emerging in Africa since the late 1970s and early 1980s hold promise as building blocks for democracy, precisely because they provide "small-scale settings for meaningful political participation," constitutional means for the transfer and rotation of power, consultative processes of decision making, and "innovative means of information collection and communication."[22] By contrast, the hierarchical, authoritarian structures of governance inside the mass organizations of corporatist states like Mexico and Egypt have discouraged autonomous political participation, depressed citizen efficacy, and, so, buttressed the cultural and social foundations of authoritarianism.

Fourth, the more pluralistic civil society can become without fragmenting, the more it benefits democracy. Some degree of pluralism is necessary by definition for civil society. Pluralism helps groups in civil society survive and encourages them to learn to cooperate and negotiate with one another. Pluralism within a given sector, like labor or human rights, has a number of additional beneficial effects. It makes that sector less vulnerable (though at the possible cost of weakening its bargaining power); the loss or repression of one organization does not mean the end of all organized representation. Competition also can help ensure accountability and representativeness by giving members the ability to bolt to other organizations if their own one does not perform.

Finally, civil society serves democracy best when it is dense, affording individuals opportunities to participate in multiple associations and informal networks at multiple levels of society. The more associations in civil society, the more likely that associations will develop specialized agendas and purposes that do not seek to swallow the lives of their members in one all-encompassing organizational framework. Such all-encompassing "parties of integration" isolate individuals from contact with competing perspectives and promote intolerance and polarization.[23] Multiple memberships, thus, tend to reflect and reinforce crosscutting patterns of cleavages.

IMPLICATIONS FOR SOUTH AFRICA

These principles have important implications for the development of democracy in South Africa after the transition. Some basis for a democratic civil society already exists in the pluralism and robustness of autonomous organizations, institutes, academic centers, and media based within the white and more developed nonwhite communities and in "the veritable explosion in associational life" that took place in South Africa's black communities during the 1980s.[24] Black trade unions significantly undermined the economic and political foundations of apartheid, and grass-roots civic associations and social movements provided the backbone of resistance to the apartheid state within the black townships. So long as they remain independent of political parties and the state, black trade unions figure to be a crucial constituent of a postapartheid civil society. However, the civic associations cannot constitute the civil society foundation for a democratic South Africa so long as they claim a popular (but unelected) "mandate" to represent a monolithic black community, denying the existence and legitimacy of a broad plurality of interests, even within the black townships.[25] "The totalist, exclusivist, violent and intimidating nature" of many popular organizations in the townships and the absence of internal structures of democracy and a culture of tolerance now loom as major obstacles to the construction of a democratic civil society.[26]

If civil society is to contribute to national reconciliation and democratic consolidation in South Africa, popular organizations within urban black communities will need to undergo a transformation, either through the adaptation of the civic association, their displacement by new forms of association, or (most likely) both. To the extent that the existing civic associations are to play a positive democratic role in the future, they must adapt:

from resistance and hostility to (apartheid) state authority to acceptance of the authority and legitimacy of the democratic state;

from seeking to displace the state as alternative authority structures to engagement with the state as watchdog, advocate, and developmental partner;

from a self-styled monolithic broad front to acceptance of democratic pluralism and competition of interests within the urban black community and to acknowledgment of the need for dialogue and negotiation among those interests (no less than between them and the state);

thus, from the representation of an undifferentiated black "community" to the representation of more discrete and internally diverse interests;

from close affiliation with the African National Congress (ANC) to autonomy from political parties and the struggle for state power;

from constituting the main outlet for black political leadership to being a continuing source of training and recruitment of blacks into the political arena and, therefore, continuously having to identify and train new organizational leaders;

from secretive and poorly institutionalized organizations with informal procedures and memberships to transparent and institutionalized organizations with formal procedures, written rules, and openly documented memberships and finances;

from blocking the plans of state authorities to initiating positive development plans and policies of their own;

from organizations dominated (for the most part) hierarchically by local activists imposing their strategies from above to more internally representative structures, better able to articulate and reconcile divergent viewpoints; and

from a disparate set of local organizations to some sort of more closely networked national structure, with a better balance between the need, on the one hand, for local autonomy and responsiveness and the need, on the other, for regional and national coordination if these organizations are to have any coherent impact on the nation's development policies.[27]

Robert M. Price sees hope in the adaptation of civic associations toward developmental tasks at the community level, such as "town planning, housing, school and clinic construction, the training of teachers and primary health care workers, and the improvement of youth recreational facilities" and in their formation of a national umbrella association, the South African National Civic Organization.[28] Kehla Shubane and Pumla Madiba suggest the most realistic path for civics may lie in their evolution into more limited local advocacy groups, "but even a change to this role would require changes to civics' approaches — in their attitudes to local government and in their willingness to scale down their claims to representativeness and influence."[29] If civic associations do follow this path of evolution, there still will remain the need for an array of "voluntary associations diverse enough to express the full range of interests and values [in society] and strong enough to influence events."[30]

Such a democratically evolving and authentic civil society cannot serve democracy by "demonising" the state and, implicitly, politics. Even as they seek to limit and scrutinize its exercise of power, subjecting it to the rule of law, the new voluntary associations of a democratic South Africa must view the state as the legitimate arbiter of political order and resources.[31] If a truly new political and social order is to be viable, the culture of resistance must give way to a shared culture of civic obligation and responsibility toward the new democratic state.

At the same time, however, it will be important for popular organizations to maintain their distance from the state. With the completion of the democratic transition and the accession to power of the ANC, there is a danger that many black organizations in civil society might not merely cease their resistance to the state but also form an organic and intimately functional relationship to it. This is especially likely at the level of local government but could take on national dimensions as well. A number of leaders of civic associations, most prominently Moses Mayekiso (the president of SANCO), have called for state funding of the civic associations after the transition and favor an institutionalized role for them in a new political order. As Oscar Dhlomo, president of the Institute for Multi-Party Democracy, has warned, this raises the "danger of some of our civic organizations being coopted by the government or becoming praise-singers for the government. This attitude would threaten a democratic culture and the ability of such groups to maintain a healthy skepticism."[32] The future integrity and democratic potential of civil society in South Africa will depend critically on it remaining financially (as well as politically) independent of the state.

CIVIL SOCIETY AND THE DEVELOPMENT OF A DEMOCRATIC CULTURE IN SOUTH AFRICA

A democratic culture of participation, moderation, accommodation, tolerance, and restraint is critical to the consolidation and long-term stability of democracy. Behavioral dispositions toward moderation and accommodation may be induced by structural and institutional incentives and constraints, absent underlying norms. However, these behavioral orientations, and, thus, democracy itself, will not be truly stable and secure until they have become internalized — deeply embedded in a coherent syndrome of beliefs and values, not only among elites but also at the mass level. This is why careful attention must be paid to the ways in which such a culture of democracy takes root and, thus, to the considerable role civil society has to play in this regard.

Civil society may contribute to the development of democratic culture in many ways. One important process is what Dankwart Rustow called "habituation" — the diffusion and internalization of democratic norms and practices as a result of the repeated successful practice of democracy over a long period. This process consists of three elements. "First, both politicians and citizens learn from the successful resolution of some issues to place their faith in the new rules and to apply them to new issues." Second, "experience with democratic techniques and competitive recruitment will confirm the politicians" — and active members of civil society organizations — "in their democratic beliefs and practices." Third, party organizations (and, it can be added, those in civil society) forge enduring and effective links that connect elites with ordinary citizens throughout the country.[33]

Civil society organizations are crucial instruments for such democratic change and socialization because they function as continuous instruments of participation and mobilization, while (after the transition) political parties involve most citizens more intermittently, during election campaigns.

In addition to these development and change-oriented civic organizations, South Africa needs a massive, multidimensional, and sustained campaign of democratic civic education explicitly designed to transmit the knowledge, habits, and values of democratic citizenship. In a period of just a few months leading up to the historic April 1994 elections, civil society organizations conducted a breathtaking crash effort in voter education, unprecedented on the African continent. As a result, despite the extraordinary levels of illiteracy and ignorance about the voting process, voter turnout was extremely high, the process was miraculously orderly, and the percentage of spoiled ballots was lower than even the most optimistic projections. A wide range of civil society organizations mobilized for this intensive voter education effort, including the Institute for Multiparty Democracy, the Institute for a Democratic Alternative for South Africa (IDASA), and the Matla Trust, as well as older groups involved in the struggle against apartheid, such as Black Sash. In addition to educating people about the substance and mechanics of the voting process, such civic education efforts had to break through the psychology of fear and suspicion that caused many blacks to doubt that their votes would be secret.[34] An example of the intensity and scale of what was accomplished was the effort of the Matla Trust, which began in 1993 by opening eight civic education centers (later expanded in number) where trainers trained tens of thousands of trainers (up to 25,000 by mid-1993) and also established numerous additional community centers. The trust (and like efforts) produced millions of pamphlets, with simple language and graphic depictions in each of eight indigenous languages; sponsored traveling theater groups to perform a play on democracy and voting; and reached out to millions of first-time voters through creatively designed (entertaining as well as instructive) radio and TV programs, songs and posters, and audio and video cassettes.[35] Matla also is launching an educational program for secondary schools in deprived areas to promote awareness of the transitional and electoral processes, understanding of democracy and citizenship, and cultural and political tolerance.[36] IDASA opened, in January 1992, a Training Center for Democracy as part of its wide-ranging efforts to educate voters and in its broader efforts to encourage "tolerance, free speech, public assembly and fundamental human rights."[37] These and many other organizations played a crucial role in helping to mobilize the more than 100,000 South Africans that staffed and monitored the April 1994 elections (along with some 4,000 international observers).

The legacy of apartheid is likely to persist stubbornly in endless petty and profound ways for many years to come. Breaking it down will require not only educating and empowering the victims of apartheid but also reeducating its former practitioners and promoting dialogue between these two groups, as IDASA has been trying to do in its policing project.[38] Civil society organizations also have a crucial role to play in helping to control political violence, through education, mobilization of community vigilance, and mediation between contending political forces. An IDASA-sponsored workshop on tolerance and voter education in KwaNdebele in January 1993 provided a neutral venue where delegates from the ANC and the ruling party of KwaNdebele were able to strike a peace agreement.[39]

Given the low levels of political knowledge and democratic understanding among the long-excluded black population, the mass media played a critical role in the intensive voter education campaign that swept the country early in 1994, and its potential to contribute to further civic education remains substantial. Around the world, independent organizations and think tanks have used the mass media to great effectiveness in their efforts to educate as wide an audience as possible about the workings and requirements of democracy. In its future reporting, the South African press not only must strive for greater professionalism, autonomy, pluralism, objectivity, and innovativeness than has been possible in the establishment newspapers and the government-controlled electronic media (the SABC) under apartheid, it also must seek in its reporting and commentary to break down cultural stereotypes and deflate rhetoric that depicts politics as a zero-sum game.[40] Such a democratic and civically enlightened evolution of South Africa's mass media could be greatly advanced, Anthony Heard has argued, by the creation of an independent foundation to train journalists, support new, independent media enterprises, defend press freedom, monitor press performance, honor journalistic excellence, and otherwise promote pluralism, autonomy, and civic responsibility within the mass media.[41]

There are many other types of civil society organizations that can contribute to the construction of a democratic culture in South Africa. Many of these will operate on the local level, either growing out of existing civic associations or emerging anew. A particular successor role for the civics may emerge in the need for new community level organizations to draw together blacks in the townships for collective, self-help development efforts that complement but do not seek to supplant the role of government. These or parallel community organizations will need to work at the grass-roots level to control violence, mediate disputes, and facilitate civic education efforts. All of this implies the need for effective linkages between national civil society organizations and independent community associations in the townships and rural areas. Wider metropolitan organizations will be needed not only to negotiate a restructuring of local government (as is being done through the Witwatersrand Metropolitan Chamber) but also to work on a continuing basis to bridge historic racial and class divides and facilitate, through dialogue and interaction in civil society, integration and reconstruction at the local level. At every level and in every functional arena of social and public life, independent organizations will need to act to mediate and facilitate dialogues like that which IDASA has been conducting "to bridge the gap of credibility between the police in South Africa and the communities they must serve."[42] Reconciliation, understanding, tolerance, and mutual respect can be fostered also through the work of cultural organizations that enable South Africans of diverse racial and ethnic backgrounds to come to appreciate the artistic beauty, historical grandeur, and distinctiveness of the country's various cultural traditions and, in so doing, give each ethnic group a sense of pride and self-confidence.[43]

Now that the urgent challenge of the "founding elections" has passed, there are massive new requirements for training, particularly among the black population: of human rights and civic education instructors, community mediators and organizers, political candidates and campaign workers, as well as managers and administrators. Comprehensive training programs also will be needed for the new elected officials in local, provincial, and national legislatures and governments. Well-established international programs and techniques exist to lend a hand in this regard, through organizations like the German party foundations and the U.S. National Endowment for Democracy, which are already giving assistance to democratic organizations like the Institute for Multiparty Democracy and IDASA.

There is real hope for democracy in South Africa in the fact that these multiple, diverse, pluralistic foundations of civil society are, in fact, developing and beginning to change and reconstruct society and culture.

However, in these myriad efforts in so many different arenas and levels, democrats should not lose sight of the big picture. The consolidation of democracy in South Africa will depend heavily on the resumption of vigorous and sustained economic growth. Broad democratic legitimacy cannot be established unless democracy can work to improve the appalling conditions of life of the vast majority of the population while providing economic inducements for wealthier and more skilled segments to keep their capital and skills in South Africa and to invest anew. President Frederik Willem de Klerk conceded that South Africa will need a minimum real economic growth rate of at least 5 percent annually in the coming years even to begin to generate the social improvements that are needed. However, this is probably the *best* South Africa can hope for and will be achieved only if the country liberalizes its economy, becomes much more productive and internationally competitive, avoids overtaxation, and promotes market-friendly policies that win the confidence of foreign investors and the indigenous business community.[44]

A democratically elected government in a new South Africa will face a formidable dilemma. To produce real and sustainable economic growth, it will need to allow exchange rates and possibly real wages to fall. It will need to increase taxes but not so much as to destroy incentives to invest and produce. It must demand payment of rents and rates while resisting pressures to overspend the country into hopeless debt or hyperinflation. Such policies for long-term growth will be difficult to square with expectations for massive, immediate, and rapid material progress. Organizations and media in civil society must help a new government to level with the people, share with them the dilemma, and preempt, to some extent, the surge of populism. Policies for economic reform, growth, and redistribution forged through such a broad societal dialogue will be more sustainable than those negotiated secretly by a narrow stratum of corporatist elites.

A final important contribution that South African civil society can make to the consolidation of democracy is in proliferating and deepening the country's ties with the rest of the democratic world. The expansion of civil society is a global phenomenon, both in that it is happening all over the world and in the rapid growth of transnational ties, networks, and exchanges among civil society organizations. By working to enhance these linkages, autonomous trade unions, professional, developmental, and democracy-building organizations in South Africa not only may reinforce democratic trends within their own organizations but also may be crucial catalysts for attracting greater international support for and investment in the process of democratic change and consolidation in South Africa.

NOTES

This is a condensed, revised and updated version of Larry Diamond, "Civil Society and Democratic Consolidation: Building a Culture of Democracy in a New South Africa," in *The Bold Experiment: South Africa's New Democracy*, eds. Hermann Giliomee and Lawrence Schlemmer (Johannesburg: Southern Books Publishers, 1996). For a similar but more comparative and theoretical treatment, see Larry Diamond, "Rethinking Civil Society: Toward Democratic Consolidation," *Journal of Democracy* 5 (July 1994): 4–16. The author is grateful for the comments and suggestions of Alex Boraine, Hermann Giliomee, Stephen Stedman, Kathleen Bruhn, and Naomi Chazan.

1. Philippe Schmitter, "Interest Systems and the Consolidation of Democracy," in *Reexamining Democracy: Essays in Honor of Seymour Martin Lipset*, eds. Gary Marks and Larry Diamond (Newbury Park, Calif.: Sage, 1992), p. 158.

2. This formulation draws from a number of conceptual treatments but has been influenced particularly by discussions with and writings of Naomi Chazan. See in particular Naomi Chazan, "Africa's Democratic Challenge: Strengthening Civil Society and the State," *World Policy Journal* 9 (Spring 1992): 279–308. I am particularly indebted to her emphasis on the partial and pluralistic nature of civil society groupings and the relationships of mutual support and legitimation, as well as conflict and scrutiny, that undergird the interaction between state and civil society. For other useful formulations, see Edward Shils, "The Virtue of Civil Society," *Government and Opposition* 26 (Winter 1991): 9–10, 15–16; Peter Lewis, "Political Transition and the Dilemma of Civil Society in Africa," *Journal of International Affairs* 27 (Summer 1992): 31–54; Marcia A. Weigle and Jim Butterfield, "Civil Society in Reforming Communist Regimes: The Logic of Emergence," *Comparative Politics* 25 (October 1992): 3–4; Philippe C. Schmitter, "Some Propositions about Civil Society and the Consolidation of Democracy." Paper presented at the conference on Reconfiguring State and Society, April 22–23, 1993, at the University of California, Berkeley.

3. The use of the term "civic organizations" here is not to be confused with its application in South Africa, where civic associations are grass-roots organizations, based largely in the black townships and forged in the struggle against apartheid, which pursue a much wider range of both national and local social, economic, and political goals. See Kehla Shubane and Pumla Madiba, "The Struggle Continues? Civic Associations in the Transition." Research Report No. 25, Center for Policy Studies, Johannesburg, South Africa.

4. Chazan, "Africa's Democratic Challenge," pp. 288–89; Lewis, "Political Transition and the Dilemma of Civil Society in Africa," pp. 35–36.

5. The definitive global analysis of democratization during this period (beginning in 1974) is from Samuel P. Huntington, *The Third Wave: Global Democratization in the Late Twentieth Century* (Norman: University of Oklahoma Press, 1991).

6. Guillermo O'Donnell and Philippe Schmitter, *Transitions from Authoritarian Rule: Tentative Conclusions about Uncertain Democracies* (Baltimore, Md.: Johns Hopkins University Press, 1986), chap. 5.

7. For a summary of recent empirical evidence, see Diamond, "Civil Society and the Development of Democracy"; Lewis, "Political Transition and the Dilemma of Civil Society in Africa"; Chazan, "Africa's Democratic Challenge"; Naomi Chazan, "Between Liberalism and Statism: African Political Cultures and Democracy," in *Political Culture and Democracy in Developing Countries*, ed. Larry Diamond (Boulder, Colo.: Lynne Rienner Publishers, 1994); Michael Bratton and Nicholas van de Walle, "Toward Governance in Africa: Popular Demands and State Response," in *Governance and Politics in Africa*, eds. Goran Hyden and Michael Bratton (Boulder, Colo.: Lynne Rienner Publishers, 1992), pp. 27–56.

8. Samuel P. Huntington, "Will More Countries Become Democratic?" *Political Science Quarterly* 99 (Summer 1984): 204.

9. Larry Diamond, "Introduction: Civil Society and the Struggle for Democracy," in *The Democratic Revolution: Struggles for Freedom and Pluralism in the Developing World*, ed. Larry Diamond (New York: Freedom House, 1992), p. 8.

10. Alexis de Tocqueville, *Democracy in America*, vol. 2 (New York, Vintage Books, 1945 [1840]), p. 124.

11. Ibid.

12. I am grateful to Stephen John Stedman for emphasizing this point to me.

13. Georgina Waylen, "Women and Democratization: Conceptualizing Gender Relations in Transition Politics," *World Politics* 46 (April 1994): 327–54. Although Waylen is correct that O'Donnell and Schmitter speak to the dangers of excessive popular mobilization during the transition, her criticism of the democracy literature as a whole for trivializing the role of civil society is unfairly overgeneralized and certainly inapplicable to work on Africa. Moreover, accepting her challenge to treat civil society as a centrally important phenomenon in democratization does not require one to accept her insistence on defining democracy to include economic and social rights as well as political ones.

14. Seymour Martin Lipset, *Political Man: The Social Bases of Politics* (Baltimore, Md.: Johns Hopkins University Press, 1979), pp. 70–79.

15. Larry Garber and Glenn Cowan, "The Virtues of Parallel Vote Tabulations," *Journal of Democracy* 4 (April 1993): 94–107.

16. Arye Carmon, "Israel's 'Age of Reform,'" *Journal of Democracy* 4 (July 1993): 114–23; Chai-Anan Samudavanija, "Promoting Democracy and Building Institutions in Thailand," in *The Democratic Revolution: Struggles for Freedom and Pluralism in the Developing World*, ed. Larry Diamond (New York: Freedom House, 1992), pp. 125–44.

17. This is a notable conclusion of a number of the papers on economic reform and democracy in the *Journal of Democracy* 5 (October 1994).

18. John Sullivan, "Business Interests, Institutions, and Democratic Development," *Journal of Democracy* 5 (October 1994).

19. Tocqueville, *Democracy in America*, vol. 2, p. 126.

20. Diamond, "Civil Society and the Struggle for Democracy," p. 11.

21. Joel Migdal, *Strong Societies and Weak States* (Princeton, N.J.: Princeton University Press, 1988).

22. Naomi Chazan, "The New Politics of Participation in Tropical Africa," *Comparative Politics* 14 (January 1982): 174–76.

23. Lipset, *Political Man*, pp. 74–75.

24.   Robert M. Price, "Civil Society, Democracy, and Political Change in South Africa." Unpublished paper, University of California, Berkeley, 1992, p. 15.

25.   Steven Friedman, "An Unlikely Utopia: State and Civil Society in South Africa," *Politikon* 19 (December 1991): 5–19. Price disputes this perspective, arguing that "the associations that mushroomed during the 1980s did not make exclusive or all encompassing claims on the allegiance of their members" but drew them "on the basis of a particular social attribute . . . into organizations with issue specific foci." Price, "Civil Society, Democracy, and Political Change in South Africa," pp. 30–31.

26.   Neville Alexander comments to the IDASA conference on The Role of a Civil Society in an Emerging Democracy.

27.   Shubane and Madiba, "Civic Associations in the Transition."

28.   Price, "Civil Society, Democracy, and Political Change in South Africa," p. 28.

29.   Ibid., p. 24.

30.   Friedman, "State and Civil Society in South Africa," p. 15.

31.   Ibid., pp. 16–18.

32.   Oscar Dhlomo, Remarks to the Conference on Consolidating a Democracy in South Africa: The Socio-Economic Imperatives, July 22–23, 1993, Johannesburg.

33.   Dankwart Rustow, "Transitions to Democracy: Toward a Dynamic Model," *Comparative Politics* 2 (April 1970): 360.

34.   The depth of popular ignorance about the most elementary features of formal democracy is suggested by the topics of the booklets the Matla Trust is planning to produce for its voter education campaign: "What Is Democracy?," "What Is a Constitution?," "What Is an Election?," and "How to Vote." Matla Trust Funding Proposal 1993–94, p. 8.

35.   Interview with Billy Modise, executive director of the Matla Trust, July 24, 1993, Johannesburg. See also Matla Trust Funding Proposal 1993–94, pp. 8–13. Translating civic education materials into indigenous languages is far from a trivial challenge. As Dhlomo observed at the above-referenced conference, many necessary terms have no exact translation within African languages. "Democracy" in the Zulu language translates into "majority rule" — which can lead to serious misunderstanding. Linguistic research and innovation, thus, appear necessary.

36.   Ibid., pp. 14–15.

37.   Alex Boraine, "Mobilising to Uphold Core Democratic Values," *Prospects (South Africa in the Nineties)* 2 (March–April 1993): 25; for the perspective of the Institute for Multiparty Democracy see Oscar Dhlomo, "Democracy Has to be *Taught* and *Learnt*," *Prospects (South Africa in the Nineties)* 2 (March–April 1993): 26–27.

38.   Boraine, "Mobilising to Uphold Core Democratic Values," p. 25. Needless to say, some of those police, military, and administrative enforcers of apartheid likely are beyond reeducation and retraining and simply will have to be removed.

39.   *Democracy in Action* (Journal of the Institute for a Democratic Alternative for South Africa) 7 (February 28, 1993): 9.

40.   Ibid., p. 28.

41.   Anthony Hazlitt Heard, "The Struggle for Free Expression in South

Africa," in *The Democratic Revolution: Struggles for Freedom and Pluralism in the Developing World*, ed. Larry Diamond (New York: Freedom House, 1992), pp. 167–80.

42.   Boraine, "Mobilising to Uphold Core Democratic Values," p. 25.

43.   Mongrane Wally Serote, "We Need the Milestones of Who We Are," *Prospects* 2 (March–April 1993): 38–40.

44.   Raymond Parsons, "Are Socio-Economic Policies Possible to Promote Growth and Consolidate Democracy? A Business Perspective." Address to the conference on Consolidating a Democracy in South Africa: The Socio-Economic Imperatives, July 23, 1993, Johannesburg.

2

The "New" Civil Society and Democratic Transitions in Africa

Edward R. MacMahon

One of the key factors in the move toward democratic pluralism in much of subsaharan Africa has been the development of a vibrant civil society. This sector, which had either not existed or been absent from the political process in the immediate postindependence period, resulted in part from the failings of the single-party system. Perhaps paradoxically, the inability of single-party states to provide adequate services such as health and education led to the development of domestic and foreign-supported nongovernmental organizations (NGOs). Restrictions on human rights and political freedoms fostered the creation of civic and professional organizations with emphasis on strengthening the rule of law, civil society, and democratic political freedoms. Many such groups played important roles in articulating interests and mediating political change in nations where authoritarian rule has given way to pluralism. Conversely, in a number of countries where democratic development is constrained and political polarization is paramount, the impact of nonpartisan civic organizations has been more circumscribed.

This chapter discusses a number of issues central to understanding the role of civil society in the African political reform process. It is divided into three main parts. First, the causes of democratization will be highlighted. Second, the different elements of civil society and the relative weight of their contributions to political pluralism will be analyzed.

Finally, the prospects for continued development of civil society and democratic institutions will be assessed.

It should be noted that our working definition of civil society does not include traditional or mainly ethnically based organizations. In doing so, it is not meant to be implied that these groups are not active or might not have a role to play in the development of democratic political institutions. The focus of this chapter, however, is on the new or rejuvenated civil institutions that make this period different from that which preceded it.

CAUSES OF DEMOCRATIC REFORM

Two of the most oft-quoted statements about African politics come from the immediate postindependence period. In the 1950s, President Kwame Nkrumah of Ghana urged Africans to "seek ye first the political kingdom." In 1960, British Prime Minister Harold Macmillan referred to the "winds of change" that were blowing across the continent.

Both quotations have been largely misunderstood by those who perceived such statements as suggesting that the transition from colony to democracy should be a rapid and relatively painless process. Both statements were a reaction more to what had transpired in the immediate past than to any precise vision of the future. Macmillan's winds of change and Nkrumah's political kingdom referred to the end of colonialism and the advent of independence, rather than to the establishment of democracy. A facile presumption, at least on the part of the soon-to-be former colonial powers, was that the end of colonialism would bring with it democracy. In fact, within a few years, authoritarianism and single-party rule had become the rule of thumb throughout the continent.

What are the differences and similarities between the 1960s and the 1990s? Why should the establishment of democratic institutions in this decade prove any different from what happened in the 1960s? This question is worthy of a chapter, if not a book, all by itself. A quick answer is that, although, in general, both periods are times of fundamental reaction against the previous period, in the case of the 1960s, it was against colonialism, whereas in the 1990s, it is against the excesses of the single-party authoritarianism of the previous 30 years.

Arguments persist regarding the proper weight to be accorded to external versus internal factors playing a greater role in the African democratization trend. These arguments miss the point, however. Each of the dozens of countries that have been affected by the process had peculiarities that make generalizations of this sort difficult. More importantly, however, it is clear that, throughout the continent, some mix of both factors was involved. The absence of one probably would have neutralized the other. For example, the demonstration effect of the fall of the Berlin wall would have meant little had African single-party regimes not already been suffering from a serious lack of internal legitimacy. On the other hand, without a supportive international environment, the pace of political change probably would have been much slower.

Constructing democratic societies is a very complex and subtle task. We should recognize the paradox that this process takes years and, indeed, is never really finished, but economic situations in these countries will not permit the luxury of long periods of fiddling with institutions.

There are many internal factors, some of which cannot be attributed to the failings of the single-party state. The growth in human capital, for example, since the immediate postindependence period has created a new class of educated opinion leaders who are less likely to accept the narrow patronage structures so familiar to many postindependence governments. These individuals served to swell the ranks of opposition to the single-party state.

Ironically, however, the track record of these governments themselves has proved to be a key contributing factor to the democratization process. In the economic sphere, the literature on Africa is rife with examples of misguided economic policies. Attempts at protectionism, import substitution, and capital-intensive development projects proved largely to be costly mistakes. Primary resources often were tapped without sufficient attention paid to their renewability or to using revenues gained from their exploitation for longer-term developmental purposes. Emphasis on socialist policies led to bloated government bureaucracies, massive budgetary deficits, and significant distortions in already-fragile economies. It is true that the prices of many commodities exported by African nations declined, especially in the 1980s. This should not camouflage the fact that the single-party state did not contribute to the economic development of its citizens.

Michael Bratton attaches considerable importance to this issue. He claims that "the economic crisis in African countries is a fundamental cause of the demand for political reform. . . . After all, the recent flush of political protests in Africa have occurred in a context where economic conditions were rapidly deteriorating but where the degree of central political control has remained constant for many years. Thus, the popular demand for political accountability seems to be largely instrumental, aimed at restoring economic equilibrium."[1]

The elements cited above tell only part of the story, however. They represent poor policy choices on the part of governments. However egregious these faults may have been, they did, at least, represent visions of the direction in which leaders wanted their countries to go and were the "fruits" of these visions being translated into policies.

A whole different set of problems resulted from the structural weaknesses inherent in the single-party state itself. There are two basic weaknesses to any system other than democracy. First, there is no system of succession guaranteed to represent the, at times admittedly ephemeral, "will of the people." Second, there is no institutionalized system of checks and balances to ensure that the excesses and mistakes of the government — or other elements of society, for that matter —can be controlled.

Too many caricatures of Africa — Uganda's Idi Amin, Equatorial Guinea's Macias Nguema, Zaire's Mobutu Sese Seko, the Central African Republic's Emperor Bokassa, to name a few — already have paid testament to the awful effects of power run rampant. On a less visible scale, however, almost every country has suffered from the same problem. Without a check on power, the essence of democracy — that those who govern are the servants of those governed — quickly becomes obscured, as it was in postindependence Africa. Corruption sapped initiative. Funds flowed out of Africa and into real estate and numbered bank accounts in the West. Government leaders used their power to benefit specific regions or supporters to the extreme detriment of other sectors in society.

THE DEVELOPMENT OF CIVIL SOCIETY

As a reflection of the interconnected nature of politics and economics, these problems were not, of course, isolated solely in the economic sphere. The detrimental effects of the single-party state on human rights and political freedoms is well-known. An argument was put forth by many leaders (and echoed by many Western academics who felt inhibited against contradicting these African "voices") that, given the communal nature of African society, it was, in fact, quite reasonable to create a system in which decisions were debated and then made within the context of a single party. These arguments rang increasingly hollow as more and more countries began to suffer from the results of economic decline and limitations on political freedoms. Over time, it became a case of the emperor wearing very few clothes indeed.

Ironically, the seeds of the single-party state downfall were sown by the system's very failings. Parallel economies sprouted, designed to avoid the economic absurdities or disincentives faced by those who attempted to function in the aboveground, or formal, economy. As the state failed to fulfill, or even abdicated, its responsibilities in the economic sphere, a growing number of organizations were created to fill the gap. In many countries, umbrella groupings of related NGOs have been organized, such as the Ghana Association for Private Voluntary Organizations in Development (GAPVOD), the Council of NGOs Supporting Development (CONGAD) in Senegal, and the Tanzanian Association of NGOs (TANGO). Thus, unlike in the 1960s, self-help groups, credit and farmers' marketing cooperatives, peasant organizations, and local private voluntary development initiatives were founded in many countries at the grassroots level.

These efforts took place against a backdrop of African society that contains many elements and traditions supportive of civic institutions. Many Africans draw their identities from collective social units. In addition, the expansion of association life has, to a significant extent, cut across class, social, and economic lines.[2]

It was only a short step to make the connection from activism in the economic sphere to focusing on issues relating to greater popular participation in the political process. Issues relating to transparency and accountability transcend economic and political boundaries. Stephen Riley writes that "Increasingly problems are seen as political in character, and political reform has been added to an already top-heavy reform agenda of economic structural adjustment, environmental conservation and new population policies. As the World Bank put it in 1989, the root cause of weak economic performance in the past has been the failure of public institutions."[3]

At the same time that the economic crisis was fostering the creation of a civil society, a similar impetus was happening on the political side. "Weary of repression and corruption and no longer convinced that authoritarian systems accelerated development, the African intelligentsia and its supporters mobilized, often at considerable risk, to demand political reforms."[4] As a reaction to the abuses of power and the lack of checks and balances, pressure groups began to develop, urging greater political freedom. Some of these organizations were reinvigorated versions of associations that had existed for years, such as bar or journalists' associations. These groups may have been appendages or mouthpieces to the government during part of the single-party era, or they may have been moribund or focused on safely nonpolitical issues.

Another set of organizations were those that developed during the single-party period in response to a particular problem or set of problems. Examples of these groups are human rights associations, democracy promotion groups, women's or regional associations, and advocacy groups. The groups were in addition to those civil society organizations that, although not formed in reaction to any problem in society, nonetheless served to bring together representatives of various elements within society. Examples of these are alumni organizations, service clubs, self-help groups, and community associations.

The politically oriented NGOs faced many challenges, some of which were symptomatic of civil society as a whole and others that were more specific to their mission. It is important to focus on these, because there is a tendency to idealize civic organizations and to imbue them with qualities that do not exist on this side of heaven. A balanced perspective should include discussion of weaknesses as well as strengths. In this regard, one problem has been, quite simply, a lack of resources with which to carry out activities.

The lack of resources poses a number of different challenges. In addition to simply constraining the range of activities possible, it has also been a factor impeding such organizations from developing across societal lines to a greater extent than they already have. It is also clear that increased donor interest in such activities as a possible source of funding, if not approached carefully, risks subverting the indigenous nature of these groups. Whether consciously or not, they may begin to orient their agendas and priorities to fit those of the donor. Another potential problem concerns the extent to which organizations have possessed infrastructural and logistical capabilities to carry out their anticipated activities.

A complicating challenge regarding resource development is that, given the level of suspicion and polarization existing in many countries, reliance on domestic funding may engender the presumption that the organization is beholden to one or another interest or political movement. NGOs can be suspected of being pro-government, for example, or, more often, of harboring antigovernment sympathies, and human rights organizations often were perceived as being oriented against a particular regime in power. The fact that civil society, by acting as a counterweight or independent actor within a national political context, invariably carries with it a certain skepticism about governmental actions, easily can be interpreted as a bias or hostility directed against the government. The perception of civic organizations as being hostile leads invariably to the presumption that such organizations are not truly nonpartisan. Experience in democratizing nations shows that one of the most difficult elements of the transition is for civil society organizations to define their role when a government that may long have been the object of their focus is no longer in power. Another perspective is that of the newly elected government that finds that its relationship with civil society, which may have been fostered by elements of a common perspective when in opposition, undergoes a significant change when it assumes power.

Another problem is the gap that exists between rural and urban perspectives regarding organizing within civil society. This problem is less pronounced than in the 1960s, when rural, grass-roots interests found little voice in either societal or governmental institutions. This facilitated the fall of the first wave of officially democratic regimes; because of the centralization of power within the political culture, the capture of the main symbols of state authority, such as broadcast facilities, was usually a sufficient gesture to impose authoritarian rule.

The problem of discord between urban and rural interests has not gone away, although more NGOs now exist that address at least part of this issue. The problem is compounded by the attitude of some African elites — although this problem is certainly not restricted to Africa — which views interaction with grass-roots rural interests as a low priority at best and something to be avoided at worst. At a conference of civic organizations held in Abidjan in February 1993, a civic organizer from the U.S.-based group Common Cause explained in detail how her organization had developed a mass membership of over 300,000. African participants (most of whom could be considered to be from the elite) reacted against this approach. Their arguments were that African NGOs working in the democratic development field had limited resources and, thus, had to rigorously prioritize their activities and that, for better or worse, elites ran African societies and were likely to do so for the foreseeable future. These groups, thus, saw their highest priority as targeting their activities in the direction of the elites and working toward ensuring that the elites internalized the key elements of a democratic political culture.

It is not surprising that economic and political NGOs found common ground in analyzing the problems of the single-party state and in searching for solutions. Shared desired outcomes — reduced corruption; creation of an environment hospitable to private enterprise; greater political, social, and economic freedoms; a rule of law; transparency in governmental actions — all fostered the development of common ground. Coming from different directions, the groups arrived at similar perspectives.

An example of an organization that embodies the two elements is the West Africa-based Study and Research Group on Democracy and Economic and Social Development in Africa, known by its French acronym of GERDDES. GERDDES was founded in Benin as that nation moved toward ending dictatorship and establishing democracy. GERDDES' membership is drawn mainly from the ranks of the professions. Its first project was to send out observers to monitor Benin's 1991 presidential elections, the first time that an African election had been observed by an NGO. GERDDES was founded and the Benin observation mission undertaken without any donor country funding, actions that helped to foster GERDDES' credibility as a legitimate start-up organization.

GERDDES now has chapters in ten countries in West and Central Africa. It has placed highest emphasis on maintaining its nonpartisan status and on disseminating information on the development of a democratic political culture. In addition to election observation, workshops and training sessions have been held in several countries on themes such as the press in a democracy, corruption, lessons learned from African elections, the role of women in a democracy, and how to organize civic groups focusing on democratic development.

THE ROLE OF CIVIL SOCIETY IN POLITICAL REFORM

The advent of formally democratic structures to a number of African countries has been well-documented. Countries such as Benin, Mali,

Niger, and the Congo held national conferences in which sovereignty and executive power passed from the authoritarian leader to the conference, which then elected a transitional government charged with the responsibility of organizing elections.

It is important to reflect upon the circumstances that led to the holding of the national conference. Although the political situations in the four countries cited above were by no means identical, they were similar in several key respects. Each country was undergoing a severe economic crisis. They all had leaders who had governed in an authoritarian fashion for a significant period. They had increasingly restive political opposition and civil societies. An important event or a series of events served as a flash point that galvanized popular mobilization through parties or civic groups against the regime.

Finally, meaningful political change — the decision to hold the national conference — occurred after the president lost the allegiance of all or part of the security forces. In the case of Mali, this took place through the vehicle of a coup d'état led by progressive military officers who subsequently handed power over to a democratically elected government. In the other cases, the loss of control over the security forces was more subtle, but the effect was similar. In the Congo, security forces sent to arrest a leading trade union activist met resistance from other elements of the security forces and withdrew. In Benin, street protests over the economic decline forced security leaders to decide between upholding Kerekou's regime and spilling the blood of fellow Beninois or responding to what was manifestly the will of the people and supporting fundamental political change.

We can see the strength and role of civil society most clearly in these types of cases, but they are not the only ones. In many other countries across the continent, civic activism helped initiate change. Analysis of institutional affiliation of participants at national conferences, not only in the countries cited above but also at other national conferences with less clear-cut results, such as in Togo, Zaire, and Gabon, attests to the role that at least part of civil society played. According to Nicholas Van de Walle, "Participation included the establishment elites of the ancien regime as well as the members of the reform coalitions associated with the social protests. Prominent politicians from both the single party and the opposition, student spokesmen, ethnic and religious leaders and public sector trade unionists dominated the proceedings."[5] He also notes that disenfranchised groups, especially the rural poor, did not seem to be as well-represented, but it remains true that participation did come from many different sectors of society.

A common thread in national conferences was the role played by the Catholic Church. As governments, opposition, and civil society groups grappled with organizational questions relating to the conduct of the national conferences, a central preoccupation was identifying a figure with sufficient authority and independent, nonpartisan status to make him acceptable to all to preside over the national conference. In Togo, Benin, the Congo, and Zaire, the country's leading Catholic cleric undertook this responsibility. In other countries, religious organizations played a key mediating role behind the scenes. In addition, churches helped form the backbone of nonpartisan election monitoring organizations in Zambia, Malawi, and elsewhere. The role of religious figures and churches in the South African liberation struggle is well-known.

Although themselves not an immediate part of civil society, international financial institutions (IFIs) also contributed a number of former personnel to the democratic transition process. In earlier days, the idea that multilateral financial institutions would enter so directly into the political process would have been unthinkable. The fact, however, that political reform was, to a considerable extent, spurred on by the international financial community's growing sense of fatigue with Africa's economic nonperformers perhaps made it inevitable that those who were championing economic reform would be called upon to assume positions of leadership in their own countries. Prime ministers who had worked for the World Bank, the African Development Bank, or other international institutions came to power in the Ivory Coast, Benin, Niger, and the Congo.

The role played by both the Catholic Church and the IFIs did not go unnoticed by those for whom the political changes posed, to put it succinctly, uncomfortable challenges. A long-time political figure who has now assumed senior government responsibilities in one Francophone country told this author in 1991 that the wave of democratization had been instigated by the church and the IFIs. Queried whether this represented a "plot" by these institutions to create their own political hegemony, the man smiled and said that he preferred to think of their roles as representing a "confluence of interests."

CIVIC GROUPS AS INSTRUMENTS OF MEDIATION

A key element in answering the question of whether democracy will survive is whether civil society can play the role it needs to in support of democratic development. In addition to representation of specific interests, which forms the core of a participatory style of government, civil society also provides an integrating and mediatory function, because its component parts include fora where individuals representing different elements of society can come together in pursuit of a larger, common interest. In countries such as Cameroon and Gabon, where the political climate has remained highly polarized, the dearth of civil society organizations is striking. Regarding Cameroon, for example, Van de Walle emphasizes that "there are simply no civic organizations with significant organizational power, in large part because the state destroyed them all in the first decade after independence."[6]

One may pose the chicken and the egg question regarding whether polarization occurs as a result of the lack of a strong civil society or vice versa; whatever the answer, it would appear that the two phenomena are inversely linked.

Without the mediating influence of civil society, political parties have little way of interacting with each other except through direct confrontation. The risk of polarization and misunderstanding through an inability to communicate, to find neutral terrain, or simply to benefit from the culture in which political opponents can share similar pursuits and nonpolitical institutional affiliations can have tragic consequences. This is equally true of the period subsequent to initial competitive elections and the period leading up to them.

RWANDA

Where does the tragedy of Rwanda fit into this discussion of civil society and democratization? Many, including a visiting African foreign minister in a May 1994 discussion with this author, suggest that opening the Pandora's box of political liberalization can give vent to uncontrollable forces within the body politic. A related, but less openly expressed, sentiment suggests that cases such as Rwanda, Somalia, and Liberia demonstrate that Africans simply are not prepared for democracy.

Those who point to the Rwandan case as proof of what can happen when a country moves toward democracy, however, have turned reality on its head. The bloody paroxysm that country has gone through is proof of what happens when moves toward addressing fundamental iniquities in a country's political structure are too-long delayed. The 1993 Arusha Accords called for the installation of a transition government charged with preparing for elections within a two-year period. Unfortunately, political violence, haggling, and a lack of flexibility on the part of the Rwandan government kept the transition government from ever being named. It was in this context of political confusion and lack of progress that the death of President Habyrimana led to widespread communal violence.

Rwandan civil society organizations had been playing a role in trying to help foster a new political equilibrium. In a gruesome testament to the influence those groups had, security forces representing regional Hutu interests, which perceived they had the most to lose in a peaceful settlement, targeted opposition Hutu political parties and civil society organizations in the early hours of the genocide. It has been suggested, although not proven, that Habyrimana's aircraft had been shot down by the same security forces that were supposed to protect him.

Skeptics of African democracy also point to the violence that erupted in neighboring Burundi in October 1993 as proof of what can transpire when poorly prepared countries move toward democracy. In the Burundi case, a minority (Tutsi) population had long governed the majority Hutu. A reformist president initiated a democratization process, which led to a victory by the mainly Hutu-backed FRODEBU party. After barely three months of a FRODEBU government, elements within the largely Tutsi military staged an attempted coup, which resulted in the death of President Melchoir Ndadaye and other leading members of government.

These events certainly provide sobering food for thought for proponents of democracy in Africa. A number of lessons must be learned, including the need for political institutions during the democratic transition to be inclusive and positive sum in nature and constructed in such a fashion so as to minimize the sentiment on the part of the electoral "losers" that they have no stake in the new system and, hence, no interest in seeing it succeed.

An equally important lesson, however, should be drawn from the fact that the coup in Burundi failed. In the "good old days" of single-party government, any coup attempt that resulted in the death of the president, several government ministers, the president of the national assembly, and other leading political figures and saw the radio and television stations occupied and the airport closed certainly would have spelled the end for the former regime. In the case of Burundi, however, the coup plotters felt a need to rally domestic support in order to legitimize their rule, only to be met with surprisingly unified resistance on the part of most of the political parties and civil society organizations. The coordinated opprobrium of the international community certainly was also a crucial factor in influencing the putchists of the hopelessness of their cause. Nonetheless, it is true that democracy had taken root in Burundi to the extent that pluralistic forces in society joined together to oppose an attempt to impose military hegemony by force. Subsequently, a coalition of civic groups, the Action Group for Social Protection (GAPS), has played a useful mediating function in the political context.

CONCLUSION

It is clear that the task of democratic development takes time and that, in Africa today, democratic institutions are only beginning to take shape. It may well be that, 25 or 50 years from now, democracy on the continent may, in some ways, take a somewhat different shape than elsewhere in the world, just as European democratic institutions differ from those of the United States in a number of important ways. The fundamental point, however, is that all such systems share the underlying, core principles of democracy.

One lesson that should be noted in comparing the tragedies in Rwanda and Burundi with the successful beginning of a transition in South Africa is the importance of crafting a positive-sum system, as opposed to a negative-sum, winner take all outcome of the initial democratic transition. Civil society can play a vital role in helping political actors focus on ways to make the process one in which most, if not all, players feel that they have a stake in the system. It is not easy for political parties alone to work out this system, even if they would benefit from it in the long run, because it necessitates them conceding some political space to others, an instinct that is not necessarily indigenous to *Homo sapiens politicus*.

What are some key issues and challenges that need to be addressed if civil society is to help foster democratic development in the years to come? Most importantly, civil society must be self-renewing. There is the risk that this fragile and tentative democratic opening may prove too ephemeral. The chances of this occurring are greatly diminished if civil society can remain an active player on the scene. The necessary elements for this to happen are many and varied, but the following are several that would appear to be particularly salient.

Civil society must have adequate human and material resources. It is axiomatic that most civil society groups operate without a level of financial resources that they would consider appropriate to accomplish their goals. Many also must face a lessening of enthusiasm and resultant membership challenges in the postelectoral period. Mobilization of people is always easier when there is a clearly definable opponent, usually taking the form of an authoritarian government. The more subtle, longer-term, and, at times, seemingly intractable challenges of postelection democratic consolidation can prove to be more difficult themes around which to arouse passion and interest. Issues such as domestic resource mobilization versus reliance on external (often donor) sources of funding and the concept of volunteer participation in organizational activities often pose challenges and have to be worked out.

Civil society must develop a clear focus of activity. This will be easier for groups with a specific mandate, such as a chamber of commerce or trade union. For others, many of which sprouted in recent years, identifying and prioritizing areas of focus can prove a challenge. What should human rights groups do, for example, in a formerly authoritarian country where human rights are now generally respected? What program priorities should a democratic development organization operating in a post-election environment adopt, given that its emphasis had been placed almost entirely on ensuring that legitimate elections were held? The question also has pertinence in countries where change may come more incrementally, if at all, and where hopes for change have been tempered by the lack of progress.

Civil society must maintain a nonpartisan stance. Civil society groups must walk an eternal tightrope of nonpartisanship. Often it is highly difficult, if not impossible, to remain free of criticism from one or more elements of the political spectrum. More often than not, this takes the form of a government criticizing the organization for being in league with the opposition. Sometimes, however, in postelection environments, civil society groups that had developed their identities by watchdogging the activities of the previous government now find themselves in the awkward position of being expected to perform the same function regarding the new government, with which they shared a common legacy of opposition. These issues, which are difficult enough in established democracies, can be especially challenging in new democracies, where concepts such as nonpartisanship and constructive opposition have yet to be internalized within the political culture.

Civil society must accomplish all these while being representative of society as a whole. For civil society to be effective, it must, in aggregate, represent a cross section of society writ large. In the 1960s, civil society did not exist sufficiently to have a significant impact; its manifestation was primarily urban and upper-class. It is not surprising to note that, even today, probably the plurality of civil society organizations are urban based, primarily in capital cities. One of the crucial challenges facing nascent or would-be democratic political cultures is how to ensure that rural and other disadvantaged interests can be factored into the equation.

Newly emergent civic groups representing the elements of society that have not been able to express themselves previously in a collective fashion must continue to be factored into the process. Of course, civil society cannot and should not act as one; diversity and independence of action are important. Nonetheless, the extent to which fissures within society, such as urban-rural, class, religious, or ethnic dichotomies, obscure basic common goals mean that the larger challenge of democratic development also can become more complicated.

It is likely that civil society will continue to play a central role in continued democratic development on the African continent. Why? First, because the past (and in some case, the present) weighs heavily in most African perspectives and will continue to do so for a long time to come. Thus, Winston Churchill's maxim — that democracy is the worst form of government except for all others — is clearly operative in the African case. Civic groups, which in most cases saw the light of day or were newly empowered as a result of the failings of the previous system, are those that are least likely to forget this lesson.

Second, given the limited power of the state in contemporary Africa, it would be very difficult for civil society to be forcibly repressed. Unlike the early postindependence period, the breadth of civil society organizations, modern means of communication, donor interest (and pressure), and domestic popular sentiment all mitigate against the idea that governments could revert to old-style single-party–state authoritarianism. Instead, would-be governments appear to be employing a more subtle divide-and-conquer strategy that includes the sponsorship of allegedly nonpartisan civic groups that, in fact, owe their allegiance and existence to their ruling party. As complicated and messy as this state of affairs may be, however, it is preferable to the former situation and, in a sense, represents an acknowledgment by the government of the current realities.

Third, we have already noted that what happens in Africa is part of a worldwide movement away from attempts at state dominance in most areas of human existence. Politics in Africa clearly do not occur in isolation from events in the rest of the world. Although the road to democratic consolidation may be rocky and result in reverses along the way, global forces mitigate toward the continuance of political pluralism, in Africa as elsewhere.

The "new" civil society has a vital role to play in fostering the development of pluralism. It cannot do everything, it is not perfect, and too much should not be expected from it. However, the potential exists for civil society to continue to contribute significantly to the process. It is, for example, relatively easy to create new or reinvigorated institutions; the difficult part is to breathe life into them and ensure that they interact in a productive and constructive fashion. Civil society can act as an overseer, or watchdog, of this process. It can provide a forum for honest discussion of sensitive issues, such as the role of the military in a democratic society. It can act as a meeting ground where erstwhile political opponents can communicate in a positive fashion. It can serve as a breeding ground for imaginative ideas regarding how democratic political institutions can adapt to more fully represent African realities. Finally, civil society can help bind together different elements of the national fabric, be they regional, ethnic, religious, or economic.

NOTES

1. Michael Bratton, "Economic Crisis and Political Realignment in Zambia," in *Economic Change and Political Liberalization in Sub-Saharan Africa*, ed. Jennifer Widner (Baltimore, Md: Johns Hopkins University Press, 1994), p. 123.

2. USAID, *An Assessment of USAID's Capacity for Rapid Response in Support of African Civil Society* (Washington, D.C.: U.S. Agency for International Development, 1994), pp. 15–16.

3. Stephen Riley, "The Democratic Transition in Africa," in *Conflict Studies* (London: Research Institute for the Study of Conflict and Terrorism), p. 9.

4. Donald Rothchild, "Structuring State-Society Relations in Africa," in *Economic Change and Political Liberalization in Sub-Saharan Africa*, ed. Jennifer

Widner (Baltimore, Md: Johns Hopkins University Press, 1994), p. 207.

   5.   Nicholas Van de Walle, "Neopatrimonialism and Democracy in Africa," in *Economic Change and Political Liberalization in Sub-Saharan Africa*, ed. Jennifer Widner (Baltimore, Md: Johns Hopkins University Press, 1994), pp. 140–43.

   6.   Ibid., p. 151.

3

Lessons to be Learned from the Angolan Elections: Reliable Guides or Misleading Judgments

William Minter

In the aftermath of Angola's return to war following the September 1992 elections, there has been much commentary on what went wrong. A U.S. State Department review in April 1993, for example, singled out errors including "winner-take-all vs. power-sharing," "elections without prior agreement on shape of political system," "premature construction of a national army," and "no neutral control of transition."[1] In slightly different wordings, other common elements often cited are the small and ineffective United Nations (UN) presence and the failure to demobilize the two armies.

Each of these critiques, although containing elements of truth, is subject to different interpretations and is often presented in oversimple and misleading terms. Like the State Department, moreover, most accounts evade the issue of the responsibility of the international community, and the United States in particular, in setting the scene for disaster and failing to respond as it developed.

This chapter looks at the lessons most commonly cited and evaluates to what extent they may be reliable or misleading guides to what happened in Angola and what might happen in future Angolan settlements or presumably comparable cases. It is not a comprehensive review of the 1991 Bicesse peace agreement, the election process, or the subsequent period of war and renewed negotiations,[2] but it is a call to look critically at "lessons" that, once examined, are much less obvious than at first glance.

BACKGROUND

In their war for independence, which began in 1961, Angolans were divided.[3] The National Front for the Liberation of Angola (FNLA) was based among Kikongo-speaking people in the north. Jonas Savimbi's National Union for the Total Independence of Angola (Unita) claimed leadership of Umbundu-speaking Angolans. The Popular Movement for the Liberation of Angola (MPLA) had a national political appeal, but its strongest base was among Kimbundu-speaking people in the Luanda area.

Once Portuguese control began to crumble in 1974, the FNLA and Unita were backed by Zaire, the United States, and South Africa. The MPLA turned to Cuba and the Soviet Union for support. War broke out in early 1975, only months after agreement on elections. U.S., Zairian, and South African intervention was matched step-by-step by Cuban advisers and troops with Soviet supplies.

The MPLA proclaimed the People's Republic of Angola under President Agostinho Neto in November 1975 and soon gained international recognition. The U.S. Congress barred further U.S. involvement in early 1976. South African troops then withdrew, leaving the FNLA exhausted as a military force and Unita struggling to survive.

Over 90 percent of the Portuguese settlers fled as Angola came to independence. Because they had monopolized almost all skilled jobs, both in the government and the private sector, the economy was devastated. State companies taking over from fleeing Portuguese lacked management skills. Only the oil sector, where the government worked together with foreign companies, prospered.

From 1976 through 1991, Angola suffered both guerrilla warfare and direct South African attacks. Angola provided support for guerrillas seeking the independence of South African-occupied Namibia, and South Africa backed Unita on a massive scale until the independence of Namibia in 1990.

Beginning in 1979, Unita occupied sparsely populated southeastern Angola with the aid of South African troops. Conflict over this area led to large-scale battles involving South African and Cuban troops as well as Angolan government and Unita forces, culminating in a military setback for South Africa in 1987–88.

Agreements in December 1988 on Namibian independence and withdrawal of Cuban troops from Angola ended large-scale South African military involvement. However, the United States, which had officially resumed funding of Unita's army in 1986, escalated its support. A military stalemate ensued. Peace negotiations between the Angolan government and Unita began in 1989. In May 1991, they signed an agreement in Bicesse, Portugal, providing for a cease-fire, demobilization of the two armies, and multiparty elections.

In formal terms, the political system under the MPLA was a one- party state on a Marxist-Leninist basis. In practice, party membership was small, and nonparty bureaucrats also had substantial influence. Factionalization within party and state, together with the inefficient Portuguese legacy, often paralyzed policy formation and implementation. Although the strongest influence within the state was the presidency, in practice, the president had to conciliate many internal factions.

Unita's administration in zones it controlled was even more autocratic, although, for public relations purposes, the movement exalted a commitment to Western democratic values. Control was highly centralized in the person of Savimbi; internal rivals and protest were brutally repressed.

Constitutional reforms in 1991 provided for a national assembly and a president, each elected by direct suffrage on a secret ballot. Although separate rights and duties were defined for both branches, the constitution retained a strong role for the president.

The electoral system provided for presidential and legislative votes administered by a National Electoral Commission, which was chaired by a former FNLA supporter. All parties were entitled to representatives at every level, down to the local polling station. Legislative seats were allocated proportionally, 70 based on the provincial vote, 130 on the national totals.

During the election campaign, none of the new small parties managed to gain much support, despite widespread disillusionment with the government and fear of Unita. Election campaigning was relatively free and open in the cities, with all parties having equal access to free television and radio time. Freedom of movement to campaign was difficult in the countryside, however, and almost impossible in areas still under Unita control.

Peace treaty provisions mandating demobilization of troops and formation of a new national army were delayed on both sides and systematically evaded by Unita. During the campaign, Angolan President José Eduardo dos Santos projected an image of peacemaker, while Savimbi's belligerent style shocked many Angolans.

The election itself was conducted in an orderly fashion, with observers of the rival parties present at polling stations, and a total of almost 800 international observers from the UN and other private and public delegations. Observers generally rated the procedures free and fair, and there was a high turnout of over 90 percent. The MPLA won 54 percent in the legislature, as compared with 34 percent for Unita. Dos Santos fell just short of 50 percent, compared with 40 percent for Unita leader Savimbi, requiring a runoff for the presidency. Unita rejected the results as fraudulent, however, and Angola returned to war.

Unita launched a series of offensives around the country in October 1992. Government forces expelled Unita from the capital in November but lost control of over 75 percent of the countryside. The fighting was more intense than at any time during the previous 16 years of war. In March 1993, Unita took the provincial capital Huambo, Angola's second largest city, with a population of over 400,000, after a two-month siege. With stockpiles concealed during the election period and with new supplies overland from Zaire and by air from South Africa, Unita held the military offensive for most of 1993. Controlling the diamond-producing areas of the northeast, Unita smuggled diamonds through Zaire for sale on the world market. The government army, weakened by demobilization before the election, took time to rebuild.

The sieges of inland cities by Unita produced casualties estimated to exceed 50,000, without counting those dying in the countryside. An estimated 1,000 people a day were dying from war-related causes in 1993; despite somewhat reduced levels of conflict in 1994, casualties were still high. Even in the capital Luanda, which did not come under direct attack, the swollen population of over 2 million (one-fifth the country's population) was afflicted by water shortages, cholera, and rampant inflation, leaving hundreds of thousands on the edge of survival. Over 2 million of Angola's 11 million people were dependent on international relief for survival. Fighting still blocked resumption of agriculture or freedom of movement in most of the countryside. Cereal production, down by almost one-third in 1993, was projected to decline an additional 20 percent in 1994.

The international community was slow to respond. In May 1993, the United States finally recognized the Angolan government, after Unita refused to accept a new internationally endorsed cease-fire agreement. In September 1993, the UN Security Council imposed an oil and fuel embargo on Unita. New peace talks then began in Lusaka, resulting in agreement on demobilization procedures, a second round of presidential elections, and other issues.

As of July 1994, Unita was still holding out for more power than the government was willing to give, despite government acceptance of a mediator-approved proposal giving Unita a number of ministries and provincial governorships. The war continued. Government forces had regained the advantage in many areas, but Unita still had a strong military position and retained its supply routes through Zaire.

LEARNING LESSONS

Drawing lessons from historical events is always an uncertain exercise. The logic is that of the counterfactual conditional: if only some decision or some factor had been different, then the results would have been different. Disaster would have been averted, or more generally, history would have taken a different course. Because, in fact, neither the if's nor the would have been's took place, definitive proof is elusive.

The purpose of drawing lessons, moreover, is to give guidance for future policy. It is no accident that the lessons drawn tend to reflect the policy preferences of those doing the drawing. That does not make the exercise irrelevant, nor does it imply that there is no scope for rational debate among those with different perspectives. However, it does mean that one should be explicit about the implications of the lessons for what parties are being blamed and what parties are being called on to learn what lesson, and one should be skeptical about claims that the lessons are objective and easily read conclusions.

In the case of the Angolan elections, for example, the focus on absence of sufficient power sharing in the electoral system can and has been used as if to justify Unita's return to war. The policy implication is that the primary way to promote future conflict resolution is to more adequately satisfy Unita's concerns. A focus on the failure to demobilize the armies, in contrast, may be used primarily to critique Unita, the party most guilty in this regard, or to castigate the international community for turning a blind eye to this failure. The policy implication is the need to limit Unita's access to the means of war.

Although most commentators and analysts criticize Unita for its decision to return to war, acknowledge that the election process was free and fair, and dismiss Unita's claims of fraud as unsubstantiated, many simultaneously draw "lessons" that imply concessions primarily from the government rather than from Unita.

Former U.S. Assistant Secretary for Africa Herman Cohen, for example, who directed U.S. African policy in the period of the Bicesse Accords and the Angolan election, commented on the Angolan situation after one year of renewed war in Angola:

There's a real dilemma here. . . . The government has right on its side, total legitimacy. They won the election. It was a free and fair election. Unita lost the election. Unita had demanded this election, and then they reneged and they went back to the bush and started fighting, so Unita is totally in the wrong. . . . [But] the only way to end the war is to have a real negotiation where all of Unita's concerns can be taken into account, and those are security guarantees, meaningful power sharing, resource sharing, and a decentralized government in which Unita could have some local authority. . . . It's more important right now to influence the government, despite the fact that they're in the right and they have a legitimacy to be willing to make concessions.[4]

In addition, the analysis of what might have been done differently and what should now be corrected often is limited to a short time horizon, implicitly putting some factors beyond question. The military balance as it stood at the cease-fire in May 1991 is taken as given, for example, blocking out the issue of how Unita gained the military capacity that enabled it to return to war. Thus, an unnamed U.S. diplomat was quoted in the fall of 1993 as saying "We didn't create Savimbi. We may have rented him for a few years. This is a messy situation but it's not our fault."[5] The message was that the United States has no responsibility for the fact that Angola returned to war and no obligation to bring its former client to heel.

Each of the reasons commonly given for failure in Angola is, at the general level, obviously correct. The existence of separate armies, lack of an adequate neutral international presence, and failure to reach sufficient political agreement before the elections all contributed to the return to war. However, each can be interpreted in ways implying very different practical lessons.

SEPARATE ARMIES

If there had been only one effective army committed to supporting the results of an election, then there could have been no return to war. This explanation is almost tautological and, in itself, explains little. The question is what alternatives may have existed to the failure to create an integrated force, as the peace plan prescribed.

The State Department's reference to "premature construction of national army" implies that the idea of constructing a national army under the circumstances was, in itself, a flawed idea. However, their positive examples (Namibia, Zimbabwe, South Africa) are all classic decolonization scenarios, providing little guidance for other countries. In each case, the only effective military force was that of the incumbent white-minority regime, while the opposition liberation forces had overwhelming popular support but very limited military capacity. In each case, after elections, the military cadres of the election victors were assimilated into existing military structures. The election losers knew that they could give up political power at the top while retaining dominant economic influence and significant control over bureaucratic institutions.

U.S. officials tended to conceive the Angolan situation in a parallel fashion, assuming that Unita had overwhelming popularity and would win and that the Angolan government would go the way of the white regimes in Southern Africa or the crumbling regimes of Eastern Europe. They were wrong. Their image of Unita as a liberating force was based on wishful thinking. Their complacency at Unita's failure to demobilize was the prelude to disaster.

The situation in Angola was quite different, much closer to parity between the contending parties in both military strength and potential votes. In the final stage of negotiations before the 1991 peace agreement, Unita argued strongly for postponing creation of a national army until after the elections and for a short time between the cease-fire and elections. The Angolan government contended that a longer period — at least three years — should be allowed, during which the armed forces would be transformed into a nonpartisan body incorporating Unita as well as government soldiers.

Unita's favored scenario was premised on elections with a credible threat of return to war if they did not win; observers talked of the precedent of the 1990 Nicaraguan election, in which many voters opposed the Sandinista government in order to avoid renewed war. The contrasting government scenario implied the dilution of Unita influence by assimilating their personnel into the existing system and postponing elections until the country had had time to reap significant benefits of peace.

Although Unita formally conceded the principle of integration at Bicesse, they won a relatively short time period before elections. In hindsight, there is little indication that they ever intended to abandon their separate army. When the elections were held, neither side had completely demobilized or disarmed, but the pattern of compliance was decidedly unequal. The attempt to blame both sides equally is an error both of fact and analysis.[6] The Angolan government demobilized more than 36,000 troops, leaving 29,000 in cantonment areas, while Unita demobilized only 5,000, leaving 26,000 in cantonment areas, not counting an alleged 20,000 more hidden in the bush or in Zaire.[7] The greater military preparedness of Unita was clearly apparent throughout the first year of renewed war.

This is an essential analytical point, because the two armies' character and openness to play a nonpolitical role were fundamentally different. The government army at the level of the rank and file was, by and large, a drafted army, multiethnic and with relatively low political commitment. At the officer level, it had previous experience of incorporating former enemies (significant numbers of former FNLA soldiers had joined in the 1970s and 1980s). Unita, in contrast, imposed a brutally tight discipline and rigid political loyalty to Unita leader Savimbi. Its troops were almost all from Savimbi's Umbundu-speaking ethnic heartland. A significant number of government soldiers went absent without leave, in a kind of de facto self-demobilization. Within Unita, fear combined with loyalty made such cases almost unheard of.

The State Department paper of April 1993 argues that military integration could have worked only if satisfactory power-sharing arrangements were agreed in advance, a point discussed below. However, it is also necessary to ask whether the presumption of parity between the two sides was not an insuperable obstacle. The Angolan government peace plan presented in 1989 offered, instead, the assimilation of Unita officers and troops into the existing government and army. The offer, clearly unsatisfactory to Unita and to its patron in Washington, was based on previous Angolan experience with the FNLA.

Acceptance of such a subordinate position for Unita would not necessarily have required an implausible total military defeat, but it would have required that the military and diplomatic balance be substantially tilted against it. For that to happen, the United States would have had to back away from its client in 1989–91, rather than stepping up support to compensate for Unita's lost supply line from South African-controlled Namibia.

Under such a scenario — which depended primarily on political options in Washington rather than in Angola — Unita might have been forced into a less advantageous agreement on military integration. It certainly would have had far less capacity to return to war even if it had held back part of its forces.

There is no way to prove that this road to integration might have worked, but it certainly is more plausible than any scenario that does not deal with the principal obstacle that did block integration of the armies: a still well-equipped Unita army with an officer corps fanatically loyal to an autocratic warlord.

INADEQUATE NEUTRAL PRESENCE

Again, this is a criticism on which almost everyone agrees in general. As UN Special Representative Margaret Anstee quipped, noting that the UN resolution laying out her mandate was numbered 747, she was "flying a 747 with only enough fuel for a DC3."[8] The numbers speak for themselves: in Angola, there were less than 600 UN officials for a population of 12 million, as compared with more than 7,000 for the elections in Namibia, with less than 1.5 million population.[9] The mandate also was restricted to observation rather than administration of the process. The three outside powers formally involved (the United States, Russia, and Portugal) were also observers. Implementation of the agreement was in the hands of the two parties themselves, or in other words, the agreement was to be "self-implementing."

This critique is correct but incomplete. It fails to ask why the mandate and the resources of the force were so insufficient and why there was little will to correct the mistake once it was clear that they were inadequate. The reasons are complex, ranging from the inadequacies of UN bureaucratic structures through U.S. concerns about budgets for peacekeeping operations to Angolan government sensitivities about sovereignty.

However, the fundamental reason lies in the context of the end of the Cold War. Dominant influence was in the hands of the one remaining superpower, beginning to waver in its unconditional support for its former Angolan client but still unwilling to admit the errors of the past and reluctant to abandon its enmity to the Angolan government.

Alex Vines notes that the UN Angola Verification Mission (UNAVEM), "failed to use effectively its only two weapons — publicity about violations and the threat of withdrawal."[10] It was generally not well-informed, and its efficacy was crippled by internal bureaucratic squabbles, lack of local knowledge, inadequate numbers of Portuguese-speaking personnel, and no strong leadership independent of the major Western powers. Delays and violations on both sides went unchallenged for the sake of moving the process along. Human rights issues involving both sides, but particularly the tightly controlled population administered by Unita, were conspicuously uninteresting to the UN team.

Most seriously, with Cuba removed from the scene and the Soviet Union collapsing into Russia, there was no outside party with a serious interest in ensuring Unita's compliance with the peace treaty. In addition to general laxity, there was a double standard most visible in the failure to insist on freedom of movement in Unita-controlled areas. The newly installed U.S. Liasion Office did move toward a more evenhanded public posture, particularly in support of election preparations, and doubts increased about Unita as the campaign went on. However, most U.S. personnel, as well as diplomats from other key countries such as Great Britain, remained more sympathetic toward Unita than toward the Angolan government. They also expected it to win.[11]

If Unita had won and there had been a revolt against the results by the Angolan government or factions within it, international pressure on the Angolan government likely would have been prompt and high-profile. It was known that the government was not really prepared for war, despite complaints about their new antiriot police. Savimbi's readiness to fight was public knowledge. At a speech at his headquarters in Jamba in July 1992, he predicted that he would win but that the Angolan government would reject the results. He said he was prepared: "What interests me is where the troops are to take over. . . . Those who will take over the country, interrupt the law . . . that's who I want with me. On the day that the election results are announced, I won't be at home. I'll be hiding in some corner in some section of the city. . . . At that point, there's going to be a two or three-week battle, and those who are in the city are going to die."[12]

Nevertheless, the UN mission and the international community in general were unprepared for the scenario of a government electoral victory and a Unita revolt. As tensions escalated in the weeks following the election, Unita threatened and then resorted to arms, and the government responded, including handing out weapons to civilians in Luanda.

The international reaction was largely passive. The election was recognized as free and fair, but there was no move to deter Unita. The United States refused to recognize the new Angolan government on the grounds that the second round of presidential elections still was to be held.

The United States eventually conceded diplomatic recognition in May 1993, and the UN Security Council imposed nominal sanctions on Unita in September. However, in general, the international response over the two years of war focused almost exclusively on relief and on a series of negotiations aimed at providing new incentives for Unita to renounce war and return to a new agreement.

The only lesson that seemed to be absorbed by the international community was the need to promote power sharing, but the power-sharing discourse by itself tended to be defined operationally as more power for Unita and alleviating Unita's security concerns. There was little attention to assuaging government security concerns or to weakening Unita to the point that it would be forced to accept the subordinate role of the loser in a democratic election.

WINNER TAKE ALL, POWER SHARING, AND POLITICAL AGREEMENT

"The winner-take-all approach did the most damage. For conflict resolution to work, multi-ethnic states need power-sharing among ethnic groups and consensus-building, rather than confrontation, between a ruling majority and opposition minorities." Thus, the State Department put it, in a comment echoed by many other commentators. The popularity of the phrase and the concept has increased only subsequently, with the South African transition serving as the model of success to contrast with failure in Angola.

Nevertheless, this recipe for conflict resolution and stability is far from sufficient and easily subject to abuse. Condemning "winner take all" in favor of power sharing makes sense if it implies simply that the rights of minorities and election losers to some share of participation, power, and privilege in the society should be guaranteed. However, what share? In proportion to what? To their ambition? To their military power? To their skill in negotiation and support from outside patrons? Or to their share of a vote? And through what mechanisms? Is a mandatory government of national unity, with proportional representation in the cabinet after multiparty competition, a universal prescription for multiethnic societies? What then of democracy, which requires the possibility of opposition having roots in civil society as well as power in the central government?

Nor is it at all clear that a different constitutional arrangement, however well-justified in theory, would have averted the return to war in Angola without, simultaneously, more adequate deterrents against one party's resort to violence to get an even larger share of power than the rules demanded.

Ironically, the Angolan government's initial proposal in 1989 for a settlement sketched a plan for negotiated power sharing that involved participation by Unita in both military and political positions, including governorships of several key provinces. There is no good reason to doubt that the offer, which would have involved a significant but clearly subordinate share of power, was real, but it was premised on the temporary retirement from politics of Unita leader Savimbi and did not include the prospect of a competitive election in which Unita would have a chance to be the winner. Unita, supported by the United States, rejected this proposal, holding out for elections that it expected to win and after which it expected to take over full control.

In the immediate runup to the election, the Angolan government was more receptive than Unita to pressure from the troika of outside observers for preelection agreement on a government of national reconciliation. Although there was no unanimity within the government as to what might be offered, a substantial share for Unita was consistent both with earlier proposals and with offers made by the government in later negotiations. When a new government was formed in December, it was after the war already had resumed. In that context, Unita was offered only the ministry of culture and four vice-ministries.[13]

On the legislative side, the proportional representation system ensured that it was more open to minority voices than, for example, the U.S. system of winner take all, excluding all but the two largest parties from representation. Many Angolans wryly commented that such election results would have been taken as a landslide in the U.S. context, surely not entitling the loser to guaranteed representation in the president's cabinet. Labeling the Angolan system "winner take all" without noting such qualifications is surely unfair.

What is true is that the history of centralization of power in Angola, both under the Portuguese and under the MPLA, and the wide authorities of the president under the constitution made the effective influence of the legislative minority problematic. Influence for other parties was not guaranteed by the constitution but was dependent on the degree of openness the election winner was willing to show.

The government that was formed under MPLA leadership after the elections included among its 53 ministers and vice-ministers 11 members of minority parties, as well as significant numbers of former members of the FNLA and of Unita. Continuing the trend of the late 1980s, which opponents scoffed at as buying off opposition, such defectors played important roles in lower ranks of government as well. The government's deficiencies in capacity for governance and democratic responsiveness to popular needs were widely and justly criticized, but it was genuinely multiethnic and politically inclusive. In sharp contrast, Unita's base of support was reduced to hard-core loyalists, because its return to war alienated even many who had voted for it.

The point is not to deny that some additional form of power sharing may have been appropriate, and it is certainly a necessary ingredient of a new settlement. It also is true that a more decentralized political order, particularly for the purpose of greater responsiveness and participation at local levels, is desirable in any case. However, the question is whether such arrangements would have been, or will be, sufficient to deter renewed war.

Although most commentators prefer to omit or evade the issue, out of continued bias toward Unita or simply from the conviction that there is no way to address it, no serious approach to conflict resolution in Angola can avoid asking a further question. Did Savimbi return to war because he did not get a *share* of power or because he did not get it *all*? In other words, what share, short of giving the election loser more power than the winner, would be sufficient to persuade him that further resorting to violence and maintaining a military capacity under his own control was unnecessary?

One response is to say that we really do not know; therefore, it is necessary to keep making offers until one works. That is the logic for seeking concession after concession from the Angolan government. A more realistic policy would not abandon the search for compromises and power sharing but would supplement it by putting substantive pressure on the party most guilty of violating previous agreements and showing least willingness to accept the results of a democratic election (see Appendix). It would entertain the plausible hypothesis that weakening Savimbi's capacity to make war may be an essential prerequisite for both stability and power sharing to work.

The record in Angola, through mid-1994, is precisely the opposite. The U.S. and UN reaction to Unita's return to war was sluggish and ineffective; at no point was there a serious effort to apply sticks as well as carrots to deter Savimbi. The only real pressures on Unita to negotiate seriously were the Angolan government's recovering military campaign and Unita's own inability to administer the territory it captured. Although an arms and fuel embargo against Unita was approved by the UN Security Council in September 1993 after a delay of almost a year, both U.S. and UN officials made it clear that they had no intention of trying to enforce it, despite blatant violations by Mobutu Sese Seko's Zaire and illegal supply flights from South African airports.

The argument that nothing could be done to enforce the embargo or otherwise to affect the military balance is either dishonest or naive. No embargo could ever be totally effective, but it is guaranteed to be ineffective when lack of will to enforce it is open knowledge. Serious pressure on

Zaire and the former South African government — closing down Savimbi's clandestine radio station, restricting international travel of Unita officials, and other similar measures — could have significantly weakened Unita's military capacity. Positive efforts to strengthen Angolan military capacity, even without any involvement of foreign troops, also could have made a difference.[14]

Such measures were not taken, partly because of lingering hostility to the Angolan government and sympathy for Unita from old Cold Warriors, such as U.S. holdover officials making Angola policy. However, few policymakers still openly defended anachronistic clients such as Savimbi or his friend Mobutu. More important was that to take any significant action to reverse the power such clients gained from decades of patronage would take high-level political will. Such will has not been forthcoming.

Although the Cold War implied apparently clear criteria for identifying friends and enemies and for intervening to alter power balances, in the new era, the still prevailing Realpolitik gives little guidance save pragmatic adjustments to realities. Politically, it is irrelevant that previous U.S. policies of support for undemocratic clients left a wake of destruction. There is little public awareness of the history and no sense of U.S. obligation to undo the damage.

In conflict situations, an interpretation of "neutrality" as staying halfway between, regardless of the relative merits of the parties, puts the process at the mercy of the most belligerent parties. Total exclusion of a group from access to power on the basis of its minority status at the polls or of the abhorrent conduct of its leadership is not a solution. However, the rhetoric of power sharing may slide easily into appeasement when the share of power is seen to be appropriately determined by firepower and bloody-mindedness rather than the ballot box or respect for human rights. Even if such a process leads to signatures on a new treaty, it is unlikely to produce results that are just, democratic, or durable.

APPENDIX: ANGOLA POLICY FRAMEWORK

The war raging in Angola since late 1992 is one of the world's most serious and most neglected humanitarian crises. As many as 1,000 are dying each day, agricultural production is paralyzed in many areas by ongoing combat, and thousands of displaced people are pouring into government-held urban areas. Diplomatic hopes for a renewed cease-fire repeatedly have been disappointed.

The international community has deplored Unita's resort to war and called on all parties to continue negotiations, finally imposing a mandatory arms and oil embargo against Unita. However, the slow international response has lacked urgency and failed to bring effective pressures to bear to restore peace. Despite what Anstee called "a conspiracy of silence by the international media," it is urgent to mobilize support for active implementation of effective policies.[15]

Premises

Any lasting solution to the conflict in Angola must build on the May 1991 Peace Accord and the legitimacy of the elections carried out under its terms in September 1992. Whatever adjustments may be necessary to achieve future settlements, they must be designed to reinforce the trust that millions of Angolans put in these guarantees of peace and democracy, rather than to entrench the cynicism aroused by the violation of these agreements by force. Respect for the democratic verdict in Angola is a test case for South Africa, Mozambique, and, indeed, the entire continent, and it is a measure of the credibility of U.S. and UN commitment to democratic initiatives they endorse.

Although no party can escape blame for incidents reinforcing mistrust, primary responsibility for the relapse of Angola into vicious warfare lies with the leadership of Unita, which systematically evaded the Peace Accord's provisions to disarm and demobilize and used its military advantage to reignite war after refusing to accept election results regarded as generally free and fair by international monitors. The UN and the three countries designated as observers (the United States, Russia, and Portugal) failed to expose and react in a timely fashion to these violations of the Peace Accord.

There can be no purely military solution to the conflict. Total military victory by one side or the other is neither possible nor desirable. All parties should resist the tendency toward attitudes of intransigence or ethnic hostility and should take measures to curb human rights abuses by their security forces. Despite repeated frustrations, negotiations must continue.

At the same time, experience to date leads to serious doubts about the good faith of the Unita leadership in negotiations. Without constraints on Unita's military power or other concrete demonstrations of good faith, appeals for talks and new opportunities for talks likely will be empty charades. Unless international resolutions are accompanied by practical efforts to curb Unita's war-making capacity, they will continue to be seen as empty gestures to be ignored in favor of the ebb and flow of the battlefield.

The United States, with South Africa as a principal sponsor over the years of Unita's military capacity, holds a special responsibility to take serious action to restrain its former client, rather than to walk away blaming the destruction it helped foster on the Angolan parties.

Recommendations for U.S. Policy

The U.S. government should take the lead in implementing the mandatory UN embargo on the supply of arms, fuel, and other war-related material to Unita.

The U.S. government should reiterate, at high levels, its warnings to Unita not to attack U.S. and other oil installations in Cabinda and off shore at Soyo. It also should make it clear that it will not recognize the legitimacy of Unita's acquisition of territory by force or recognize any government that might be established on that basis.

The U.S. government should express its willingness to support a greatly expanded UN presence in the case of a renewed settlement.

The U.S. government should continue and expand active support of UN and other efforts to deliver humanitarian aid to Angola. It also should immediately initiate programs of development aid in conjunction with the Angolan government and nongovernmental organizations in those areas of the country where security considerations permit. Plans for both private- and public-sector economic cooperation, through trade and investment, should not be held hostage by the war.

The U.S. government should stress to both parties the urgent imperative for respect for the laws of war, particularly concerning attacks on civilians, kidnapping, summary executions, and lack of respect for humanitarian relief operations.

The U.S. government should recognize that stability in Angola depends on completion of the democratic transitions underway in Zaire and South Africa and urgently address itself to the obstacles threatening those transitions.

NOTES

1. U.S. State Department, Bureau of Intelligence and Research, "Conflict Resolution in Africa: Lessons from Angola," Washington, D.C., April 6, 1993, pp. 1–4.

2. Two well-informed accounts that begin to deal with these issues in more detail are Alex Vines, *One Hand Tied: Angola and the UN* (London: Catholic Institute for International Relations, 1993); Anthony W. Pereira, "The Neglected Tragedy: the Return to War in Angola, 1992–3," *The Journal of Modern African Studies* 32 (1994): 1–28. See also Anthony W. Pereira, "Angola's 1992 Election: A Personal View," *Camões Center Quarterly* , Winter 1993/1994. The report of the International Foundation for Electoral Systems (IFES) observation mission was prepared by Tom Bayer, *Angola: Presidential and Legislative Elections* (Washington, D.C.: International Foundation for Electoral Systems, 1993).

3. For more extensive background, see William Minter, *Apartheid's Contras* (London: Zed Books, 1994).

4. The MacNeil/Lehrer NewsHour, December 1, 1993, transcript No. 4810.

5. *Washington Post*, September 20, 1993.

6.   A typical example is the statement by former U.S. Assistant Secretary of State Chester Crocker, *Washington Post*, October 13, 1993: "Cheating was so commonplace that the military provisions of the 1991 agreements were basically never implemented."

7.   Vines, *One Hand Tied*, pp. 17–18.

8.   *Financial Times*, May 11, 1992.

9.   Vines, *One Hand Tied*, p. 19.

10.   Ibid.

11.   Toward the end of the campaign, official and unofficial observers had very diverse predictions about the election results, and those most familiar with Angola said it was far too close to call. There were different views even among U.S. officials, but the dominant expectation in those circles was for a Savimbi victory.

Two days before Angola's multiparty elections in September 1992 the top U.S. diplomat in the country boasted to Antonio da Costa Fernandes, a former Unita party official, that his old boss, Jonas Savimbi, could not fail to win. Fernandes, who with Savimbi had been a founding member of Unita thirty years before . . . had defected earlier that year to form another party. . . . [He] denounced Savimbi's past human rights record, his current strategy of hiding a 20,000-man army from the United Nations, and his plans to return the country to war if he should fail to win the election. Everyone in the Western intelligence fraternity working on Angola knew Fernandes' information was true, but Washington chose to ignore it and stuck with Savimbi.

Victoria Brittain, "Savimbi, Bloody Savimbi: Angola Betrayed," *The Nation*, July 11, 1994, pp. 50–53.

12.   Transcript of speech, July 17, 1992.

13.   This often is cited as evidence of lack of openness by the Angolan government to power sharing, but most of those who cite it fail to note that this offer came just *after* Savimbi had already resumed the war and that better offers were on the table both before and after.

14.   Reports that the United States was supplying military support to Angola, as it had to Unita in the previous war, were almost certainly disinformation or misunderstandings.

15.   This alternative policy framework was developed by the Washington Office on Africa, in consultation with other groups, in the fall of 1993. It was released in December 1993, after being endorsed by representatives of over thirty U.S. churches and other organizations, including the Africa Faith & Justice Network, African-American Institute, the American Committee on Africa, American Baptist Churches, Association of Concerned Africa Scholars, Bread for the World, Center of Concern, Church of the Brethren, Community Action International Alliance, Episcopal Church, Interfaith/Impact, Disciples of Christ/United Church of Christ, Maryknoll Fathers & Brothers, Maryknoll Sisters, Missionaries of Africa, Mozambique Solidarity Office, the National Association for the Advancement of Colored People, Africa Office of the National Council of Churches, National Rainbow Coalition, Presbyterian Church, Progressive National Baptist Convention, Society of African Missions, Southern Africa Action Network, TransAfrica, United Methodist Church, U.S. Catholic Conference, U.S./South Africa Sister Community, and Women Strike for Peace, as well as a number of groups in other countries.

II

THE POLITICS OF
ECONOMIC REFORMS

4

Labor, Structural Adjustment, and Democracy in Sierra Leone and Ghana

Alfred B. Zack-Williams

Contrary to the impression in sections of the literature on adjustment, Africa's experience of economic adjustment predates the 1980s, the now-recognized decade of structural adjustment programs (SAP) in Africa. In the case of Sierra Leone, this initial contact could be traced back to 1966 when the contradictions in the "postcolonial model" forced the government to take measures to restore macroeconomic stability with a series of stabilization programs supported by standby arrangements with the International Monetary Fund (IMF). Similarly, in the case of Ghana, this relationship goes back to the statist epoch of the Kwame Nkrumah regime, when he was able to utilize loans from the fund while ignoring much of the conditionality in order to overcome the crisis of accumulation that, by then, had beset the Ghanaian economy.[1]

Both countries share a number of socioeconomic and political features in common: accumulation has been financed via monocultural economies and state-derived rent-seeking activities via produce marketing boards and other buying agents; by the late 1970s, not only was the postcolonial model showing signs of crisis of accumulation, but also the very legitimacy of the state was being questioned. A prolonged period of economic decline was accompanied by a series of military interventions leading to the reification of political authoritarianism.

Despite these similarities, there are a number of major differences between these two formations, reflecting not only the development and intensification of the class struggle but also the degree of internal accumulation that the indigenous bourgeoisie has been able to effect. For example, the degree of proletarianization has been relatively low in the case of Sierra Leone, reflecting the dominance of peasant production, as well as tributariness within the diamond industry, one of the major sources of employment outside of agriculture.[2] The net effect of these developments is reflected in the uneven development of working-class organizations. Thus, in Sierra Leone, labor institutions have remained weak for most of the postcolonial period, and nothing resembling either the vibrant Trade Union Congress or the Workers Defence Committees have emerged under the civilian or military regimes.

In what follows I will look at the conditions under which SAPs have been implemented and the impact on labor and the latter's responses and will point to the antidemocratic propulsion in SAPs.[3] The approach will be historical and identify dominant themes within each period.

SIERRA LEONE IN CRISIS

In Sierra Leone, the early postcolonial years were marked by the import-substitution strategy, with an open-door policy designed to attract foreign investors. Government embarked on infrastructural construction and offered tax concessions to would-be investors.[4] For a while, this policy seemed to be paying off, as capital entered the country, destined for the booming mining sector. Between 1950 and 1972, average annual growth rate was 7 percent, one of the highest in the West Africa subregion,[5] but the benefit of this growth was narrowly distributed. The period also was marked by a low rate of inflation. By the early 1970s, the crisis of accumulation had started manifesting itself, as internal and external forces triggered off spiraling inflation and economic decline.[6]

Between 1966 and 1986, in their drive to restore macroeconomic stability, successive governments embarked on a series of stabilization programs supported by standby arrangements with the IMF. Government policies included the "triple zappers": devaluation, liberalization of the economy, and credit squeeze. There are a number of points to be noted about stabilization programs during this period. In 1967, there was the first military intervention in Sierra Leone, and this junta, the National Reformation Council, led by Major Juxon-Smith, lasted for a year. This was a corrective authoritarian regime, determined to put the country on a firm political and economic basis. This regime was able to implement a series of austerity measures accompanied by a clampdown on organized labor in his silent war against lack of discipline.

The National Reformation Council was succeeded by the All People's Congress (APC), which ruled the country for the next 24 years, initially under the leadership of Siaka Stevens and from 1985 to 1992 of his force commander, Joseph Momoh. Stevens formed a coalition government in which other parties were represented. However, Stevens, who was widely acclaimed to have won the disputed elections that impelled military intervention, was aware that one reason for his good showing in the elections was the economic mismanagement of the civilian regime of Albert Margai. As a result, he was cautious about any short-term stabilization measures that might worsen the economic situation. Stevens' action was very similar to that of Nkrumah, who utilized loans from standby agreements but was very reluctant to fully implement the conditionality. He prided his trade-union links and, therefore, was concerned about widespread unemployment that would pitch the unions against the government. Furthermore, after the formal ending of the coalition government, Stevens was worried about opposition from the military (he had to fight off a series of attempted coups) as well as the opposition.

As the 1980s progressed, it soon became clear that the stabilization programs alone were not sufficient to deal with what was increasingly seen as a long-term problem. With this in mind, the government of Sierra Leone concluded two SAPs between 1981 and 1985. The agreement was canceled by the IMF in the first case before the first tranche was drawn and in the second case after the first tranche. The cancellation was partly because of the unwillingness of the government to go whole hog with the IMF's conditionality and partly because of the government's inability to keep up payments of arrears. As we have seen, Stevens always was mindful about the potential for social upheaval stemming from full implementation.

In 1985, Stevens announced to the country his intention to resign, and the following year, he handed power over to his force commander, Major-General Joseph Momoh. The new president decided to distance himself from the excesses of Stevens by announcing a new order regime, which was less hostile to the IMF and World Bank and by showing a greater determination to work fully with these institutions. A year's standby arrangement was made with the IMF in 1986; however, by the following year, the IMF suspended the agreement because of the government's failure to adhere to the conditionality. The country was declared ineligible for further credit, and in March 1987, the government embarked on a "shadow" program, whereby the conditionality was gradually implemented but without the loans to ameliorate the negative effects of SAP.

By early 1990, the labor force in the public sector had been reduced significantly to the point at which the wage bill of the civil service was reduced by 40 percent. These policies caused widespread unemployment and poverty and increased the numbers of those Sierra Leoneans who had to depend on the informal sector for their survival. This structured impoverishment provoked strikes from public workers, especially teachers. The rebel incursion in the south of the country provided the pretext for further clamping down on all forms of opposition. Soon, there were demands for a multiparty political system and an end to what was seen as "dictatorship of the party." The clamor for democracy started with university students who, through a series of seminars, argued that a return to democracy was sine qua non for economic regeneration. The government's initial response was to draw attention to the fact that any demand for political pluralism was a criminal offense, because the congress was the only legitimate political party in the land. Political stalwarts were dispatched to the provinces to spread the message. However, in opposition strongholds such as the southern province, these party cadres met strong opposition, which resorted to intimidation and political thuggery.

After much agitation, which included a series of strikes led by students and schoolteachers and pressure from donor agencies, the government set a commission of inquiry to advise on the desirability of returning the country to multiparty democracy. The Tucker Commission recommended that the country be returned to multiparty democracy. A number of political parties were registered, and a small number of newspapers were legalized. The government promised to hold fresh elections once the electoral register was updated. The congress hoped to play on the weakness of a fragmented opposition. It claimed that it was the only party that could save the country from ethnic cleavage. The leadership still believed it could win through manipulating voting figures.

However, before this plan could be hatched, in April 1992, junior officers of the armed forces struck to remove the regime of Momoh, whom they described as corrupt, and a government that had heaped misery upon the mass of the Sierra Leonean people. These officers set up the National Provisional Revolutionary Council, with Captain Valentine Strasser as its leader. He sought to establish a populist agenda and an image as a revolutionary and the "redeemer" of the nation. His immediate tasks included ending the rebel war, ridding the country of corruption, and putting the economy right.

The National Provisional Revolutionary Council struck an accord with the International Financial Institutions (IFIs) whereby the former decided to implement a number of economic recovery and reform programs to which the defunct APC administration had agreed but had gradually implemented without loan support from the IMF. The accord with the IMF and World Bank heralded a flow of capital into the country, with aid coming from the African Development Bank, European Union, and the International Labor Organization. Central to this program is SAP, which was based on the Policy Framework Paper 1990/91–1992/93, approved by both the IMF and the World Bank in August 1990, the aims being to create macroeconomic stability, particularly, lowering inflation to facilitate sustainable growth; to restore government's capacity to provide basic services; to create the conducive economic institutional and regulatory environment for private sector development; and to bring social problems and poverty issues to the forefront of national policy agenda, incorporating concrete actions to address directly the impact of SAP on vulnerable social groups and poverty.[7]

This was quickly followed by a Rights Accumulation Programme by the board of the IMF in April 1992 and a disbursing of a Reconstruction Import Credit (RIC) of U.S.$43.4 million with the World Bank. These agreements signaled the rehabilitation of the country's credit worthiness as loans resumed disbursement from other donors that had withdrawn their support to the country in 1987 because of accumulation of arrears in debt payment. This was followed by the preparation of a rolling three-year public investment program. This points to how multilateral institutions such as the World Bank and IMF can take over the bureaucracy of a weak Third World country and restructure its organization to suit the policies of these institutions.[8]

This main focus of the Reconstruction Import Credit was fiscal management, including streamlining the civil service and public enterprise management reform, that is, privatization of viable concerns and the liquidation of nonviable ones. The program also sought to enhance revenue collection and provide for the supply of much-needed petroleum products. This meant an end to petroleum queues and a return of electrical power to the country's capital. However, privatization simply led to a tighter hold on the economy by the minority Lebanese commercial class, who alone had the capital to buy former state enterprises.

Nonetheless, the availability of these essential commodities bolstered the popularity of the regime, and Sierra Leoneans were quick to contrast the effects of the policies of the young officers with those of Momoh and the APC. They failed to realize that these were desensitizing sweeteners for the tough policies ahead. Thus, by July 1993, subsidies had been removed from a number of essential commodities as market forces were being allowed free reign. Also, more than 30,000 daily-wage workers had been laid off, mainly by the public works department, which, by then, had become "privatized." Indeed, in their callous way, the "new-right" bureaucrats blamed the daily-wage workers for the inefficiency of the service, and the effect on their salaries smacked of a class project. These helpless workers had to carry the can for the bad policies of successive administrations in Sierra Leone. As if losing their jobs was not bad enough, many of these workers did not receive their terminal benefits for months after they had been laid off. Similarly, for those who were destined for retraining, by late August 1993, the infrastructure for such training through the Social Action for Poverty Alleviation was not in place.

GHANA AND THE INTERNATIONAL
MONETARY FUND AND WORLD BANK
STRUCTURAL ADJUSTMENT PROGRAMS

By the mid-1960s, the Ghanaian economy had begun showing signs of major structural weakness. This was triggered by the policies of state-sponsored rapid industrialization after 1960, when Nkrumah embarked upon a policy of consolidating the state sector. The huge expenditure that this demanded was not accompanied by a similar increase in government expenditure. Indeed, the period between 1960 and 1966 was marked by a gradual worsening of the terms of trade of the country's major export item, cocoa, which accounted for 68 percent of total value export earnings by 1955.[9] This meant that funds for the development efforts had to come from the country's foreign reserves as foreign investment gradually dried up. This is shown by the fact that, the ratio of net reserves to gross domestic product fell from 35.3 percent in 1955 to –1.8 percent in 1966.[10]

In order to arrest the trend toward economic decline, the Nkrumah government tried to diversify the country's trading partners to reduce dependence on Western capitalist economies, embark on bilateral barter trade pacts with socialist countries, and impose import licensing and foreign exchange policies; to check the decline in the economy, the government had to abandon the policy of nonintervention. The net effect of these policies was that a significant proportion of the commercial and manufacturing sectors were brought under state control. Furthermore, by mid-1965, Ghana's trade with the rest of the world had shown a marked diversification; trade with the then-socialist countries accounted for 26 percent of imports and 21 percent of exports,[11] as compared with 5 percent in 1957.[12]

THE CONVENTION PEOPLE'S PARTY
AND THE INTERNATIONAL MONETARY
FUND: SEEKING A MODUS VIVENDI

By 1962, the structural weakness of the economy, such as "a fragile external sector, heavy debts, a delicate fiscal structure, an export sector,"[13] impelled the government to conclude a standby agreement with the IMF for U.S.$14.25 million to overcome the balance of payment problems. One feature of this early encounter between the Convention People's Party (CPP) government of Nkrumah and the IMF, was the former's reluctance to abandon its socialist policies in favor of the IMF's conditionality. This resistance led to growing tension between the government of the CPP and the fund, and by the mid-1960s, Ghana had been declared ineligible for Western sources of credit. This, together with a further slump in the price of cocoa, led to more economic difficulties and the coup that overthrew the government of Nkrumah.

His refusal to implement the conditionality was based on his perception of the role of the state in a dependent capitalist economy. To implement the conditionality, he argued, would lead to the abandonment of certain development efforts beneficial to the mass of the people, which private capital would be unwilling to undertake. He was mindful of the weak position of the domestic capital vis-à-vis metropolitan capital. He felt that, without state intervention, the accumulation that was needed to modernize the infrastructure would be lost, thus, binding Ghana even more strongly to the apron strings of imperialism. Finally, not only was there the need to protect "the socialist gain," but he also was mindful of unleashing hostile social forces through widespread unemployment. Nkrumah himself had, by the mid-1960s, survived a number of assassination attempts.

THE NATIONAL LIBERATION COUNCIL
ACCOMMODATION WITH THE FUND: 1966–69

The military junta (National Liberation Council — NLC) that succeeded Nkrumah sought accommodation with the IMF by repudiating the CPP's policy of state intervention. The regime reached an accord with the fund, and under the rehabilitation program, Ghana received a standby credit of U.S.$36.4 million, as well as a further four year standby credit of U.S.$78.4 million. These credits were accompanied by full implementation of the usual conditionalities. This period was characterized by confrontation between the state and organized labor. The austerity that followed in the wake of the conditionality undermined further the living conditions of working people as measures were taken that seriously impacted on labor. This included the retrenchment of some 60,000 workers from the state sector within one year "and as the austerity hit the private sector, unemployment spread to this sector. These policies provoked widespread industrial unrest as workers embarked on a series of strikes which were among the most violent in the recent labor history."[14]

BUSIA'S PROGRESSIVE PARTY AND THE
INTERNATIONAL MONETARY FUND: 1969–72

The civilian regime that succeeded the NLC continued the policy of promoting private inward investment but regarded most of the stabilization efforts of the NLC as having had an excessively contradictory effect on the economy that must be reversed.[15] "This points to the difficulty elected civilian regimes face in trying to implement SAP. In order to ensure compliance with Fund and Bank policies, it was necessary to place a network of representatives from the Fund and Bank in the Ministry of Finance and Cabinet Secretariat."[16]

The economy under Busia stagnated with worsening balance of payment and a debt burden rising to $65.1 million by June 1971. The authorities were worried by this growing indebtedness, which they had identified as part of the main problems of the economy under Nkrumah. An attempt was made to secure a long-term concessionary loan of $360 million in order to pay off the short-term debt that, by then, stood at $100 million. This meant that the government had to resort to the IMF for assistance. Indeed, "the decision to devalue became the highlight of the economic experience of the Busia period, and was reported to have brought down the Government."[17]

The indecisive nature of the Busia period points again to the problem of democratically elected governments finding the political will to make the unpopular decisions necessary to put the economy right. As J. H. Frimpong-Ansah put it: "The lesson from this experience was that . . . Ghana needed a leader who was sufficiently courageous politically to take unpopular but appropriate measures and enforce them."[18]

ACHEAMPONG AND THE SMC I: 1972–78

The regime that overthrew the government of Busia started off with a strong but brief defiance against any cooperation with the IMF, including a reversal of the devaluation decision of the previous administration, and the reimposition of restrictive trade policy. Acheampong saw himself as the bearer of the Nkrumahist mantle, with widespread state intervention and state ownership of mines and timber concessions. This period has been described as "the most militant expression of economic nationalism."[19] Despite these outbursts of economic nationalism, foreign creditors were quite accommodating as the regime obtained what K. Jonah has called the best debt rescheduling terms the country had ever received.

After an initial period of economic growth, the economy took a turn for the worse as inflation grew because of the decline in export earnings and the rise in the price of petroleum products. Meanwhile, pressure grew for the administration to reach a compromise with the creditors in order to facilitate the importation of consumer goods that were becoming scarce. Negotiation was started with the creditors in Rome, and in 1973, an accord was reached, though this did not trigger increased inflow of capital. Even the subsequent rise in cocoa prices did not prevent the imposition of an austerity program, which was contrary to the original stance of the regime. The inflation, corruption (Karabule), and declining standard of living of the mass of the Ghanaian people triggered nationwide strikes by workers and agitations by students and other professional bodies, led by the Association of Recognized Professional Bodies, People's Movement for Freedom and Justice, and the Front for the Prevention of Dictatorship.

Acheampong was removed by junior officers and replaced by General Akuffo, whose strong adherence to the austerity of adjustment provoked widespread urban unrest. The fact that only the head of state was replaced points to the fact "that no major political ideological differences were involved."[20] The new stabilization program involved a year's standby credit for SDR53.0 million. This was followed by the usual conditionalities. In order to see the reforms through, a state of emergency was declared, signaling to workers that the regime was not going to tolerate any "subversive" actions. The hostility to adjustment was so intense that the day a team from the IMF arrived in Accra for talks with members of the regime was the day that junior officers struck to remove what was seen as a pro-IMF regime, after only the first tranche had been drawn. These officers formed the interim government, the Armed Forces Revolutionary Council, which ruled for four months until power was handed over to Limann's Peoples' National Party (PNP).

THE PEOPLES' NATIONAL PARTY: CAUTION AND NONCOMPLIANCE

Once the civilian regime assumed power, pressure increased for Ghana to comply with the conditionality of the IFIs, especially because the IFIs had invested over $208 million in the country since 1975. Furthermore, there were serious shortages of essential commodities and spare parts. The government remained resilient in its effort to hold out against SAP, and in 1980, the World Bank closed down its Accra office and ceased all lending activities in the country. Limann was concerned about unleashing social chaos. He had seen the unrest triggered by the conditionality in the late Acheampong and Akuffo regimes. He argued that devaluation had failed in the past, that cocoa was not responsive to devaluation, and that labor retrenchment would not help reduce government spending. The shadow of Jerry J. Rawlings the avenger deterred Limann from implementing the conditionality.[21]

THE PROVISIONAL NATIONAL DEFENCE COUNCIL

In the midst of this indecisiveness, the expulsion of more than a million Ghanaians from Nigeria, famine, and a bushfire that destroyed crops, junior officers struck once more to remove Limann to mark the second coming of Rawlings. This time, Rawlings and the Provisional National Defence Council (PNDC) seemed to have a long-term project. The bureaucracy that the PNDC inherited was quite an expansive one following the nationalization of Acheampong. Between 1982 and 1983, through its defense committees, the PNDC sought to mobilize workers. This period marked the triumph of the left wing of the PNDC over its right wing, as factory occupation and strikes spread.[22] Organized labor and the PNDC worked closely to challenge "reactionary and anti-socialist" elements within society. Once the reactionary elements had been coerced and it became clear that funds were not coming from the socialist block or the Libyan Jamariya, it was time to subdue radical elements within the left, thus, removing the main opposition to SAP.

In 1983, the PNDC used the budget speech to announce its intention to implement the IMF's Economic Recovery Programme (ERP). Toye argued that this volte-face was not induced by the IFIs but emerged from conflict within the PNDC. The first ERP, which lasted from 1984 to 1986, was designed to control inflation, increase output, increase international creditworthiness, and rehabilitate the country's infrastructure using both internal and external sources. The second ERP continued the theme of improving the balance of payment while increasing savings and investments.

During the two ERPs, Ghana received an additional $1 billion, 60 percent of which was provided by the IMF.[23] The implementation of the conditionality created widespread misery as retrenchment continued in the public sector and the accompanying austerity measures created unemployment in the private sector. The alternative unions that had emerged from the "anti-imperialist" struggles of the 1979–83 period now were locked in battle not only with the more established unions but also with the PNDC, who denounced them as reactionary. In 1984, the government moved from denunciation to reorganization, renaming the defense committees and bringing them under more centralized political control.

In direct response to the demand for adjustment with a human face, the government set up the Programme of Actions to Mitigate the Social Costs of Adjustment in 1987 to help such vulnerable groups as low income, unemployed, and underemployed urban households and retrenched workers to cope with "adjustment fatigue."

CONCLUSION

First, we can see tension between the demand for democratic politics and the antidemocratic milieu that favors full implementation of SAPS. The recent history of both countries shows that the regimes best suited to implement SAPs are military or authoritarian regimes that do not have to seek election or need to seek consensus but can easily resort to the oppressive state apparatus. In a situation in which organized opposition can exploit disenchantment with SAP, civilian regimes always will show reluctance to adjust if this is going to threaten their very existence. Second, it also is seen that fragile states (overladen with crisis) like Ghana and Sierra Leone easily can submit themselves to the wishes of the multilateral agencies and that their bureaucracies can be easily hijacked. Third, the stronger reaction of Ghanaian workers to structural adjustment is a clear reflection of the relatively high level of industrialization and proletarianization of the peasant producers. Finally, it is shown that organized labor in Ghana was more independent than their Sierra Leonean counterpart. This reflects the relatively high levels of clientism and corporatism that characterized APC rule. Stevens, like Momoh after him, incorporated labor leaders into the power structure of the APC; even so, full implementation of SAPs was not feasible.

NOTES

1.   E. Hansen and K. A. Ninsin, eds., *The State Development and Politics in Ghana* (Dakar: Codesria, 1989).

2.   A. B. Zack-Williams, *Tributors, Supporters and Merchant Capital In Sierra Leone: Mining and Underdevelopment in Sierra Leone* (Aldershot: Gower-Avebury Press, 1995).

3.   For a similar conclusion, see M. Mamdani, "A Critical Analysis of the IMF in Uganda," in *African Perspectives On Development*, eds. U. Himmelstrand, Karibu Kinyanjui, and Edward Mburugu (United Kingdom: James Currey, 1994), pp. 128–36.

4.   For a detailed discussion of the nature of this sector, see A. B. Zack-Williams, "Some Comments on the Manufacturing Sector in Sierra Leone," *Africa Development* 10 (1985): 128–36.

5.   A. B. Zack-Williams, "Sierra Leone: Crisis and Despair," *Review of African Political Economy* 49 (Winter 1990): 22–33.

6.   J. Weeks, *Development Strategy and the Economy of Sierra Leone* (London: Macmillan, 1992). Also, for full discussion of the etiology of the crisis, see Zack-Williams, "Sierra Leone"; A. B. Zack-Williams, "Sierra Leone: The Deepening Crisis and Survival Strategies," in *Beyond Structural Adjustment in Africa: The Political Economy of Sustainable and Democratic Government*, eds. J. E. Nyang'oro and T. M. Shaw (Westport, Conn.: Praeger, 1992).

7.   United Nations Development Program, "Development Co-Operation in Sierra Leone, 1992 Report," July 1993.

8.   This also is emphasized in the case of Ghana in K. Jonah, "Changing Relations Between IMF and the Government of Ghana," in *The State Development and Politics in Ghana*, eds. E. Hansen and K. A. Ninsin (Dakar: Codesria, 1989).

9.   J. H. Frimpong-Ansah, *The Vampire State in Africa: The Political Economy of Decline in Ghana* (United Kingdom: James Currey, 1991), p. 84.

10.   Ibid., p. 94.

11. E. Hutchful, *The IMF and Ghana: The Confidential Record* (London: Zed Press, 1987), p. 38.

12. Jonah, "Changing Relations," p. 97.

13. Frimpong-Ansah, *The Vampire State*, p. 97.

14. K. A. Ninsin, "State, Capital & Labour Relations," in *The State Development and Politics in Ghana*, eds. E. Hansen and K. A. Ninsin (Dakar: Codesria, 1989), pp. 15–42.

15. Frimpong-Ansah, *The Vampire State*, p. 97.

16. Jonah, "Changing Relations."

17. Ibid.

18. Frimpong-Ansah, *The Vampire State*, p. 103.

19. Jonah, "Changing Relations," p. 183

20. Ibid.

21. J. Toye, "Ghana," in *Aid and Power: The World Bank and Policy-Based Lending*, vol. 2, *Case Studies*, eds. P. Mosley, J. Harringan, and J. Toye (New York: Routledge, 1991).

22. Kwame Ninsin, an interview, Legon, September 1993.

23. Ibid., p. 16.

5

Privatization in a Transitional Society: A Kenyan Case Study

Rukhsana A. Siddiqui

This chapter addresses two issues: what are the constraints of privatization in Kenya and what are its effects, if any, in this country. The relationship between the two also is brought out wherever necessary.

In most developed and developing countries, state ownership of enterprises expanded rapidly in the 40 years following World War II. Most public enterprises (PEs) were created in response to a variety of economic and political problems. Most of the countries wanted to provide services that the private sector was either unwilling or unable to offer. In the developing countries over the years, PEs became not only instruments of channeling investment flows, supplying adequate social and economic infrastructure, pursuing development programs, and redistributing income but also a means for politicians to create independent bases of power by rewarding supporters through job allocation and investment.

As late as the 1960s, few questioned the central role of the state in affecting income transfers and promoting social objectives. It was during the 1970s and 1980s that the role of the state-owned enterprises came under scrutiny because of widespread mismanagement, deficits, and political abuse.

Strong arguments were made in favor of privatization, claiming that it would improve economic performance and economic growth. During the Reagan and Thatcher administrations, privatization became the main slogan. This became evident not only in the economic policy of the industrialized countries but also in developing countries like the Philippines, Venezuela, Brazil, Turkey, Kenya, and Pakistan. This trend toward privatization has not been without controversy. Although some of them debated in favor of the pragmatic concerns of the private sector, others were concerned with its efficiency and effectiveness.[1]

Much of the above debate was not without ideological overtones. Many argued that development can best be achieved through freeing up markets and letting the impersonal forces of supply do their work or that "developing countries that relied on market forces experienced much more rapid growth than planned economies."[2] Success stories of the "Asian Tigers" — Japan, Taiwan, Hong Kong, Singapore — were cited as paragons of development through private enterprise while being juxtaposed with cases of failures of centralized planning, like Tanzania and India. Furthermore, the former Soviet Union and China, who previously were ideologically disposed against free enterprise, today endorse privatization, which gave a certain credibility to this trend.

Critics of this trend argued against the reliance on the free market as an avenue for development. They claimed that, in low-income countries, markets deviate substantially from the basic assumptions of a competitive environment and, therefore, this environment is unsuitable to the needs of lesser developed economies. Less developed economies cannot afford to risk their limited resources on unsuccessful ventures or "trends" or waste them on luxury goods.[3] Such criticisms also made a case for a detailed national development plan as an important prerequisite for obtaining foreign assistance and also a factor that could influence the bringing together of diverse and fragmented populations in developing countries.

The question still remains, is privatization the answer to development. The purpose of this chapter is to examine privatization in the case of one developing country — Kenya.

METHODOLOGY

This study takes as its framework Luigi Manzetti's model of privatization that he uses in the study of Latin America.[4] According to Manzetti, privatization can be seen as policy substitution, which, under the conditions of willingness and opportunity, can lead to policy implementation. It is under these three categories that he analyzes the role of privatization in Argentina. He hopes that the findings presented in his research can be applicable to other developing countries facing similar challenges. This chapter attempts precisely to evaluate such a possibility.

PRIVATIZATION AS POLICY SUBSTITUTION

Privatization as a policy alternative can be conceived as a substitute for previous public policies that policymakers no longer consider viable.[5] In developing countries, the concept of "substitutability" can be useful in understanding the adoption of drastic policy departures, like privatization, as contrasted with previous policies like economic protectionism and import substitution industrialization (ISI). In most developing countries, policymakers turned to ISI as a means to promote self-sufficiency and steady employment levels as necessary conditions for political stability. In the 1980s, many developing countries, particularly in Africa, experienced large foreign debts and fiscal deficits, high inflation and unemployment rates, unstable terms of trade with industrialized nations, and sluggish growth. Many African countries responded to this in the late 1980s by substituting ISI and state interventionism with free market economics and state divestiture of PEs.

OPPORTUNITY AND WILLINGNESS

The conditions that shape and determine the likelihood that a decision maker will substitute state interventionism with privatization policies are shaped by two related events: willingness and opportunity.[6] Manzetti focuses his attention at a microlevel — on the decision of a country's top policymaker, that is, the president, to privatize. In Africa, this is particularly relevant because the executive branch enjoys much greater de facto powers than the legislature and the judiciary. "The decision maker's willingness is influenced by the perceived margin of advantage, that is the degree to which the expected results of privatization are preferred to available advantages. Willingness to privatize can come mainly from two types of calculations: ideological and pragmatic" (Table 5.1).[7]

Several factors that are most common to induce a decision maker to decide in favor of privatizing rest on pragmatic grounds; these include the need to reduce the fiscal deficits under which many African countries operate. Transferring state operations to private companies can make an important contribution to balancing the budget. Sales bring money into the government's coffers, and by the same token, privatized companies will no longer burden the state with deficits.[8] Another most crucial pragmatic factor triggering privatization is that international lending agencies and foreign governments have made it a precondition in order to receive loans and discounts on the foreign debts. Privatization has, in this sense, become a chief source of attracting foreign capital by showing an improvement in state-business relations. However, according to Manzetti, willingness is only one requisite; opportunity must accompany it. For instance, governments often want to dispose of deficit-ridden

TABLE 5.1
Decision to Privatize and Implementation

STAGE I: DECISION TO PRIVATIZE
Ideology   1.   Affinity with leader's goals and ideological standing
                      2.   Free market economics regarded as superior to state
                           intervention
                      3.   Emasculation of labor power
WILLINGNESS
                      1.   Deficit reduction
                      2.   Improvement of business climate
Pragmatism   3.   Rationalization of state operations
                      4.   Improvement of economic efficiency
                      5.   Support of foreign banks and governments
                      6.   Positive result of past experience
                      7.   Lack of alternatives
OPPORTUNITY   1.   Availability of tenders
                      2.   Favorable public mood

STAGE II: IMPLEMENTATION

                           GOVERNMENT CAPABILITIES
                           1.   Government cohesiveness
                           2.   Central financial control mechanisms
                           3.   Bureaucratic management cooperation
                           4.   Control of legislative agenda

                           POLITICAL RESPONSES (opposition)
                           1.   Civil servants and PEs employees
                           2.   Labor unions
PRIVATIZATION REFORM   3.   PEs suppliers
IMPLEMENTATION   4.   Military
                           5.   Lack of political support

                           TECHNICAL DIFFICULTIES
                           1.   Market failure
                           2.   Inadequate financial markets
                           3.   Difficulty in valuation of assets
                           4.   Lack of deregulation mechanisms

Source: Luigi Manzetti, "The Political Economy of Privatization through Divestiture in Less Developed Economies," *Comparative Politics* (July 1993): 429–54. Reprinted with permission of *Comparative Politics*.

enterprises but cannot find buyers or encounter strong public opposition. A favorable public mood and availability of buyers, thus, become opportunities in this respect. Whereas opportunity represents macrolevel (environmental and structural) factors, willingness represents the choice processes that occur on the microlevel, that is, the selection of a behavioral option from a range of alternatives.[9] Thus, opportunity and willingness enable us to discern a decision maker's policy priorities and the environmental factors that circumscribe these priorities.

POLICY IMPLEMENTATION

Although willingness and opportunity are essential in identifying the conditions leading to policy substitution, they may not suffice to successfully implement a privatization scheme. Past experiences indicate the probability that a privatization program may be abandoned or seriously diluted in midcourse because of lack of governmental capabilities or interest group's lobbying.[10]

KENYAN PRIVATIZATION: A CASE STUDY

Privatization in the African context, as elsewhere, can be thought of as a substitute for previous public policies that policymakers no longer consider viable. In the case of Kenya, it can be argued that the failure of ISI as a main economic policy led the government to abandon it (and replace it with a new one).

From the 1960s to mid-1970s the Kenyan government supported industrialization through import substitution on the assumptions that ISI would provide employment facilities, bring in needed skills and technology, and create a process of domestic-capital formation necessary for long-term industrialization.

In 1972, an International Labor Organization (ILO) mission report found that Kenya's economic growth manifested great imbalances that led to unemployment and poverty, slow growth of employment opportunities in the industrial sector, deteriorating terms of trade, and an absence of a general policy.[11]

Parallel to growing unemployment and poverty, then, could be witnessed the emergence of a small elite in both manufacturing and agricultural sectors. Land ownership became more concentrated, and those who had high incomes, either as state functionaries or as employees of multinationals, did not use their income for investment in private enterprise. Instead, many of them engaged in conspicuous consumption — a behavior quite familiar to the nouveau riche. Consequently, domestic capital formation through saving failed to occur, because those with large incomes also tended to be wasteful spenders. This nonproductive expenditure also could be attributed to the state.[12]

As expected in such a situation, an economic crisis soon hit the country. Also, in 1973, as the oil crisis hit the capitalist world, Kenya's balance of payments situation sharply deteriorated. The international terms of trade for all commodities shifted decidedly away from Kenya, from 120 in 1977

(1973 = 100) to 66 in 1981.[13] For example, the oil bill increased so much that 40 percent of Kenya's export earning — equivalent to the value of the country's coffee and tea exports — went to pay for oil. The balance of payments current account deficit tripled between 1973 and 1977.[14] In order to deal with this situation, the government resorted to more external borrowing, thereby worsening the economic situation through debt-reservicing expenses. According to one estimate, whereas external debt servicing accounted for a relatively low 3 percent of exports throughout most of the Kenyatta period, the proportion reached 10 percent by 1981.[15]

The crisis was just beginning to have its toll when Daniel Arap Moi took over the presidency from Kenyatta.

A new regime was in power. And following the character of "pacts of domination" that have typified such regimes in Africa, real social crises are interpreted as being conspiracies by certain individuals to destabilize the regime, or as the result of these individuals within the pact not being as loyal to the president as would be expected. The policies of the regime are not put to question, what is questionable is the sincerity and loyalty of the individuals who apply them. Thus the disease exists but the proper cure is not prescribed because no proper diagnosis has been made.[16]

According to some researchers, ISI in Kenya led to the artificial differentiation of products and distortion of domestic demands, the undermining of local firms, and the penalization of agriculture.[17] Uncontrolled importation of machinery and different types of equipment under ISI agreements limited the domestic value-added. Local industrialization also was discouraged by the huge numbers of different types of vehicles locally assembled or imported into Kenya. Government shareholding in multinational subsidiaries led to very little state control of multinational corporation (MNC) activities; if anything, it weakened the state by compromising it with the fortunes and misfortunes of MNCs.

Another adverse effect of ISI was the extent to which such industries penalized agriculture.[18] The problem involved making the agricultural sector depend on high-cost inputs produced by import substitution (IS) industries while producer prices of agricultural commodities were kept down artificially by the state in the interest of urban dwellers. Simultaneously, rural dwellers who relied on incomes from the sale of agricultural commodities were faced with deteriorating terms of trade between agriculture and industry, thereby enduring the declining standards of living. "The poverty of the rural masses is thus explained by the profit havens that the IS industries carved out for themselves in LDC's."[19]

According to some observers, IS industries significantly contributed to the economic crisis in Kenya by not providing the employment opportunities that were expected from them, not only because they were capital intensive but also because they expanded very slowly, served a very small market, and had very little linkage with the domestic economy.

One study argues that IS industries did not transfer technology to the Kenyan economy in any significant way and that technical skills could not be transferred because Kenyans usually did not occupy administrative positions in MNC subsidiaries even if they had technical qualifications. Because major decisions were made by MNC headquarters, the personnel are trained to apply already-made decisions rather than to initiate, experiment, and operationalize their field decisions.[20]

It is in the aftermath of the above that the Kenyan government published the 1980 sessional paper that was, in reality, a mid-plan revision of its earlier development strategy.[21] The paper, in so many words, sent a signal to international donors asserting that:

Kenya continues to receive substantial support from the World Bank, the International Monetary Fund and various bilateral agencies in the forms of grants and loans on concessional terms to assist Government in the efforts it is making to cope with unfavorable developments in world markets. Such assistance provides the time and resources necessary to permit an orderly adjustment of the Kenyan economy to the changing international environment. It is the intention of Government to continue its co-operation with those international agencies that are helping to ensure the success of the efforts being made to achieve financial stability and to maintain Kenya's reputation for credit-worthiness.[22]

The sessional paper of 1980 explicitly recognized the limits to further import substitution in the country. "Highly dependent upon imported raw materials, intermediates and capital goods, the domestic import substitution sector was seen as too often a drag on domestic efficiency and foreign exchange resources."[23]

In the 1982 sessional paper, a further list of policy reforms were articulated in the areas of agriculture, energy, balance of payments, monetary and fiscal policies, government operations and budgeting, and foreign aid.

Furthermore, the World Bank criticized African countries that had tried ISI for overconcentration on production for the local market rather than production for export. In 1981, a World Bank report asserted that, for the countries that had nearly completed the first stages of import substitution, such as Kenya, the Ivory Coast, and Tanzania, few import substitution opportunities existed based on internal markets. It advised countries like Kenya, among other things, to engage in more processing of raw materials for export so that they can gain more local value-added before export and engage in production for export by first making African manufactured goods price competitive in the international market; to achieve this, local production costs have to be lowered through currency devaluation and less protective wage policies.[24]

In the mid-1980s, the World Bank made increased import liberalization and reduced price control a condition for continued funding for Kenya. Although, for many products, import liberalization was considered appropriate, caution was required not to flood the market with imports and, thus, stifle local production. The World Bank advocated a shift toward export promotion and away from substitution. Some other general political and economic recommendations by the International Monetary Fund and the World Bank to Kenya included decontrols, devaluations, and other stabilization measures.

KENYAN GOVERNMENT'S POLICY SUBSTITUTION: WILLINGNESS AND OPPORTUNITY

Kenyan experience with the structural adjustment programs (SAPs) launched by the World Bank began in 1980. In assessing Kenya's compliance with the conditionality of SAPs, it is argued by some that the country performed best on policy parameters subject to change by decree, for example, interest rates, exchange rates, and ceilings on price and wage increases. However, Kenya was less successful with those terms and conditions that required institutional changes. Thus, whereas variables like exchange and interest rates could be altered at a stroke of a pen or a government decree this was not true in the realm of institutional changes that required management of external debt, control of public expenditure, promotion of exports, implementation of population programs — areas that required agreement and implementation by agencies within the government. Friction arose between officials who believed in complying with SAP conditionality and those who advocated domestic self-sufficiency.

Although it became evident in the 1980s that SAPs had been embraced as official government policy in Kenya and that specific commitments were made to their implementation through policy change, there was a clear dichotomy between those who favored SAPs and those who opposed them. The former included government officials interested in maintaining access to donor assistance flows (even at the cost of being forced to make far-reaching structural reforms), small and new producers in agriculture and industry (who expected to accrue rewards from efficiency-based foreign and domestic sales), and the poor rural masses (dependent upon stronger national growth promoting higher levels of income and employment). In the latter group were included those government officials who were opposed to an open economy approach to Kenya and were concerned that SAPs would disrupt social and political balances and commercial and industrial groups whose interests had been protected for a long time in a closed economy.[25]

POLICY IMPLEMENTATION:
WILLINGNESS AND OPPORTUNITY

As mentioned above, the policy substitution from ISI to liberalize the economy through SAPs faced a dichotomous situation. For the most part, success in implementation of policy was confined to "decrees." Other areas of SAP conditionality requiring extensive administrative implementation were not met adequately or in time.

The varied experience with compliance is evident when areas of conditionality are compared with policy changes actually implemented. Walter Hecox uses such a comparison to emphasize the very broad array of policies that were supposed to be changed in such areas as trade and industry; agricultural compliance; public expenditure reforms; policies for energy pricing, substitution, and observation; population control; external debt management; and domestic resource mobilization.[26]

Although, in 1983, Kenya succeeded in starting a multiyear set of tariff reductions in the fiscal budget, attempts to free imports from administrative delays and controls were hampered by shortages of foreign exchange and lingering opposition by powerful groups to a dismantling of administrative rationing. Lack of commitment and administrative inertia impeded strategies aiming toward higher efficiency and lower protection. Absence of concrete action to make policy reforms effectively delayed export-promotion policies.

Government implementation of planning, budgeting, and project administration in agriculture was easier. With considerable technical assistance, the Ministry of Agriculture and Livestock succeeded in introducing some major reforms. Little progress, however, was made in determining effective ways to grant individual land titles for cooperative and group-owned farms that had been subdivided. The 1984 drought in Kenya made the grain marketing reform a problem area for the government and delayed many promised reforms.

Policies for energy substitution, observation, and pricing were pursued adequately, though an investment plan for energy substitution and conservation was proposed but not implemented. With regard to population control, Kenya's progress vis-à-vis its extremely high growth rate was slow in implementing programs intended to meet specific targets. Public expenditure reforms also were implemented very slowly and, in some cases, failed to meet the targets of conditionalities as laid down in SAPs because of adverse revenue conditions during the period, lack of adequate expertise to implement the reforms, and opposition by bureaucrats and officials to tight controls.

STRUCTURAL ADJUSTMENT PROGRAMS
AND KENYAN PRIVATIZATION

The 1980s were rife with the paradox in the relations between Kenya and the World Bank. At the level of policy statements, the approach of both parties seemed to be harmonious, that is, a consensus on an approach toward the removal of long-term constraints to growth. However, the actual implementation of policy was another matter.

The World Bank in the early 1980s was venturing into "policy based lending" to Kenya. This was to be accomplished on "sectoral basis." Among many other sectors were included conditions related to budgetary control and the monitoring of external borrowing. It has been argued that the SAPs sharpened incentives to the industrial sector (which accounted for less than a quarter of Kenyan gross domestic product in 1979), which was not an accurate assessment of priorities for dealing with the growth and balance of payment problems of an agricultural country.[27]

However, in the course of time, it became apparent that the Kenyan economic crisis was to be more protracted than expected. The Working Party on Government Expenditure (WPGE), which has senior civil servants and economists as members, drew attention to waste and over-spending within the government sector and made recommendations for stricter budgetary control and selective privatization.

By early 1982, in spite of evidence that the Structural Adjustment Loan (SAL) I was proceeding slower than hoped, the World Bank launched SAL II, which was much more demanding than its predecessor, including an "agricultural condition" by asking the government to consider the privatization of the marketing of maize. "In asking, as a centerpiece of the conditions of the second SAL, that the Kenya Government should 'undertake a review of maize marketing in order to develop recommendations on the appropriate roles of the public and private sector . . . and implement its recommendations,' the World Bank was therefore attempting, from outside the country, a feat of political muscle which had defeated all liberalizing pressures from inside for over forty years."[28]

It has been questioned whether the SALs promoting privatization in Kenya were politically feasible and sensible in the sequence that they were launched. Also, was it possible to administer them? Many have criticized the World Bank for inserting the issue of maize control in SAL II, while others criticize the Kenyan government for having begun the adjustment process by liberalizing imports in the face of a large fiscal and balance of payments deficit. The World Bank criticized its own efforts on the level of administrative feasibility, arguing that SAL II was so wide-ranging that it was difficult for the country to implement unless it consisted almost entirely of policies already firmly rooted.[29] According to one estimate, the World Bank is opting for a more pragmatic approach and "acknowledges the minor importance of privatization and import liberalization in the revitalization of low-income economies, and acknowledges the very real political and economic achievement of a relatively resource-poor country."[30]

According to one study, Kenyan experience with the SAPs teaches some lessons: that the economic crisis facing Africa has been caused by both internal and external factors; that the programs need longer periods for their impact to be felt; that there is more need in the SAPs to include the human welfare dimension; that the pace of implementation must be carefully considered, along with the question of political stability; and that mobilization of domestic resources is vital to Kenya's development and SAPs must emphasize this.[31]

According to F. M. Mwega and J. W. Kabubo, SAPs in Kenya have adversely affected employment in the public sector, the largest source of employment in the country.[32] The SAPs had an impact on the health sector by the devaluation of the Kenyan shilling, cuts in public spending, high taxation on mass consumption goods, removal of subsidies on basic foodstuffs, and so on. The situation is aggravated by the lack of drugs in government health institutions. In the education sector, the SAPs have led to massive increases in school fees and other charges, a reduction in the quality of educational programs, and an increase in the number of dropouts from the school system. This has skewed educational opportunities away from poor people and marginalized them in a way that may worsen social inequalities.

KENYAN PRIVATIZATION:
THE POLITICS OF EXPERIENCE

A general set of broad policy guidelines for privatization in Kenya was adopted by the cabinet. Under these, though, the privatization program was decentralized so that individual ministers were "required" to pursue privatization within these guidelines only as they saw pertinent. It is argued by some that these guidelines were essentially the principles set out by the WPGE and that the decentralization of the privatization initiative has served to dilute the policy's significance (and to enhance the capacity of unsympathetic ministers to block sale moves); that those enterprises were considered for privatization in which the government participation was through equity participation on the part of the domestic finance institutions (DFIs) and that there was not much indication of government willingness to tackle privatization in the large-scale infrastructure sector; and that there was no systematic program to identify and prepare candidates for privatization. On the contrary, privatization emerged as a residual response to financial and operational failure on the part of government-owned commercial enterprises.[33]

In terms of direct sales of PEs, the first and most widely publicized privatization initiative was the Uplands Bacon Factory, a totally government-owned body involved in meat processing since 1946 that had never shown a profit. Throughout 1986 and 1987, the government actively sought a buyer, but the factory could not be sold and continued its public ownership as of 1991, even though it fitfully remained closed.

By mid-1990, there were a number of PEs identified as possible candidates for privatization. Some of them were KENATCO, Kenya Fishing Industries Ltd., and Yuken Textiles Ltd. Apparently, the government was pursuing privatization through what is referred to as the "receivership method," whereby the government, its holding company, or, often, a third creditor would initiate foreclosure. The company concerned would be put in the hands of the "receiver," but no acceptable private operator was found. Long delays would ensue, and the costs of delay were borne by the relevant DFIs; however, in occasional cases, enterprises were sufficiently rationalized and management improved under the receivers for starting up the operations, which improved performance to a certain degree.[34]

This method of privatization was argued by the World Bank as a "halfway measure to divestiture."[35] Others argued that, by pursuing this method, the government had "distanced itself from privatization and has developed a mechanism to achieve the basic aim of privatization without conflicting with the politically sensitive issues of Kenyanization."[36]

According to one analysis, a real racial barrier to privatization in Kenya has been the fear of Asian control of the economy. "Full-scale open privatization would probably have the result of transferring state assets to Asian entrepreneurs. Such transfers would likely improve firm-level performance, but the government fears the overall economic and political repercussions."[37] Kenyan-Asians are considered dynamic entrepreneurs providing high-quality managerial, financial, and technical inputs in the economy. "The Kenyan-Asian community has, however, been the target of considerable antagonism, not least following the attempted coup d'état in 1982, and, though they remain the one group most able to acquire and manage industrial public enterprise profitably, their direct participation in the privatization program is likely to be discouraged."[38]

It also is argued that, in the past, the Kenyan government has worried that privatization also would favor the Kikuyu, the most privileged ethnic group in the country. The Kikuyu were politically dominant in the nationalist struggle and had benefited from several postcolonial land distribution schemes. Moi wishes to check the Kikuyu power. "By stalling privatization, Moi has kept both the Asians and the Kikuyu from expanding their influence in Kenya."[39]

IMPLEMENTATION: PROBLEMS
AND POLICY DEFICIENCIES

According to Peter Coughlin, the failure to properly implement agreed policies in Kenya arose from four major and interrelated factors: the lack of centralized or coordinated decision making, inadequate staffing of strategic management organs dealing with economics, political interference, and bribery.[40]

If malfunctioning, certain governmental organs dealing with strategic aspects of economic policy can pervert that policy completely and do exceptional damage to the economy. Understaffing of many vital government departments and mistakes or corruption in these can cost the nation dearly. Too often, mediocre bureaucrats are designated to perform key functions. Officers frequently resign, destroying continuity.[41]

Discussing the problems encountered during privatization in Kenya, Karanja argues that state corporations have acted as a deliberate training ground for most of the country's manpower requirements.[42] It is not clear whether the disposal of these corporations also will mean the demise of this crucial facility. Moreover, the question that still exists is whether divesting will be a total solution to the problem or a mere transfer or postponement of the problem. Doubts have been expressed as to who would eventually acquire the state corporations. It has been the intention of the government that any divestiture of public investment should be carried out in such a way that the investments do not end up in the control of foreigners. The issue of indigenization, which is crucial to Kenyan politics, cannot be ignored. Another issue at stake has been the regional distribution of state corporations. In some cases, divestiture may mean withdrawal in a region of the only forum of economic investment, which may be viewed as a move that will destabilize the regional balance in the country. Perhaps for these reasons, privatization has received resistance from political fora.[43]

Table 5.2 is an attempt to translate Manzetti's framework in the Kenyan context.

CONCLUSION

Drawing upon the literature on Kenya, this chapter argues that the privatization process in a country can be understood in terms of policy substitutability. Thus, privatization in Kenya can be conceived as a policy alternative to others that the government no longer considers feasible. By using Luigi Manzetti's concept of opportunity and willingness, an attempt is made to show how pragmatic, ideological, and environmental factors interact in shaping the decision to privatize when decision makers are presented with a variety of available and potentially

TABLE 5.2
Kenyan Decision to Privatize and Its Implementation

STAGE I: DECISION TO PRIVATIZE

Ideology	1.	1980 Kenyan Government Sessional Paper and the Task Force on Divestiture set up by WPGE
	2.	Government endorsement of free market reforms in Kenya
	3.	IMF and World Bank advocate a shift to liberalization
WILLINGNESS		
	1.	Kenyan government "decrees" on exchange rates
	2.	Several government officers endorse SAPs
Pragmatism	3.	Rationalization of government operation through sessional pragmatism papers
	4.	Desire to improve efficiency in Kenyan trade, agriculture, public expenditure reforms, population control, debt management through the Industrial Promotion Center (IPC) in 1986
OPPORTUNITY	1.	World Bank and IMF loans and support of Kenya in 1980s
	2.	Policy-based sectoral lending by the World Bank

STAGE II: IMPLEMENTATION

GOVERNMENT CAPABILITIES AND
POLITICAL RESPONSE

1. Split in Kenyan government officials on issues of privatization
2. Opposition by powerful groups against dismantling of administrative rationing
3. WPGE's senior civil servants favor "selective privatization"

PRIVATIZATION
REFORM
IMPLEMENTATION

4. "Decentralization" of privatization by the cabinet leading to the "dilution" of privatization
5. Use of "receivership method" to PEs, which became a "halfway method" to privatize
6. Moi stalls privatization to prevent Asian and Kikuyu expansion in Kenyan economy
7. Lack of political support because of the issues of Africanization and indigenization of the Kenyan economy

TECHNICAL DIFFICULTIES

1. Weak regulatory structures and payment and trading systems, for example, Nairobi Stock Exchange is in the process of being regulated by CMDA.
2. Lack of financial sector reform
3. Concentration of savings in the hands of Kenyan-Asians
4. Lack of coordinated and centralized decision making
5. Inadequate staffing of strategic management organs in Kenyan economy
6. Bribery
7. Mediocre bureaucrats in top Kenyan policy positions
8. Destruction of "continuity" in policymaking

suitable alternatives. By no means is this attempt conclusive; it is merely an exercise to employ a framework used in Latin America in an African context. This also is an attempt to discuss how the privatization debate in Kenya raises some important implications for privatization not only throughout Africa but also in other third world countries. Kenya enjoys an economy that would be conducive to a positive program of privatization concentrated in the industrial and commercial sectors. The country enjoys relatively high levels of management skills, good international market access, and a comparatively benign macroeconomic environment.[44]

The process of privatization in Kenya is far from being complete. Other scholars have drawn varied conclusions on the subject. Arne Bigsten argues that the government has started a process of privatization, but the sales of publicly owned corporations have been slow to start; it seems as if Kenya has found it easier to implement price-related reforms.[45] Barbara Grosh examines the issue of Kenyan privatization by comparing quasi-public versus private firms, public versus private firms, and public versus quasi-public firms and concludes that the case for privatization is far from proven. Privatization would make more sense, for example, to mobilize domestic savings rather than the complete abandonment of PEs.[46] Instead of parastatal reform, Grosh argues that the best candidate for privatization would be manufacturing. She also argues in support of addressing the causes of the parastatal's failure, rather than privatization per se.[47]

Some argue to the contrary, asserting that a 1986 study of 16 major agro and agro-industrial state-owned enterprises found aggregate losses equivalent to $186 million between 1977 and 1984. Furthermore, they show that the sector was still inefficient and a loser and that the organizational reforms had not involved any major transfer of equity or managerial control to the private sector.[48]

Regardless of its success or failure, the privatization debate in Kenya raises several important questions for privatization throughout Africa. In some respects, it was even expected that Kenya would have set the pace for privatization in the subsaharan region. However, the implications that the policy remains low-key and attitudes to it remain hostile sharply underlie the fact that privatization is essentially a political process. Although some technocrats in the civil service advocated a broader PE reform package, there has been little support on the political level. Privatization, for some, remains a betrayal of the basic control function of the government. Large generalizations, then, about how to evaluate privatization in Kenya are likely to prove of only limited value because different stakeholders are likely to be looking for different results from privatization. Any attempt to reach a consensus on what should constitute a successful privatization is, thus, likely to fail.

Under the circumstances, searching for some degree of consensus at the level of individual PEs is more useful than searching for general rules applicable to all cases. It is, then, recommended that the merits or faults of privatization be approached on a case by case basis. It may not be forgotten that the largest impact of privatization may come in subtle and indirect ways. For instance, where privatization is widely believed to make a difference, it may prove a self-fulfilling prophecy. The expectations of government agencies, the public, the labor force, and the managers themselves may be altered by the changes in ownership of the enterprises concerned. Those changes in expectations may prove more important in the long run than the measurable economic consequences.[49]

NOTES

1. Raymond Vernon, ed., *The Promise of Privatization: A Challenge for US Foreign Policy* (New York: Council for Foreign Relations, 1988); Emanuel S. Savas, *Privatization: The Key to Better Government* (Chatham, N.J.: Chatham House, 1987); Paul T. Bauer, *Reality and Rhetoric: Studies in the Economics of Development* (Cambridge, Mass.: Harvard University Press, 1984); World Bank, *World Development Report, 1988* (New York: Oxford University Press, 1988); Mary Shirley, "The Experience with Privatization," *Finance and Development* 25 (September 1988).

2. Mancur Olson, "The Development Dilemma," *New Republic*, July 16–23, 1984; M. Peter McPherson, "The Promise of Privatization," in *Privatization and Development*, ed. Steven Hanke (San Francisco, Calif.: ICS Press, 1987).

3. Peter Nunnenkamp, "State Formations in Developing Countries," *Intereconomics* 21 (July–August 1986); Michael P. Todaro, *Economic Development in the Third World*, 3rd ed. (New York: Longman, 1985).

4. Luigi Manzetti, "The Political Economy of Privatization through Divestiture in Less Developed Economies," *Comparative Politics* (July 1993): 429–54.

5. Ibid., p. 431.

6. Ibid.

7. Ibid., p. 432.

8. Ibid., p. 433.

9. Ibid., p. 434, cites Randolph Silverson and Harvey Starr, "Opportunity, Willingness, and the Diffusion of War," *American Political Science Review* 84 (1990): 4 in support of his arguments.

10. Ibid.

11. International Labor Organization, *Employment, Incomes and Equality: A Strategy for Increasing Productive Employment in Kenya* (Geneva: International Labor Organization, 1972).

12. P. Anyang' Nyongo, "The Possibilities and Historical Limitations of Import-Substitution Industrialization in Kenya," in *Industrialization in Kenya: In Search of a Strategy*, eds. Peter Coughlin and Gerrishon K. Ikiara (Kenya: Heinemann, 1988), p. 37.

13. M. Cowen, "Change in State Power, International Conditions and Peasant Producers: The Case of Kenya." (City of London Polytechnic, 1983), Mimeograph, p. 26.

14. Kenya Government, *Economic Survey, 1977 & 1982* (Nairobi: Government Printer, 1982), Tables 6.9 and 6.11.

15. Cowen, "Change in State Power."

16. Anyang' Nyongo, "The Possibilities," p. 39; for a detailed account of this, also see P. Anyang' Nyongo, "State & Society in Africa," *Africa Development* 8 (1984).

17. Cf. R. Eglin, "The Oligopolistic Structure and Competitive Characteristics of Direct Foreign Investment in Kenya's Manufacturing Sector," in *Readings on the Multinational Corporations in Kenya*, ed. R. Kaplinsky (Nairobi: Oxford University Press, 1978), pp. 117–18; Steven Langdon, "Multinational Corporations, Taste, Transfer and Underdevelopment: A Case Study from Kenya," *Review of African Political Economy* no. 2 (1975): 12–35; Steve Langdon, "The Multinational Corporations in the Kenyan Political Economy," in *Readings on the Multinational Corporations in Kenya*, ed. R. Kaplinsky (Nairobi: Oxford University Press, 1978), pp. 172–77.

18. Anyang' Nyongo, "The Possibilities," p. 43.

19. Ibid.

20. Steve Langdon, "The Multinational Corporations in the Kenyan Political Economy," pp. 172–77.

21. Cf. Walter Hecox, "Structural Adjustment and Industrialization in Kenya," in *Industrialization in Kenya: In Search of a Strategy*, eds. Peter Coughlin and Gerrishon K. Ikiara (Kenya: Heinemann, 1988), p. 198.

22. "Economic Prospects and Policies," Kenya Government Sessional Paper No. 4 (Nairobi: Government Printer, 1980), pp. 10–11.

23. Walter Hecox, "Structural Adjustment," p. 199.

24. World Bank, *Annual Report, 1981* (Washington, D.C.: World Bank), pp. 93–94.

25. Walter Hecox, "Structural Adjustment," p. 215.

26. Ibid., pp. 212–13.

27. Paul Mosely, *The Settler Economies* (London: Cambridge University Press, 1983), p. 275.

28. For details on the politics of maize control in Kenya, see Mosely, *Settler Economies*, p. 285.

29. World Bank, *Program Performance Audit Report: Kenya Second Structural Adjustment Loan and Credit* (Report No. 5682) (Washington D.C.: World Bank Operations Evaluation Department, 1985).

30. Mosely, *Settler Economies*, p. 302.

31. "Kenya," in *The Human Dimension of Africa's Persistent Economic Crisis*, eds. Adebayo Adedeji, Sadig Rasheed, and Melody Morrison (New York: Hans Zell Publishers, 1990), p. 50.

32. F. M. Mwega and J. W. Kabubo, "Kenya," in *The Impact of Structural Adjustment on the Population of Africa* (Kenya: Heinneman, 1988), pp. 35–39.

33. C. Adam et al., *Adjusting Privatization* (London: James Currey, 1994), p. 340.

34. Ibid., p. 342.

35. World Bank, *Kenya Industrial Sector Policies for Investment and Growth* (Report No. KE-6711) (Washington, D.C., World Bank, 1987).

36. Adam et al., *Adjusting Privatization*, p. 342.

37. T. M. Callaghy and E. J. Wilson, III, "Africa: Policy, Reality or Ritual," in *The Promise of Privatization: A Challenge for U.S Policy*, ed. Raymond Vernon (Washington, D.C.: Council of Foreign Relations, 1988), p. 193.

38. Adam et al., *Adjusting Privatization*, p. 344.

39. Callaghy and Wilson, "Africa," p. 193.

40. Peter Coughlin, "Towards a New Industrialization Strategy," in *Industrialization in Kenya: In Search of a Strategy*, eds. Peter Coughlin and Gerrishon K. Ikiara (Kenya: Heinemann, 1988), p. 296.

41. Ibid.

42. Karanja, "Privatization in Kenya," in *Privatisation in Developing Countries*, ed. V. V. Ramanadham (New York: Routledge, 1989), p. 280.

43. Ibid.

44. Adam et al., *Adjusting Privatization*, p. 349.

45. Arne Bigsten, "Regulations Versus Price Reforms in Crisis Management: The Case of Kenya," in *Economic Crisis in Africa: Perspectives on Policy Responses*, eds. M. Blomstrom and M. Lundahl (London: Routledge, 1993), p. 73.

46. Barbara Grosh, "Comparing Parastatals and Private Manufacturing Firms: Would Privatization Improve Performance," in *Industrialization in Kenya: In Search of a Strategy*, eds. Peter Coughlin and Gerrishon K. Ikiara (Kenya: Heinemann, 1988), p. 263.

47. Barbara Grosh, *Public Enterprise in Kenya: What Works, What Doesn't, and Why?* (Boulder, Colo.: Lynne Rienner, 1978), pp. 165–66.

48. Callaghy and Wilson, "Africa," p. 193.

49. Yair Aharoni, "On Measuring the Success of Privatization," in *Privatization and Control of State-Owned Enterprise*, eds. Ravi Ramamurti and Raymond Vernon (Washington, D.C.: World Bank, 1991), p. 83.

6

"The End of History or the Beginning of the End?": Prospects for Botswana in the Twenty-First Century

Larry A. Swatuk

Botswana's postindependence transformation from colonial backwater to Africa's fastest growing economy is a "success" story not to be denied. All conventional indicators of "human welfare" and "economic growth" show marked improvement in the macroeconomic performance of Botswana, a deepening of its material base, and a spreading of the generated wealth throughout Batswana society.[1] Moreover, Botswana has managed to maintain a functioning, multiparty democracy throughout its 26-plus years of independence — a situation unheard of in postcolonial Africa.[2] Perhaps most remarkable of all is the fact that these achievements have come in the face of extremely hostile regional geopolitical and international politico-economic contexts.

Botswana's "success" is not an unequivocal one, however. In this chapter, an attempt is made to demonstrate that, although pragmatic approaches to security and development have, thus far, paid substantial dividends to both elite and mass, pragmatism in the form of a neoliberal approach to capitalist development in a marginal political economy like Botswana's is ultimately destabilizing. The neoliberal commitment to capitalist development throws up contradictions whose potential negative consequences for the social formation are more far-reaching and long-lasting than South Africa's policy of regional politico-military destabilization. This path to economic "development" serves to heighten internal contradictions between, for example, the needs of elite and mass, market and environment, and burgeoning human population and limited carrying capacity of the land. In this way, it is suggested here that Botswana's recent and relative economic "success" is accompanied by serious costs. These costs, if left unattended, will threaten not only the long-term prospects for Botswanan democracy but also the very existence of the social formation itself.[3]

DANGER SIGNALS

Although these structural challenges loom ever larger, however, they remain in the background of Botswana politics, shunted aside by more immediate prospects and problems. Recently, the government has come in for serious criticism in a number of areas; heightening corruption, widening income disparities, and increasing ill-advised developmental expenditures are but three of the more recent targets.[4]

For example, in a recent issue of *Barclays Botswana Economic Review*, University of Botswana economist J. S. Salkin had this to say about future economic prospects: "The revised macro-economic projections for the remainder of the decade paint a sombre picture of very little improvement in per capita incomes and standards of living. And even this picture is predicated upon fairly rapid growth in manufacturing, tourism, financial services, and exports of non-traditional goods."[5] Salkin places most of the blame for Botswana's present troubles squarely upon the shoulders of its policymakers:

In contrast to the record Botswana had acquired over the years for sound economic management and prudent government expenditures, in recent years there have been misplaced priorities and wasteful spending resulting in unproductive investments with low or negative returns as are manifest in prestige projects, such as the national airline, the national railway, the international hotel, the convention centre, the University science complex, the Government jet, luxury accommodation for politicians and military expenditures.[6]

Interestingly, then, much of this criticism comes from hitherto staunch supporters of the government: Western donors and international financial institutions.[7] This is significant because, in the past, perspectives on Botswana tended to fall into one of two camps: the neoliberal camp, which has been highly supportive of government in Botswana, or the radical or neo-Marxist camp, which has been highly critical of government policy.

That the neoliberals now, too, are increasingly critical of government performance in Botswana suggests that not all may be right with this African "success story." To be sure, the sorts of criticisms leveled at the government by the neoliberals and neo-Marxists differ. Nevertheless, this unlikely confluence of criticisms bears closer scrutiny.

CONTRASTING ANALYSES

To better assess the long-term prospects for Botswana's political economy and to gain insight into the reasons behind the generally critical analysis now being leveled at government there, it is necessary to locate the roots of the present economic malaise. As noted above, perspectives on Botswana tend to cleave around the issue of government performance and politico-economic philosophy. On one side are the neoliberals, who regard Botswana's success as due to the prudent management of the country's main economic asset, diamonds. Granted, there are persistent inequalities within the Botswana social formation, but according to the neoliberals, over time, these ineqalities will smooth out as economic growth broadens the middle class and creates new opportunities — via education and small business and rural development projects — for those at the margins of society to better themselves. Demands for massive developmental expenditures are, therefore, to be resisted, no matter how ethically sound they may appear to be.

According to the neoliberals, this pragmatic approach to economic development has allowed Botswana to avoid the so-called "Dutch Disease," whereby capital accruing to *rentier* economies is spent as though it will continue ad infinitum. The perils of the Dutch Disease are only too well-known in the African case, Nigeria being a particularly good example. Given Botswana's limited prospects for self-generating development, then, these scholars tend to be highly supportive of the market-led approach to developmental policy formation.[8]

On the other side are the radical scholars who reject the "modernizing and self-regarding state in a world of like-performing states" model of the neoliberals, preferring instead to situate the Botswana "state" within the more holistic and historically contingent context of the world capitalist system. Using a wide variety of analytical constructs (e.g., *dependencia*, world systems, other variants of neo-Marxism), these scholars tend to see exploitation where neoliberals see rational choice.[9] This neo-Marxist perspective, broadly defined, regards southern Africa as an integrated region whose various parts are characterized by uneven development fostered by capitalist penetration and exploitation of both human and natural resources. In Botswana's case, this perspective takes colonial neglect and the deliberate incorporation of the protectorate into the regional political economy as a labor reserve as its point of departure. The colonial government's later support for the Botswana Democratic Party (BDP), to the exclusion of more radical pan-Africanist-oriented parties, and Seretse Khama's unbridled support for economic and political liberalism are seen as evidence of the emergence of a comprador elite. Patrick P. Molutsi, for example, illustrates how a "cattleocracy" has instituted policies that have dispossessed peasants of land, thus, further marginalizing them, rather than helping them acquire the means for their own reproduction.[10]

Moreover, the capital-intensive development of Botswanan minerals has, to this time, provided the means by which Botswana's ruling elite can offer palliative care to the rural poor but cannot ensure their reproduction, let alone an increased standard of living, in the long run.

Given this capitalist alliance, the radical perspective is unconvinced of Botswana's economic "success." Instead, it sees any such success as narrowly defined within Western capitalist parameters and narrowly distributed among a few already privileged groups in Batswana society: the bureaucratic bourgeoisie, settlers and other large cattle owners, petty agricultural commodity producers, and multinational capital, which some critics define as the "grande bourgeoisie."[11]

Although each of these approaches, or theoretical perspectives, provides us with a number of important insights, it seems to me that each "school" lacks nuance in its analysis. The neoliberal approach, with its emphasis on states, markets, and policymakers, is both ahistorical and overly dependent on "agency." Also, although neo-Marxist approaches help us get beyond the myth of self-contained political economies engaging in similar activities with varying capabilities, as generally articulated in the third world context, they tend to be somewhat heavy-handed in their analysis, privileging the economic sphere above all else. In the Botswana case, for example, leadership is then equated with compradorism: the structure, particularly the prevailing mode and relations of production, becomes everything.

Neoliberals seek to redress this growing inequality primarily through the market. Radical scholars, on the other hand, seek a significant redistribution of wealth. What both fail to recognize is the fundamental structural transformations taking place in the global economy that render each perspective simplistic and self-defeating: neither strategy, particularly as articulated within the confines of the Botswana nation-state, can succeed in the long term. Minerals are a wasting asset, and the global economy has, for the most part, no desire to deal with a small, landlocked political economy located far from major global markets. A fundamental rethinking of "development" in the southern African context is needed, and this is an issue to which I will return below.

At the same time, and contrary to what the radical critique says, there exists widespread support for this approach among Batswana. Unlike most African countries, Batswana are able to express this support through the ballot box. The BDP's consistently high percentage of votes (between 70 and 80 percent) and seats (from 28 of 31 in 1965 to 31 of 34 in 1989) over the course of seven elections is testimony in this regard.[12] The question remains, however, will "pragmatic" capitalist development yield the same beneficial results for the stability of the social formation as have pragmatic, status quo–oriented, high-political decisions?

"SUCCESS," FOREIGN POLICY, AND SECURITY

Part of Botswana's success is because of the way in which the country's leadership has defined and approached its security problematique. At independence, Khama and his "new men" found themselves as governors of a state that shared borders with two hostile, racist regimes. The regime to the north — Rhodesia — found sympathizers among Botswana's white settlers in the Francistown region. The regime to the south — South Africa — had created a homeland for Setswana speakers along the border with Botswana, which included the former administrative center for Bechuanaland at Mafekeng. Fully two-thirds of all Setswana speakers found themselves resident not in independent Botswana but in the Bophuthatswana Bantustan, which gained nominal independence in 1979. Thus, in addition to being surrounded, except for its "technical border" with Zambia, by hostile sovereign and renegade states, newly independent Botswana, historically and currently little more than a transport corridor, inherited juridical borders that did not reflect the reality of regionalism in southern Africa. Weak, surrounded, and penetrated, Botswana's leadership chose a pragmatic course that clearly defined the security problem in realist terms.

Botswana's main threats struck at the integrity of the social formation. Externally, the very existence of the state was challenged by politico-military threats from South Africa and Rhodesia, by an irredentist movement among white settlers in the northeast, and by South African designs for incorporation of the former High Commission territories.

Internally, the weakness of Botswana's economic base and the lack of indigenous control over what little physical plant and capital investment did exist brought into question the capacity of the social formation to reproduce itself without handouts from the international community. Faced with an incredibly harsh climate and an equally forbidding geostrategic situation, Botswana policymakers found little room to maneuver at independence.

In such a situation, it is hardly surprising that the Batswana political elite pursued regime-survival–oriented foreign and domestic policies. The regime has been careful not to alienate South African capital, in fact, entering into numerous agreements and joint ventures with South African firms in the areas of minerals, services, manufactures, and so on. The government has emphasized negotiation over confrontation, sought to maintain Botswana's complement of foreign labor in the republic, and fostered embourgeoisement at home. At every step, both multinational and national capital have been supported by government. In turn, the governing elite have been well-rewarded by these sources of capital. In Gramscian terms, then, Botswana's leaders have not only internalized but also have successfully maneuvered within the admittedly restrictive parameters laid down by the dominant paradigm: defense of statehood through careful global and regional political alignments and economic development through allegiance to the tenets of liberal capitalism.

The congruence of state and regime security defined in terms of defense against South African destabilization has allowed policymakers to put off dealing with the structurally embedded contradictions inherent in neoliberalism as practiced at the periphery of the global economy, at least so far. Because of its geographical position as a "road to freedom," Botswana has faced a sustained politico-military threat, which preceded formal independence. Nevertheless, this unenviable geopolitical position helped create a confluence of interest between elite and mass that otherwise might not have emerged or played itself out as it did. However, as in the rest of the region, the move to a postapartheid period is likely to unmask cleavages previously hidden by the mutual need for state survival and shared perception of the South African threat.

With the question of whether liberal economics and politics will provide national security and development to Botswana still unanswered, it becomes necessary to turn to a fuller exposition of these issues and events in order to better assess this issue.

CAPITALISM, DEVELOPMENT, AND INCREASING INSECURITY

Botswana's economic growth and, hence, the very viability of the present social formation is purely a postcolonial phenomenon. Although there is a revisionist movement afoot that suggests that the Bechuanaland colonial administration began a systematic if modest development program as far back as the 1930s, most realist and radical studies of Botswana's colonial history suggest that Britain's role was one of near-total neglect.[13]

At independence, Botswana was one of the world's 25 least developed countries, having a per capita gross national product of approximately U.S.$75. In 1964, only 73,000 of a total population of 580,000 were in formal employment, with an estimated one-third of these being outside the protectorate as labor migrants.[14] Though Botswana historically had been coveted as a potential source of minerals, a missionary road, and a dumping ground for blacks,[15] by independence, it had been reduced to little more than a labor reserve and a transport corridor.

PREINDEPENDENCE SOCIAL DIFFERENTIATION

Not everyone within Batswana society suffered from this condition, however. The series of ecological disasters and colonial, settler, and South African interventions helped some to prosper, while others became worse off. According to Lionel Cliffe and Richard Moorsom, "economic stagnation" fostered "social conservation" — that is to say, traditional rulers were able to maintain and, in some cases, augment their social and economic standing by virtue of their control over land allocation; tribute labor via age-regiments; stray livestock; the use of serfs and squatters; and native treasuries, which they often used as their own personal accounts. Many peasants, on the other hand, saw migrant labor as their only means of household reproduction beyond the subsistence level.[16]

With each succeeding natural disaster (e.g., drought, rinderpest), human-made intervention (e.g., the demand for labor, the choking off of Batswana petty bourgeois development by colonial-settler conspiracy), and technological innovation (e.g., the introduction of the plough, oil-powered boreholes), those at the top of the social hierarchy became ever more capable of surviving, adapting, and prospering, while those at the bottom were more marginalized. Clearly, "the tendencies towards class polarisation and social inequality now evident [in Botswana] have long historical roots."[17]

ACCELERATED GROWTH AND
SOCIAL DIFFERENTIATION

Botswana's postindependence experience saw "old tendencies being accelerated while new forces have entered the stage."[18] The immediate postindependence period was characterized by a combination of careful government and favorable climate. Good weather led to large harvests and the growth of the rapidly commercializing cattle industry; the Southern African Customs Union renegotiation helped fuel public sector expansion; and the discovery of copper-nickel matte at Selebi Pikwe, diamonds at Orapa, and the aggressive courtship of mineral-related foreign investment had numerous spin-offs — increased employment, construction, capital investment, Customs Union revenue, and a surplus in Botswana's balance of payments. Moreover, the development of an efficient civil service served as a further attraction to foreign capital.

More than anything else, however, diamonds helped sustain this early period of growth and have since carried Botswana through the more difficult period of the 1980s and early 1990s. Thus, by the 1980s, a scant 15 years beyond independence, Botswana had been transformed from a "potential real estate annex" into an "African success story."[19]

This firm commitment to capitalist development in the liberal, individ-ualistic economic tradition has paid handsome dividends to the Batswana elite. It has at the same time, however, made it increasingly difficult for Botswana's poor to take advantage of postindependence economic growth. Although the rural poor have come to regard migrant labor as the principal means where "marginalised peasants could escape their impov-erishment," the top 3 percent of the rural population have become a "cattle aristocracy."[20] It is this group of individuals, coupled with an emergent "bureaucratic bourgeoisie," who have been best placed to take advantage of postindependence governmental development policies.[21]

COALITION BUILDING IN
SUPPORT OF THE STATUS QUO

Though it is this group that profits most and is, therefore, most supportive of Botswana's status quo–oriented policies, support tran-scends both class and category within Batswana society. Perhaps no economic tool has drawn a tighter net around the Batswana populace than development capital and planning. Foreign aid, initially, and mineral-based government revenues, latterly, have been channeled into a series of well-publicized and oft-criticized development programs. These "tentacles of capital" have extended into every corner of the state, strengthening and broadening the coalition of vested interests in present BDP policy directions.

No doubt Botswana's democratic and capitalist orientations are behind most, if not all, of this support. The influence of major donors like the European Union, Britain, and France, all of whom have "friendly and profitable relations with South Africa . . . reinforces major capitalist inter-ests" in Botswana.[22]

These capital interests came together in a powerful demonstration of the dominance of capitalist economic philosophy and its expanding web in the Shashi copper-nickel mining project. There, a consortium of inter-national capital (AMAX of the United States and Anglo American of South Africa), combined with Botswana government and international multilateral (World Bank) and bilateral (Canadian) donor assistance to finance the construction of the Selebi Pikwe mining complex. Although the mine continues to be unprofitable, barely covering its operating costs, its importance to ordinary Batswana cannot be underestimated. This can be seen in the phenomenal growth of the urban population there: from zero in 1964 to 4,900 in 1971 to 29,469 in 1981 and an estimated 55,384 in 1991. Selebi Pikwe is now the third largest urban area in Botswana, behind only Gaborone and Francistown.[23]

Total mining sector employment (i.e., including all mining centers) in 1990 was 7,800; a small number, granted, but the growth of manufacturing, construction, services, transportation, and communications; government employment; and informal economic activities that have grown up around this sector is quite large.[24] Moreover, the number of rural Batswana whom these wages are supporting is larger still. Clearly, the number and variety of interests in support of capitalist development in Botswana, and, by extension, South African capital investment constitutes a significant portion of the total population.

In summary, the Botswana government has parlayed its command over diamond and other natural resource revenues into a dominant position within the social formation: the extension of financial assistance and development aid to rural areas; increased formal sector employment via government and foreign investments, particularly in the mineral sector; and prudent foreign policy decision making in a hostile geopolitical environment leading to increased foreign aid and international political support have combined to strengthen the role and legitimacy of the state vis-à-vis civil society in Botswana.

RECENT ECONOMIC PERFORMANCE

Botswana's numerous state-supported social improvements stem from mineral-based development, particularly in the growth of diamond exports. The percentage contribution of the mining sector to total gross domestic product (GDP) went from zero to 47 percent in the period 1966–86, helping to offset the precipitous decline in both agricultural production and agriculture's contribution to GDP.[25]

Revenues deriving from diamond exports have risen from P3 million in 1970 to P243 million in 1982 and P3,301 million in 1993.[26] The percentage contribution of diamonds to total Botswana exports, thus, rose over this time period from 14.8 percent (0.7 percent of total CSO sales) to 52.0 percent (18.9 percent of CSO sales) and 79 percent (over 40 percent of CSO sales).[27]

Diamond revenues have, therefore, fueled growth in all sectors of the economy. The percentage contributions of manufacturing, government, and trade and hotels to total GDP have all remained relatively constant since 1966 in spite of the dramatic growth of mining. This is indicative of their mineral-fueled expansion. Overall GDP increased 11 times in the 20 years since independence, that is, from P118 million in 1966 to P1,316 million in 1986. Per capita GDP grew from P191 in 1966 to P1,144 in 1986 despite rapid population growth.

Although this growth has meant a dramatic rise in imports (from P468 million in 1980 to P2.1 billion in 1989), exports rose at an even faster rate: an average of 19 percent per annum over the course of the 1980s for imports and 34 percent per annum for exports. Unlike the rest of (southern) Africa, Botswana has no domestic debt, and its balance of payments surplus has risen from 3 percent of GDP in 1979–80 to roughly 15 percent of GDP in 1988–89. Its debt service ratio was a meager 3.9 percent in 1992. Further, its international reserves have risen from P255 million in 1980 to P10,160 million in 1993, the equivalent of 30 months of import cover.[28]

Increased imports also have meant increased revenue from the Customs Union, which, along with mineral revenues and nonmining income taxes, continue to be the main sources of government revenue. Customs revenues increased from approximately P104 million in 1981 to P174.8 million in 1986–87 and a projected P709 million in 1994–95.[29]

Botswana policymakers have been very prudent, to say the least, regarding development fund and recurrent expenditures. The bulk of development fund and recurrent expenditure is directed toward the creation of an "enabling environment" for private sector and complementary profitable government or parastatal expenditure. So, infrastructural (e.g., roads, water resources, thermoelectric power), human resource (e.g., education, health), and private and parastatal (e.g., mining, export-oriented manufactures, job reservation and creation, expanded slaughter capacity, and upgrading of Botswana Meat Commission investments) development have absorbed the bulk of government spending and policy planning.

As discussed above, this focus on expansion of existing leading sector development coupled with encouragement of new investment has drawn much criticism from radical academics. Recent criticisms have focused less on peasant marginalization, however, than they have on environmental degradation. Expanding wealth strains the environment by expanding cattle holdings beyond sustainable limits and by fostering migration to crowded urban areas, straining already limited services and jeopardizing water and land resources.[30] It is not so much specific governmental policies to which these critics object but the general capitalist philosophy driving Botswana's development policy.

Supporters of the government's approach to economic development remain unapologetic, however, arguing that socialism and central planning have failed, bringing untold hardship to the peoples of southern Africa; Angola, Mozambique, Tanzania, and, to a lesser extent, Zambia are their preferred cases in point. Government spokespersons argue that their approach to development planning, like their approach to foreign policy, is based in realism, not idealism. For example, in his 1987 budget speech, then Vice-President and Minister of Finance and Development Planning Peter Mmusi stated that employment creation and rural development were to be added to the existing goals of national development: rapid economic growth, social justice, economic independence, and sustained development. He cautioned, however, that, "while government's policy was to take advantage of the wide range of possibilities that the country's mineral wealth has opened up . . . we have done [this] in a disciplined fashion, within a coherent system of economic planning. This maintenance of discipline even when times are good, will hold us in good stead for the future, when we may be operating in more difficult conditions than in recent years."[31] Mmusi's resignation in the wake of corruption charges suggests that ordinary Batswana have been operating within difficult conditions for years.

THE INSECURITY DILEMMA:
SUBSTRUCTURAL CONSTRAINTS AND
SHARPENING SOCIAL CONTRADICTIONS

To this point in time, radical critiques have been neutralized by "buoyant" economic growth. So long as the economy continued to grow, belief in the "miracle of the market" and its ability to smooth out inequalities over time could be sustained. However, recent economic indicators suggest that the Botswana "miracle" already may have come to a halt. According to Salkin:

The economy has been decelerating rapidly since the 6.3% rate of growth achieved in 1991/92. Gross Domestic Product (GDP) in 1992/3 is estimated to have increased 1.8% in real terms. . . . With the population of Botswana still estimated to be growing over 3% per annum, this implies that per capita GDP (and average incomes) declined over the year. Botswana has not recorded declines in real per capita GDP since the early 1980s. . . . The projected level of GDP in 1993/94 . . . shows a further real increase of 2.0%; but again this is below the estimated rate of growth of population.[32]

Although neoliberals can claim that these are merely short-term trends, more serious problems suggest longer-term difficulties. This chapter now turns to a brief examination of some of these emerging stressors.

MANUFACTURING AND UNEMPLOYMENT

In Botswana, the prospects for increased manufacturing are poor. As Andrew Murray and Neil Parsons point out, Botswana faces "almost insuperable barriers to manufacturing." In 1966, manufacturing contributed merely 8 percent to total GDP (GDP being a mere P118 million). In the attempt to create a manufacturing base, the Botswana Development Bank, Botswana Small Enterprises Development Unit, Botswana Development Corporation, and the Financial Assistance Policy were established through the 1970s and early 1980s. Many of these have since been brought together to form the Division of Integrated Field Services. The importance of Botswana policymakers vested in manufacturing to Botswana's future economic growth should not be underestimated, despite its present small contribution to GDP. According to Charles Harvey and Stephen Lewis, "the absence of large new mining prospects, and the various problems of livestock and arable agriculture, meant that the continuation of economic growth in Botswana depended to a considerable degree on the manufacturing sector."[33]

Harvey and Lewis point out that as much as 40 percent of the manufacturing increase in Botswana Meat Corporation products and upward of 50 percent of all other manufacturing is because of increased domestic demand. However, "further rapid growth of manufacturing depended therefore on increasing import substitution and, since the domestic market would always be relatively small, on increasing manufactured exports. It was thus essential for manufacturing in Botswana to be competitive internationally."[34]

Clearly, one strategy Botswana policymakers have employed is to take advantage of their proximity to both South Africa and Zimbabwe to export largely South African or Zimbabwean products that meet specific value-added requirements to other markets in the region.[35] Further, because of the history of South African restrictions upon and embargoes of Botswana beef and other products, often in the effort to protect South African producers and in contravention of the Customs Union Agreement, Botswana policymakers have sought to avoid similar actions in the future by maintaining a very open and inviting investment climate.[36] Botswana policymakers have been very aggressive in the pursuit of new investment, both externally (via, for example, more liberal exchange controls) and internally (via, for example, unflinching control over labor and, therefore, the costs of production).[37]

Batswana labor's increasing outspokenness, in spite of its status as a labor aristocracy in a country hard-pressed to provide employment to its citizens, seems indicative of the onerous conditions under which workers labor in order that business become internationally "competitive." It also is suggestive of emerging difficulties in state–civil society relations.

Initially, these policies, even with their heavy-handed treatment of labor, seemed to bear fruit. Between 1985 and 1991, despite a prolonged drought and regional instability, formal sector employment grew from 116,800 to 222,700, an increase of 12.5 percent per annum. Although this growth was spread throughout the economy, it was most striking in the manufacturing sector: 19.2 percent average annual growth. The "boom" was short-lived, however. Again, according to Salkin: "The performance of the manufacturing sector over the past few years has perhaps been the most disconcerting, since much of the Government's development strategies for economic diversification and employment creation were focused on the expansion of this sector. Since 1990/91, economic growth has decelerated rapidly and output in 1992/93 is estimated to have declined by 11.8% in real terms with the prospect of only a marginal improvement in 1993/94."[38] This has led to widespread retrenchment in the private sector. Between September 1991 and March 1993, for example, private sector employment decreased by 8.8 percent. This leads Salkin to conclude, "in whatever hue one might paint the picture, the spectre of high and rising levels of unemployment, with all the suffering and social ills it entails, has come back to haunt the economy and shatter the image of Botswana's success as a developing country."[39]

With a democratic South Africa moving toward accession to the tenets of the General Agreement on Tariffs and Trade, Europe probably moving toward an end to beef quotas and concessions by the end of the century, and Botswana's neighbors all undergoing varying forms of structural adjustment, it is not unreasonable to wonder how long it will be before mine labor and the service sector are the only forms of formal sector employment outside government left in Botswana.

AGRICULTURE: SCRATCHING FOR HANDOUTS

Cycles of drought and disease have made accumulation a difficult process. For those few Batswana who practice subsistence agriculture, intermittent rainfall has forced them into patterns of shifting cultivation — in Batswana scholar Molutsi's words, "chasing showers."

Botswana's limited ability to create formal sector employment — irrespective of its "meaningfulness" — in both the manufacturing and mineral sectors poses a serious threat to the long-term stability of the country. Endemic drought and the de jure and de facto privatizations of grazing land have forced many peasants either to migrate to the towns of Botswana or South Africa in search of work or to remain on the land, marginally employed by large cattle owners or working for government handouts.

Aside from largely freehold agriculture in the southeast, around Baroleng, and in the Tuli Block area, Botswana cannot produce enough food to feed even a small fraction of its population. According to one estimate, crops provide approximately 6 percent of total rural incomes. Even in nondrought years, one-half of all foodstuffs consumed must be imported.[40] This puts Botswana in a somewhat ironical position of being less vulnerable to drought than its southern African neighbors, because crop loss is limited.[41]

Drought is the major contributor to the lack of crop production in Botswana. According to the *Midterm Review of NDP VI*, "since 1960 there have been two major droughts in Botswana and only one uninterrupted period of five years of good rainfall." Yet, the same review suggests, optimistically: "Over time, the subsistence subsector will progressively become smaller compared to the commercial subsector. Commercial cattle and crop production (both small and large) will rely increasingly on modern highly productive technology and management methods, and the bulk of the nation's agricultural output will be produced predominantly by an enlarged and highly efficient commercial subsector."[42] Granted, this statement came on the heels of a break in the drought cycle that saw good rains for the first time in six years. However, it also failed to anticipate the subsequent four years of drought (1989–92) that reduced Botswana's meager agricultural base even further.

Government has been forced to divert a large amount of its development expenditure toward drought relief. A variety of programs established in the early 1980s — Inter-Ministerial Drought Committee, Early Warning Technical Cooperation, Supplementary Feeding Program for Children, Labour Based Relief Programme, and the Agricultural Relief Programme — successfully combated the worst effects of drought. However, all programs, like the Agricultural Relief Programme, which was tantamount to giving farmers seeds and paying them to plant them even though there was next to no chance of producing a crop, failed to address a contributing factor to drought and crop failure in Botswana: the expansion of commercial cattle farming.

CATTLE, POWER, AND THE ENVIRONMENT

Perhaps most indicative of the long-term threats to security facing Botswana is the expansion of cattle ranching and the "attack" on the Kalahari. Overgrazing and peasant land alienation, as pointed out above, are problems of increasing seriousness in Botswana, yet, few, if any, government reports devote more than a few paragraphs to these issues.[43] More than anything else, this is indicative of the nexus of power in Botswana. As elsewhere in the region, cattle serve a dual role in Batswana society: as economic investment and symbol of political power, each reinforcing the other.

Varied but long-established routes to the means of status and production — cattle — have created a complex web of vested interests in Botswana. Cattle provide the point of intersection for numerous groups normally antagonistic toward one another, from migrant laborers who purchase cattle on the basis of their "stored value" to presidents, kings, and freehold ranchers.[44] These also are groups whose only other unifying characteristic tends to be gender, because most cattle owners are men. So, continued access to cattle — no matter how varied one's purchasing power — is a powerful drive toward status quo–oriented policies in Botswana.

This conservatism is inherently destabilizing, however. Nowhere is this more clearly in evidence than in Botswana. Mineral-based development has facilitated the growth in both cattle and human populations. However, access to the former is being limited to wealthy class fractions, that is, those individuals in and around state power. The vast majority of the population is, therefore, cut off from the means of production, land, and cattle and forced to work for sub-subsistence wages within Botswana or in the Republic of South Africa.[45] Reasonably waged jobs, like those in South Africa's mining industry, are limited and contracting. At the same time, a cattle population close to 3 million must be sustained on land ravaged by drought and exacerbated by the unwillingness of powerful cattle owners to restrict grazing areas.

CONCLUSION: AN OSTRICH WITH ITS HEAD IN THE SAND?

In an advertisement for BGI Tanning Company (Pty) Ltd. of Botswana, an ostrich appears with its head out of the sand, eyes wide open above the caption "We've nothing to hide."[46] One wonders if this may not be an appropriate metaphor for policymaking in Botswana. On the one hand, planning appears to proceed carefully, policymakers seemingly fully aware of the many shortcomings of Botswana's economy. Clearly, pressures are building at many levels within the Botswana social formation, with no clear solutions and seemingly no real options other than the careful husbandry of capital resources.

Government has demonstrated a ready willingness to restructure the economy at the first sign of danger without the overt assistance or prodding of either the International Monetary Fund or World Bank. Results from five democratically held elections show support for present policies, but from a shrinking active electorate and an increasingly disaffected urban sector.

Perhaps "success" in this context hinges upon a postapartheid southern African regional division of labor. Although Botswana policymakers do not hint at this possibility, their actions indicate a belief that state-centric developmental possibilities for Botswana may be short-lived. Botswana's steady support for the Southern African Defence Cooperation, as well as its keen pursuit of bilateral trade agreements (particularly with South Africa and Zimbabwe), seem to suggest that it does. The free flow of goods, labor, services, and capital within a greater southern African region may reduce population pressures, as Botswana "exports" its economic and ecological migrants, and increase productivity, as Botswana would be better able to exploit its position as the regional nexus between two industrial powers.

There remains the issue of the web of the status quo, however, that is, those individuals who survive, some of whom even prosper, from the present organization of the region's political economy. Would they be willing to restrict their abilities to accumulate wealth even if the links with environmental decay and peasant impoverishment could be forcefully demonstrated? At the same time, would Botswana policymakers and others tied to the state with access to capital via their "nearness" to the center of power be willing to give up their positions in a restructured regional political economy?

To both questions, it would seem the answer is "no." Given the numerous positive reinforcements at global and local levels, Gramscian analysis suggests that the most likely scenario is maintenance of the status quo — an ostrich with its eyes wide open but ever ready to plunge its head in the sand at the nearest sign of danger. As Salkin points out, however, "inaction amounts to a further constraint on development, making matters worse and further eroding the economic prospects of Botswana."[47] Put starkly, denial heads Botswana down the road toward a Kaplanesque "coming anarchy," rather than Fukuyama's overly optimistic, neoliberalist valhalla.

NOTES

1. See, for example, *Barclays Business Guide to Botswana*, 1987; and 1993/94, Gaborone; UNDP/UNICEF, 1994, Botswana Country Report for *Human Development Report 1994*, mimeo, Gaborone; and UNDP, 1991, *Human Development Report 1991*, New York: United Nations.

2. See, for example, Ken Good, "Interpreting the Exceptionality of Botswana," *Journal of Modern African Studies* 30 (1992): 69–95; Charles Harvey and Stephen Lewis, *Policy Choice and Development Performance in Botswana* (London: Macmillan and OECD, 1990); Thomas Ohlson and Stephen John Stedman, with Robert Davies, *The New Is Not Yet Born: Conflict Resolution in Southern Africa* (Washington, D.C.: The Brookings Institution, 1994); Stephen John Stedman, ed., *Botswana: The Political Economy of Democratic Development* (Boulder, Colo.: Lynne Rienner, 1993).

3. Compare the arguments made in Ken Good, "At the Ends of the Ladder: Radical Inequalities in Botswana," *Journal of Modern African Studies* 31 (1993); with Michael Niemann, "Diamonds are a State's Best Friend: Botswana's Policy in Southern Africa," *Africa Today* 40 (1993): 27–48.

4. See, for example, *The Midweek Sun*, September 21, 1994; *Southern African Economist*, September 1994; *Southern Africa Political and Economic Monthly*, September 1993.

5. Jeremy Salkin, *Barclays Botswana Economic Review* (Gaborone: 1994), pp. 1–16, particularly p. 16.

6. Ibid.

7. Ibid.

8. See, for example, Charles Harvey, *Papers on the Economy of Botswana* (London: Heinemann, 1981); Harvey and Lewis, *Policy Choice*; Willie Henderson, "Seretse Khama: a Personal Appreciation," *African Affairs* 89 (January 1990): 27–56; Willie Henderson, "Independent Botswana: A Reappraisal of Foreign Policy Options," *African Affairs* 73 (January 1974): 37–49; Ohlson, Stedman, and Davies, *The New Is Not Yet Born*; Stedman, *Botswana*.

9.   See, for example, Lionel Cliffe and Richard Moorsom, "Rural Class Formation and Ecological Collapse in Botswana," *Review of African Political Economy* 15–16 (1979): 35–52; Christopher Colclough and Stephen McCarthy, *The Political Economy of Botswana: A Study of Growth and Distribution* (Cambridge: Cambridge University Press, 1980); Patrick Molutsi, "The State, Environment, and Peasant Consciousness in Botswana," *Review of African Political Economy* 42 (1988): 40–47; "Book Review" of Louis Picard, *The Politics of Development in Africa*, in *Review of African Political Economy* 47 (Spring 1987): 126–28; Jack Parson, "The Peasantariat and Politics: Migration, Wage-labor and Agriculture in Botswana," *Africa Today* 31 (1984): 5–25; Balefi Tsie, *Destabilisation and its Implications for Botswana*, Destabilisation in Southern Africa No. 2 (Roma: National University of Lesotho, Institute of Southern African Studies, 1989).

10.   Molutsi, "The State."

11.   See, for example, Nadia Kostiuk, "Botswana," in *The Political Economy of African Foreign Policy*, eds. Timothy M. Shaw and Olajide Aluko (New York: St. Martin's, 1984); Stephen J. Morrison, "Botswana's Formative Late Colonial Experiences," in *Botswana: The Political Economy of Democratic Development*, ed. Stephen John Stedman (Boulder, Colo.: Lynne Rienner, 1993).

12.   For informed analyses of Botswana's various elections, see John Holm, "Botswana: A Paternalistic Democracy," in *Democracy in Developing Countries, (Africa)*, eds. Larry Diamond, Juan Linz, and S. M. Lipset (Boulder, Colo.: Lynne Rienner, 1988); John Holm, "Elections in Botswana: Institutionalization of a New System of Legitimacy," in *Elections in Independent Africa*, ed. Fred M. Hayward (Boulder, Colo.: Westview, 1986), pp. 121–47; John Holm and Patrick Molutsi, "State-Society Relations in Botswana: Beginning Liberalization," in *Government and Politics in Africa*, eds. Goran Hyden and Michael Bratton (Boulder, Colo.: Lynne Rienner, 1992); Patrick Molutsi and John Holm, "Developing Democracy When Civil Society is Weak: the Case of Botswana," *African Affairs* 89 (July 1990): 323–40.

13.   Compare the arguments made by Phil Steenkamp, "'Cinderella of the Empire?': Development Policy in Bechuanaland in the 1930s," *Journal of Southern African Studies* 17 (June 1991): 292–308; with Colclough and McCarthy, *The Political Economy*.

14.   Andrew Murray and Neil Parsons, "The Modern Economic History of Botswana," in *Studies in the Economic History of Southern Africa*, vol. 1 *The Frontline States*, eds. Z. Konczacki, J. Parpart, and T. M. Shaw (London: Frank Cass, 1991), p. 167.

15.   Kostiuk, "Botswana," p. 62.

16.   Cliffe and Moorsom, "Rural Class Formation," pp. 36–38. In spite of the long traditions toward migrant labor and conditions of drought and economic failure, the "myth" of precapitalist economic self-sufficiency in southern African societies is a persistent one. See, for example, Murray and Parsons, "The Modern Economic History," p. 161.

17.   Cliffe and Moorsom, "Rural Class Formation," pp. 36–38.

18.   Ibid.

19.   See Richard Dale, "Between Pretoria and Praetorianism: Drafting a National Security Establishment and Policy for Botswana." Paper presented at the annual meeting of the African Studies Association, October 28–31, 1988, Chicago,

p. 3; Philip Morgan, "Botswana: Development, Democracy, and Vulnerability," in *Southern Africa: the Continuing Crisis*, eds. Gwendolen Carter and Patrick O'Meara (Bloomington: Indiana University Press, 1982).

20.   Cliffe and Moorsom, "Rural Class Formation," pp. 39, 42.

21.   Good ("At the Ends of the Ladder," pp. 1–2) points out that, contrary to other rapidly developing countries (e.g., Singapore, Taiwan) "income distribution in Botswana lately . . . has been changing in favour of the rich. On the Government's figures, the income going to the top 20 per cent rose over the period 1974–75 to 1985–86 to 61 per cent, while that which went to the poorest 40 per cent fell from 12 to 11 per cent."

22.   See Phil Saunders, "The Foreign Policy of Botswana." Master's thesis, Dalhousie University, Halifax, 1982.

23.   Harvey and Lewis, *Policy Choice*, p. 35; *Barclays Business Guide to Botswana*, 1993, p. 14 .

24.   Government of Botswana, *The Mid-Term Review of NDP VI*, (Gaborone: Ministry of Finance and Development Planning, 1988), p. 22; *Barclays Business Guide to Botswana*, 1993, p. 13.

25.   According to Harvey and Lewis (*Policy Choice*, p. 32), agriculture as a percentage of total GDP has fallen continuously since 1966: from 39 percent in 1966 to 24 percent in 1976 and to 4 percent in 1986.

26.   Government of Botswana, *Midterm Review*, p. 5; *Barclays Business Guide to Botswana*, 1994, p.10.

27.   *Southern African Economist* (August–September 1990): vii; *Barclays Business Guide to Botswana*, 1994, p. 10.

28.   Ibid.

29.   *Barclays Business Guide to Botswana* (Gaborone, 1993), p. 22.

30.   On environmental degradation see, for example, M. H. Abucar and Patrick Molutsi, "Environmental Policy in Botswana: a Critique," *Africa Today* 40 (1993): 61–73; Jap Arntzen and Elmar Veenendaal, *A Profile of Environment and Development in Botswana* (Gaborone: University of Botswana, National Institute of Development Research and Documentation, 1986); Rodger Yeager, "Governance and Environment in Botswana: The Ecological Price of Stability," in *Botswana: The Political Economy of Democratic Development*, ed. Stephen John Stedman (Boulder, Colo.: Lynne Rienner, 1993), pp. 123–37; Rodger Yeager, "Democratic Pluralism and Ecological Crisis in Botswana," *The Journal of Developing Areas* 23 (1989): 385–404.

31.   Quoted in *Barclays Business Guide to Botswana*, 1987, p. 14.

32.   *Barclays Business Guide to Botswana*, 1994, p. 2.

33.   Harvey and Lewis, *Policy Choice*, p. 159. This was reiterated in the 1994 budget speech presented to parliament by Festus Mogae, the present vice-president and minister of finance and development planning (see *Barclays Business Guide to Botswana*, 1994, p. 19). The importance of export-oriented manufacturing also was emphasized to me in a conversation with Keith Jefferis, professor of economics, University of Botswana, September 21, 1994.

34.   Ibid.

35.   This may be negatively affected by the recent reciprocal trade agreements concluded between Zimbabwe and South Africa and Zambia and South Africa.

36. See, for example, Alan Whiteside, *Industrialisation and Investment Incentives in Southern Africa* (Pietermaritzberg: University of Natal Press, 1989).

37. *Southern African Economist*, August–September 1990, p. vii; on labor crackdowns, see *Southern Africa REPORT*, March 1992, p. 22.

38. *Barclays Business Guide to Botswana*, 1994, pp. 4, 13.

39. Ibid., p. 15.

40. Victoria Quinn et al., "Crisis Proofing the Economy: The Response of Botswana to Economic Recession and Drought," in *Adjustment With a Human Face: Country Case Studies*, eds. Giovanni Andrea Cornia et al. (UNICEF, 1988), pp. 5–39.

41. According to Quinn et al., ("Crisis Proofing," p. 11), in 1983, of 83,000 households surveyed, fully 85.7 percent (70,250) produced no crops at all, while another 9.6 percent (7,840) harvested less than 250 kilograms in total (1,500 kilograms is estimated to be necessary to meet household needs). These statistics corroborate those offered by Cliffe and Moorsom ("Rural Class Formation," pp. 41, 42), which pointed out that, in 1971, 62 percent of rural households produced less than the necessary minimum for their own subsistence. Thus, roughly 54 percent of rural households were forced to depend on wage labor to augment their rural sub-subsistence production.

42. Government of Botswana, *Mid-Term Review*, pp. 83, 84.

43. This is not to say that government is ignorant of the problem, however. To the contrary, on several occasions, commissioned reports submitted to government have highlighted the seriousness of these problems. Pierre du Toit, *State-Building and Democracy in Southern Africa: A Comparative Study of Botswana, South Africa and Zimbabwe* (Pretoria: Human Research Council, 1995), p. 120, likens these criticisms to a process he terms "gelding," that is, the use of outsiders (hence, those "neutered" of national power) by the state to impart information and give advice without posing a fundamental threat to the bases of power within the state. Hence, expatriate reports provide useful information for government, but expatriates do not make revolution.

44. On the notion of stored value, see James Ferguson, *The Anti-Politics Machine: Development, Depoliticization, and Bureaucratic Power in Lesotho* (Cambridge: Cambridge University Press, 1990).

45. At a seminar at Rhodes University in August 1994, Professor Ken Good provided some useful statistics gleaned from the Ministry of Agriculture and Central Statistics Office (*1990 Agriculture Statistics* [Gaborone: 1991]): although 18,200 cattle farms (32 percent of all farms with cattle) held an average of 6 beasts each, 35 commercial farms (0.06 percent of all holdings) averaged 4,117. Good also points out that, in 1981, 19 farms owned on average more than 10,000 cattle each.

46. See *Southern African Economist*, August–September 1990, p. xiv.

47. *Barclays Business Guide to Botswana*, 1994, p. 16.

III

THE PROBLEMS OF
DEVELOPMENT MANAGEMENT

7

Nongovernmental Organizations and Government-Organized Nongovernmental Organizations: Opportunities for Development Management in Africa in the Twenty-First Century

Peter Koehn and Olatunde Ojo

After more than four decades, the overall picture of development performance in Africa remains dismal. Today, donor fatigue coexists with loss of confidence in the ability and capacity of African governments to deliver on development. In the eyes of many Western donors, African states have lost their legitimacy. Donor frustration is reflected in the economic and political conditionalities that characterize structural-adjustment programs and debt-repayment reschedules as well as in the insistence on "good governance," code words for liberal democracy.

A rollback of the state in the African political economy is being systematically enforced by the International Monetary Fund–World Bank duo. The official contention is that the private sector and its market forces will fill the breach by becoming the agent of economic growth, thereby strengthening civil society and civil institutions and making democracy and human rights observance possible. In practice, structural-adjustment and related reforms, policies, and programs have tended to undermine governmental capacity and capability, creating instability and further weakening the legitimacy of the state. Africa has been unable to attract substantial private investment — foreign or domestic. The net outflow of capital continues on a continent-wide basis.

The poor record of governmental performance in Africa lends ammunition to calls for privatization, that is, for the transfer of authority and

resources to capitalist institutions.[1] Nevertheless, diminishing the role of
the state via privatization and simply getting the price right alongside
other such macropolicies have proven insufficient to put development on
course. Market forces and the private sector have failed to rise to the occa-
sion in spite of donor insistence on privatization measures that place
resources cheaply in that sector. Africa's economic conditions continue to
worsen. This is reflected in the continent's increasing reliance on grants
and loans and in the worsening debt that has risen to some 110 percent of
the gross national product, compared with Latin America's 42 percent
and South Asia's 31 percent.[2]

The explosion of nongovernmental organizations (NGOs) and small-
scale self-help undertakings across the continent constitutes the major
change in the landscape of developmental management over the past 25
years. Failure in the public (state-owned, coercion-impelled) sector and
lackluster responsiveness of the private (profit-oriented, market) sector
jointly have led donors to shift attention to the voluntary, collective-action
sector. They seek to energize civil organizations and to enhance the development performance of the voluntary sector. Instead of "wasting" more
aid and assistance on "incompetent" states and their agencies, donors
now often promote NGOs as alternative channels for delivering developmental services. Indeed, some of the most impressive and sustainable
development achievements have occurred largely or entirely outside
formal structures of government in Africa.[3] For instance, the number and
monetary value of community self-help projects initiated in the Kwara
state of Nigeria during the late 1970s and early 1980s far outstripped the
combined undertakings of local, state, and national governments.[4] In
short, the prevailing wisdom today is to funnel aid through NGOs. In the
1990s context of demand for "diminishing states," NGOs are receiving
even greater attention than in the past.

This chapter explores the role of NGOs in Africa, focusing on community empowerment as a critical factor in their success as agents of local,
grass-roots development and on ways that NGOs can be made stronger
and more effective contributors to development management in Africa
without further undermining state legitimacy in the process. The vital
link between refugee-related assistance and contemporary African development issues also is pursued. Our analysis includes a critical discussion
of Goran Hyden's proposed Development Fund Model (DFM) for overcoming foreign-aid shortcomings. We attempt to modify and build on
Hyden's model in ways that will optimize the goal of community empowerment while strengthening the legitimacy and development performance of both the state and civil institutions. The conclusion returns to
training as the critical continuing need in development management.

THE ROLE OF NONGOVERNMENTAL ORGANIZATIONS AND GOVERNMENT-ORGANIZED NONGOVERNMENTAL ORGANIZATIONS IN AFRICAN DEVELOPMENT

In Africa, NGOs long have played a major (if underestimated) role in local development. Recognition of this fact has led governments — colonial and postcolonial — to promote cooperative associations and to sponsor community-development projects. However, most of these officially sanctioned associations and the more formal government-organized NGOs (GONGOs) floundered for lack of the critical ingredient for success — community empowerment. Governments simply did not permit empowerment out of fear that this step would undermine or reduce their own authority or power. Yet, it is such a reduction in the role and influence of the state that is needed if development is to proceed and be sustainable. Before dealing with this issue, it is pertinent to define the terms used for differentiating the diversity of NGO types encountered in Africa in order that we remain clear about what sort of NGOs we are talking.

A NONGOVERNMENTAL ORGANIZATION TYPOLOGY

The term "NGO" itself almost always is taken literally to mean any and every organization that is not in the public sector of the economy. Thus, it is seen as a residual category that includes market (private, profit-oriented) enterprises. This perspective is misleading and dangerous. How dangerous can be seen in the current structural-adjustment debate over the best path to African economic health. That debate is couched in state versus market terms, as if those are the only two sectors of the political economy. The importance of the voluntary (neither public nor market) sector is overlooked, although the earliest and, increasingly, the more relevant organizations for local development are found there.[5] In this chapter, we limit the term "NGO" to those found in the voluntary, collective-action sector of the economy where the dominant instrument of control and compliance is voluntarism based on value commitment and shared belief in collective mission in contrast to coercion in the public sector and profit or monetary reward in the market sector.

With slight analytic variations, we join others in identifying four NGO types that are found in Africa. All are involved in one way or another in promoting development at one level or another. The first subtype is the grass-roots organizations (GROs), what Alan Fowler[6] calls "membership organizations" and M. Esman and N. Uphoff[7] early termed "local organizations." They are voluntary membership organizations operating at the level of the group, the community, or the locality, up to and including the village, town, or the subdistrict. They are set up by, and meant to benefit, the members themselves and are controlled by and accountable to them. They are the organizations usually associated with bottom-up development, in contrast to the top-down style of decision making and implementation. Two examples are rotating credit associations and traditional cooperatives.

The second type of NGO, what we refer to as the modern indigenous nongovernmental organization (MINGO), resembles Fowler's private-service organizations.[8] We refer to them as MINGOs because they are formed, controlled, or directed by Africans themselves (though they may be partially financed from outside the continent) and tend to originate by inducement, demand, or the initiatives or demonstration effect of others external to the communities concerned. MINGOs operate at all spatial levels, including the local (and, thus, overlap GROs), but generally are found more at district, regional, and national levels. They are more formal and more institutionalized than GROs and employ personnel, though they also may possess a large volunteer staff. Their objective is to promote self-help organizations (including GROs), to champion charitable causes, and to support whomever or whatever else they choose as beneficiaries of their activities. The vast majority of NGOs belong in this category and include church development-outreach organizations, nonprofit research outfits, advocacy groups like the Campaign for Democracy and Human Rights, village and town improvement unions, and regional and ethnic welfare associations.

A third category comprises external, or northern nongovernmental organizations (NONGOs), which have their parent bodies outside Africa with southern branches or sponsored groups engaged in charitable and development work on the continent. Examples are OXFAM, CARE, Save the Children Fund, Church World Service, the International Foundation for Education and Self-Help,[9] United Support of Artists for Africa, and Live Aid–Band Aid.

The fourth and final type of NGO is, paradoxically, created, sponsored, or taken over by the government or its agencies for the purpose of encouraging self-help or assisted self-reliant development. Termed "GONGOs," examples at the local level include Nigeria's Better Life for Rural Women societies and the Cameroon's village cotton-production associations. Both are monitored and manipulated by the respective governments, the one to mobilize women to use credit facilities and to enhance their organizational capacity to increase the productivity of their rural enterprises, the other to undertake input distribution and marketing functions for SODE-COTON for a small fee. In the current poststructural-adjustment context, African governments increasingly are facilitating the establishment of shadow GONGOs under the guise of GROs.

THE NONGOVERNMENTAL ORGANIZATION
COMPARATIVE ADVANTAGE

As a class, NGOs, especially the MINGO, GRO, and NONGO components, possess valuable potential strengths and are predisposed to play a
significant role in development management. Many analysts, notably
Judith Tendler,[10] Alan Fowler,[11] and John Clark,[12] among others, list and
discuss the qualities and characteristics that give NGOs potential comparable advantage over governments in this regard. Prominent on the list
are reaching the poor, popular participation, flexibility and innovativeness, commitment of staff, smallness and simplicity, effectiveness and
efficiency, and the ability to create intrasectoral linkages with other
voluntary associations at the project level and to forge federated umbrella
organizations (including north-south NGO partnerships). Above all,
NGOs possess the capacity to mobilize communities to receive and utilize
government-provided technical services and to "bulk" their market transactions (e.g., ordering agricultural inputs or selling agricultural produce).
Such intersectoral partnerships often form the basis of an integrated
approach to rural poverty alleviation.

Clark,[13] and Fowler[14] explain the NGOs' comparative advantage in
terms of those features that distinguish them from governments. Unlike
governments, they possess no particular need to organize along bureaucratic lines (their interaction with the populace is not order maintenance
and, therefore, does not require control and uniformity), nor do they need
or possess formal, coercive authority over people whose involvement in
NGO activities can be invited only voluntarily. Moreover, their international linkages enable them to construct global networks of citizen pressures; their unique vantage point ideally places them to study and
describe how contemporary crises affect the poor; their size and flexibility
allows them to experiment with new approaches and, through demonstration effect, to serve as catalysts for government action; and because
they do not stand to make personal profit, they tend to be trusted by the
public at large.

Not only do MINGOs and GROs exhibit most of these general characteristics; their sustainable-development performance also already often
rivals or surpasses that of local governments in many localities. Examples
are legion, but the rotating savings and loan associations found throughout Africa, the hometown associations (*associations des originaires*) that
flourish in west Africa and in Zaire and Zambia, and learning-process
organizations deserve special mention. Unhampered by bureaucratism,
organized in units that rarely go beyond the village or town level, and
unencumbered with social overhead, traditional rotating credit associations have been more effective than state-organized credit institutions in
many countries. They have been more responsive to members' needs,

have been much easier to hold accountable for the management of funds, and have limited free-rider problems. Many have been transformed into more formal credit unions. In some countries, like Cameroon and Tanzania, these credit unions have federated in recent years, regrouping scores of thousands of people into an effective social force that controls millions of dollars in savings. Though overtly nonpolitical, these and similar associations are contributing to the process of strengthening political pluralism in the classic sense of enhancing the power of independent groups vis-à-vis the state.[15] Hometown associations, a holdover from the welfare and mutual-aid associations of ethnic and clan groups resident in the burgeoning urban areas during the colonial era, have become the major means of mobilizing resources for the development of their natal villages and towns. Invariably called "progressive union" or "improvement union" of the town or village concerned, each of these MINGOs establishes branches wherever there are sizable numbers of members, sends delegates to the natal town or village for scheduled meetings, acts as a link to and pressure group on governments, and takes the lead in financial contributions and launchings of developmental projects such as the building of roads, hospitals, clinics, and schools and the provision of electricity, boreholes, and pipe-borne water supply.[16]

In sum, efforts to link with voluntary associations attract attention in Africa today because many NGOs already have mastered processes such as participatory management and self-reliance that are touted by the donor community as essential for sustainable development. However, the key to unleashing the full development potential of NGOs in Africa rests with diminishing the role of central government institutions. This means that, first, devolution must be taken to the level that is closest to the people who are dependent upon and responsible for sustainable development.[17] Second, governments at all levels must reward, rather than discourage or ignore, any impetus for self-reliance that is initiated from below.[18] Empowering villagers and urban dwellers will continue to present the principal challenge for development management in Africa into the twenty-first century. Building the capacity of GROs to analyze alternative approaches and to formulate small-scale projects that address their own needs are critical dimensions of this process.

NONGOVERNMENTAL ORGANIZATIONS, REFUGEES, RETURNEES, AND DISPLACED PERSONS: LINKING DISPLACEMENT AND DEVELOPMENT

Over the past two decades, involuntary population displacement has become an endemic problem in Africa. At the end of 1993, nearly 6 million official refugees and asylum seekers required protection or assistance outside their homeland.[19] The burden of hosting the vast majority of these refugees fell on poverty-stricken neighboring African countries.

No serious discussion of development management in Africa can avoid the growing phenomenon of population displacement. Michael M. Cernea reminds us that "in the context of the global refugee problem, Africa stands out as the region with the largest proportion of uprooted people relative to the total population, the most pressing human tragedies, and the hardest to solve reestablishment problems."[20] Ironically, millions of people are displaced each year in the name of development — particularly by massive dam-construction and transportation-infrastructure projects.[21] From the host-country perspective, moreover, "to the extent that refugees worsen economic [and environmental] conditions for the local population and frustrate local development, they must be viewed as a component of the wider development crisis facing Africa."[22]

The development challenges faced by displaced persons —including refugees, returnees, and the internally ousted — are, in many ways, even more intractable than those confronted by impoverished, but locationally stable, populations. The additional barriers to sustainable development that beset the displaced in Africa are likely to include lack of interest on the part of the host or home government; resentment and hostility on the part of the surrounding population; lack of access to land, employment opportunities, and other resources required for long-term self-reliance; the general failure on the part of donors, governments, and international agencies to link refugee assistance with development efforts; and the disintegration of social-support systems.[23]

NGOs have a vital role to play with regard to the relief and development needs of displaced persons in Africa. In the sustainable-development arena, their involvement has ranged from management of the Eastern Sudan Refugee Program by the Sudan Council of Churches to the initiation of development projects for villagers displaced by war across Eritrea by the Eritrean Relief Association. In practice, few of the NGOs involved with refugees possess "the skills needed for development of long-term sustainability" and some "have little commitment to sustainability as opposed to relief."[24] There are notable exceptions, however. In spite of serious material limitations and disruption by armed conflict and drought, the Eritrean Relief Association, an indigenous organization led by returning refugees that emphasized self-reliance and popular participation, introduced many successful sustainable-development initiatives prior to Eritrea's independence.[25]

The overall experience with refugees and development projects reveals several promising approaches to the management of sustainable-development projects in the future. First and foremost, refugees themselves must be in the forefront of decision making if sustainable development is to have any chance of becoming a reality. Too often, refugees have been excluded from participation in project planning and staffing and in the making of important administrative decisions. The consequences have been increased powerlessness, diminished self-confidence, and greater dependency.[26] NGOs are well-positioned to facilitate movement in the direction of greater refugee involvement in development work. The participatory approach must be accompanied by increased attention to the management-training needs of refugees. The promotion of managerial capacity must be viewed as an integral part of linking refugee aid and development.[27]

Second, assistance to the displaced and to returning refugees must be directed toward the impacted area so that benefits are shared with the local poor who have not moved.[28] Such assistance should be based on the principle of "additionality," that is, it must be in addition to development aid that otherwise would have been forthcoming.

Third, the factors that prevent a coordinated attack on the development constraints that simultaneously afflict both displaced and stable populations must be overcome. One promising approach along these lines, the cross-mandate operation introduced in some situations by the United Nations High Commission for Refugees (UNHCR), pools the efforts and resources of all United Nations (UN) agencies operating in a country. When coupled with community-based assistance in impacted asylum areas and in areas experiencing repatriation and with cross-border programs where feasible, the cross-mandate approach has the potential to avert local conflicts by "assisting the entire population of an area including returned displaced persons and stayees" along with returning refugees and drought victims.[29] It is interesting in this connection that the 1992 cross-mandate agreement between the governments of Sudan and Ethiopia and UNHCR specifically addressed putting in place "longer-term, sustainable rural development projects in the areas of agriculture and water resources" and required that "NGOs, including national agencies, be invited to participate in all stages of the work of the central and regional task forces from planning through implementation."[30] In addition to cross-mandate operations, or as an alternative when other approaches are not feasible, greater reliance upon NGOs is a useful strategy for overcoming the mandate constraints faced by UNHCR and bilateral aid agencies.

Sizable numbers of African refugees have sought asylum in Europe and North America. Most have received training and acquired experience there that would be valuable for development management back home. These refugees constitute a reservoir of talents and diverse skills that are needed sorely on the continent. They could play a critical role in development management in Africa now and in the near future. One role of the returning refugee could be to provide MINGOs and GROs with expertise regarding development planning, proposal preparation and advocacy, network building, and human rights awareness. They also could provide the leadership and impetus necessary for community empowerment to take place. These vital potential roles indicate the importance of refugee training and preparation in advance of return to the homeland. An international conference on Refugees and Development Assistance: Training for Voluntary Repatriation held in March 1994 at the University of Montana set forth specific recommendations along these lines.[31] To facilitate realization of these objectives, a Global Refugee Corps (GRC) should be established in association with UNHCR. The GRC would match exile skills, capacities, and motivation with relief and development needs in the sending continent. It should be supported by funding from a new UNHCR/UNDP trust fund for refugee-related development projects.[32] The GRC should be conceptualized, designed, budgeted, and managed by refugees themselves.[33]

NONGOVERNMENTAL ORGANIZATIONS AND COMMUNITY EMPOWERMENT

Not all NGOs are able to translate their potential comparative advantages into reality. Much depends on how deliberately they pursue community empowerment, conceived as the application of a series of management skills and techniques at various intervention points — entry, flow, and consolidation withdrawal — in the ongoing lives of the community. The essential elements of this approach[34] are a decentralized structure with semiautonomous, self-managed, "federated" units, coupled with what Clark calls "conscientization"[35] — information sharing and cooperative learning designed not simply to improve living standards but to help the poor perceive their exploitation and realize the opportunities they have for overcoming it through mass organization. The overall strategy will vary with each NGO's unique situation and role, but clear and simple objectives, a high level of awareness and commitment, and support from senior political and governmental leaders are essential. KENGO in Kenya and the Nambian Development Trust (NDT) are examples of MINGOs that operate along these lines. Among NONGOs moving in that direction are the Christian Children Fund, PLAN, and Action Aid.[36] The NDT's "organizational workshop programme" approach is particularly instructive for its initial emphasis on constituent organization, education, lobbying and negotiating, and training. External NDT actors provide resources only in response to specific requests from organized members of the local community and set an early date for the complete withdrawal of outside actors from roles that might exert any influence on GRO decision making.[37]

That community empowerment is critical for success is confirmed by NGOs that lack it; these generally have failed to realize development objectives. Studies show that early attempts by colonial and postcolonial governments to foster and promote voluntary associations yielded a "cooperative poor harvest" because the co-ops so established were "more related to state-building rather than nation-building" and were closer to being "coercitives" than cooperatives as the result of being mandated from above and lacking empowerment and self-generation.[38] Esman and Uphoff later found that of 24 NGOs scoring highest in overall development contribution to rural communities, only 4 were established under government auspices (i.e., were GONGOs that lacked concern for community empowerment).[39]

Governments have been reluctant, however, to empower or to allow empowerment of communities, because this undermines their overriding concern for control and influence on most aspects of national life and might promote factionalism. For the same reason, the state nearly everywhere in Africa has failed to devolve full governmental authority, including taxing and spending powers, to local governments. In Nigeria, for example, much of the unending debate on reform of local government has been over whether or not to increase their powers and authority over financing. The last in the series of "solutions" put forth on this issue is to have the Nigerian federal government allocate a proportion of federally collected revenue to local governments rather than concede taxing powers. Paradoxically, the ostensible reason for the government position is that grass-roots people are too illiterate or fiscally irresponsible and corrupt to be allowed such powers! Instead of empowering local governments and grass-roots organizations and people, the governments of many African countries have increasingly resorted to establishing their own nongovernmental organizations or to the takeover and coaptation of existing private ones.[40]

In an attempt to achieve greater integration and influence, African NGOs increasingly have moved to organize themselves into a federation, an umbrella organization through which they liaise and negotiate with government agents, share resources and ideas, and coordinate their development activities. An example is the Namibia Non-Governmental Organizations Forum (NANGOF). With its own staff and a budget, an NGO federation typically publishes bulletins that report on its own and members' activities, important developments in government or society, and potential external funding and support sources. Sometimes, the staff helps indigenous groups formulate and present project proposals for external funding, including rendering the proposals in the required foreign language.

LIMITATIONS

It is important not to romanticize NGOs as the cure-all for every level of development situation. For one thing, NGOs are not suitable for certain national-level development needs that the state and only the state can and must provide — for instance, dealing with external constraints on development and with the institutions and agents of multinational capital. For another, some NGOs operate with the same social logic as state institutions. They, too, may be run by individuals who lack a popular mass base and whose main preoccupation is self-enrichment; their officials may no more distinguish between private and public spheres than state officials; some NGOs may even be bogus or carry out fraudulent activities.[41] Furthermore, we cannot accept the blanket assertion that, because GROs and MINGOs contribute to local development, they ipso facto contribute to the emergence of a civil society.[42] Performance by self-encapsulated communities of functions the state does not, or can no longer, carry out effectively is a far cry from the rise of political pluralism in the classic sense of enhancing the power of such communities vis-à-vis the state via popular participation and influence. Finally, NGOs lack the revenue-raising authority possessed by the state and typically operate without public scrutiny and accountability.[43]

Realism demands, then, that we eschew the tendency to view MINGOs and GROs as alternatives to the state in delivering development services.[44] Rather, as Uphoff and Michael Bratton suggest, we should begin with acknowledgement of the complementarity and interrelatedness of MINGO and GRO strengths with those of the state and the market.[45] The role of donors should be to assist in the task of capacity building for the state, MINGOs, and GROs.

SOUTH-NORTH TENSIONS

The task of capacity building for MINGOs and GROs and the role of donors in this project are complicated by tensions between NONGOs and their African counterparts and between NGOs as a group and African governments, all a by-product of the ways donors work with and through NGOs. Two patterns of working with NGOs are evident. In the first, donors work through NONGOs, usually via contracts and expert intermediaries in the field, to aid those MINGOs and GROs whose activities fit into the national development priorities of the host state. U.S. government contributions to CARE, Catholic Relief Services, Pathfinder Fund, and the Agricultural Cooperatives Development Institute, constituting between 80 percent and 95 percent of the NGOs' resources, fall in this category.[46] In the second model, NONGOs, on their own initiative and in accordance with their own objectives, directly fund MINGOs and GROs, though by arrangement with, or permission of, host governments. Save the Children Foundation's pilot Extended Program of Immunization project in Mali is one example.

Behind the scenes, however, there often is tension. NONGOs, though fewer in number (but growing), are the dominant intermediaries and retailers of foreign aid between donor wholesalers and local development organizations and people. It is calculated that, worldwide, the amount of aid they handled increased from $2.7 billion in 1970 to about $5.2 billion in 1988 — representing 11 percent of total Organization for Economic Cooperation and Development aid that year.[47] As a result, NONGOs have become extremely powerful. The unparalleled funding opportunities that made this possible also increased the NONGOs' search for collaborative associations with MINGOs and GROs, resulting in rapid growth in numbers and in tensions among them.

One reason for this situation is the tendency of NONGOs to be influenced by the foreign-policy and aid objectives of their home governments, from which the bulk of their funding derives and for whose aid programs they often serve as subcontractors. Thus, they plan projects in accordance with the interests of their donors. At best, this leads to organizational forms more suited to the business of raising and accounting for money than for microdevelopment.[48] At worst, they distort the development priorities of the African NGOs or of the host state itself. For example, there is a tendency by some NONGOs to focus on wealth-producing rather than wealth-distributing projects, on relief rather than development, on production for export rather than environmental protection, or on utilization of capital-intensive (and debt-creating) technologies rather than more appropriate labor-intensive ones.

These tensions and conflicts came into the open at the UN Non-governmental Liaison Service meetings in Geneva in late 1985. The African and other southern MINGOs in attendance made it clear that third world development is their responsibility. Although they welcome NONGO collaboration in the process, they do not want their initiative; rather, NONGOs should concentrate on public education, advocacy, and fund raising in their home countries. Tensions and differences in perspective continue to exist in some situations. Thus, the executive director of a Nigerian MINGO (OFAD — Future) recently charged that "many Northern NGOs require Southern NGOs to be primarily accountable to them, an external body, and not to the beneficiaries."[49]

Another aspect of the question of organizational integrity and conflict over roles is what African MINGOs see as misrepresentation of Africa. NONGOs, they claim, tend to project Africans as passive, helpless, and pathetic beggars for whom the NONGOs are the only savior, instead of portraying them as resilient, capable human beings with enormous endurance and ingenuity.[50] Clark recounts the case of one NONGO that had used "starvation pornography" in fund-raising advertisements during the African famine of 1984–85.[51] This occurred in spite of constant warnings from the MINGOs about the long-term disastrous consequences of using degrading images that reinforce racist prejudices.

Attempts have been made to work out some modus vivendi that would bring into balance conflicting interests and views and create genuine partnerships among northern and southern NGOs. The formation of the Forum of African Voluntary Development Organizations in 1987 stemmed from the needs to stress collaboration among African NGOs and a new understanding and framework for north-south cooperation and to establish dialogue with African governments in order to secure official recognition of NGO participation and partnership in development.[52]

Another more provocative approach is embodied in Hyden's recent thoughtful proposal to reform the donor-aid system and allow NGOs to serve in the frontline of development management in Africa. In light of the promise of this proposal, we next critically assess and build on it in presenting an approach to development management for the twenty-first century.

THE DEVELOPMENT FUND MODEL

Hyden's thoughtful proposal, termed the "development fund model," aims to transform development management in Africa by introducing "the principle of marketing aid among competitive bidders within systems that are insulated from partisan politics."[53] The decisional center-piece would be an independent accountable body that allocates capital resources from an intermediary vantage point between donors and recipients. To be effective, Hyden maintains, the new body must "(1) have legal and political autonomy, (2) be national in scope, and (3) not discriminate among clients."[54]

We find much to applaud in Hyden's articulation of the DFM. Establishment of an independent and accountable body that generally allocates capital for social- and economic-development projects according to national priorities and on an impartial basis would go a long way toward restoring citizen confidence in the development process. It is particularly important, in our view, that the board of the funding body not be controlled by the head of state or any other political figure(s) or organization(s) and that the public consequently possess confidence that funding decisions will be based on the power of the ideas set forth in one's proposal rather than on the relative influence of one's connections. Hyden's suggestion that a limited number of board members consist of respected international figures has promise in terms of external scrutiny of fund operations and in terms of building donor confidence in the

DFM.[55] The healthy competition among NGOs, GONGOs, and government agencies for project support envisioned by the DFM also carries the potential to generate an infusion of new energies into the development process throughout the continent and to tap the latent enthusiasm for development that African countries need to mobilize.

There are weaknesses in Hyden's proposal that need to be addressed, however. For instance, the recommendation that members of the governing board select their own replacements[56] is fraught with the danger of nepotism, ethnic favoritism, and other non–merit-based considerations. Moreover, we question Hyden's proposal that multiple funding bodies be established on a sectoral basis within a country.[57] The artificial assignment of projects into exclusive categories such as public health, education, and agricultural development fails to recognize the cross-sector or sectoral nature of underlying constraints on development and might well lead to the exclusion of promising innovative proposals as well as those that incorporate a useful holistic approach.

Based upon the African experience with development management, we suggest several modifications in Hyden's DFM that are intended to enhance prospects that it will be successful. Funding bodies should advertise and distribute available capital in independent tranches that are differentiated by funding levels. One division that is easy to understand and administer is large scale, medium scale, and small scale.

It is not sufficient to establish an independent and impartial funding body. African experience has shown that the criteria used in evaluating project proposals are equally critical. In assessing and selecting competitive development-funding proposals at all levels of funding, board members responsible for disbursing capital need to adopt appropriate and easy-to-implement evaluative criteria that focus on key impact-related considerations.[58] One of the most important dimensions of such impact analysis should be identification of project consequences and benefits for various elements of the poorest and most exploited population groups.

Sustainable development rests upon community empowerment. Inherent in the DFM is the potential to promote this most fundamental objective. The initial key is to create and maintain a level playing field. The single most important step in this direction would be for funding bodies to focus attention and concentrate resources on small-scale projects, because even federations of GROs with NONGOs are unlikely to be competitive for or interested in large-scale project funding. A second requirement should be that participation by NONGOs in proposals to the fund must be in collaboration with one or more indigenous partners. Furthermore, the board and its professional staff should seek to ensure the widest possible publicity regarding the resources and services available and current application policies and procedures and that virtually every initial proposal submitted by a GRO is successful in securing some funding. Any deficient initial proposals involving a GRO should not be rejected outright;[59] instead, the funding body's staff should assist in whatever reworking and networking is required to prepare a winning proposal upon resubmission. Training in proposal writing would result in valuable payoffs in this connection. Many initial GRO proposals are strong on ideas for projects that would address critical needs but are poorly articulated and presented in terms of implementation design, budget, and evaluation plan. Short training courses coupled with intensive individual assistance can overcome these barriers and allow GROs to submit competitive proposals. The opportunities suggested in this discussion also should be open to refugee communities, returnees, and NGOs that work with displaced persons. One encouraging development along lines similar to those proposed above is the commercial debt-reduction program for Zambia launched in May 1994. This program enables GROs, MINGOs, and NONGOs to convert eligible debt acquired through donation or purchase to finance approved development projects that promote health, education, production capacity, environmental protection, or general social welfare in Zambia. To facilitate such involvement, the Debt-for-Development Coalition has made available technical advisory services and support without charge to interested NGOs.

The DFM must not ignore indigenous government structures — especially at the local level. African governments need to be strengthened to perform their assigned functions responsively and responsibly as a vital precondition for the emergence and sustenance of civil society. Consequently, the key to long-term success of the DFM involves the total amount of resources available. Donors must be prepared to reward success with additional, rather than diminished, capital transfers.

On their part, African governments at all levels must view the new competition for development funding as an opportunity, rather than a burden, and must respond with creative and responsive proposals that are attentive to community empowerment and to innovative ways to network with NGOs of all types. In this way, the DFM can be made consonant with trends toward "diminished states" as opposed to the unreal and unfortunate "withering state" image. With the modifications and elaborations set forth here, then, the DFM promises to balance the interest of donors in promoting NGO involvement in small-scale local projects with GRO and MINGO interest in playing more prominent and direct roles in development-planning processes.

Finally, fund boards must ensure that rigorous standards of accountability are built into operational procedures and funding processes. Performance evaluations should be required on *all* funded projects. Applicants that fail to satisfy minimum performance standards on a prior project award should forfeit their eligibility for technical assistance from fund staff and for guaranteed favorable treatment in future awards. Applicants that exceed minimum performance standards on prior projects should be granted preference in subsequent competitions.

CONCLUSION

Donor frustration over the failure of aid and technical-assistance programs to bring about Africa's development (and anger at the role of African states in this failure) has produced a shift of focus toward funding aid through NGOs. Many NGOs have performed well in promoting development on the continent in spite of problems, not least with respect to conflicts between NONGOs and their African counterparts. However, MINGOs and GROs cannot perform their roles effectively without a strong, effective state and without developing capacity on the demand as well as the supply side of the public policy process (i.e., shaping and deciding the content of development policies). In short, both the state and civil society must be strengthened, not one at the expense of the other.

This conclusion points to the crux of the matter — training as the critical need in development management in the 1990s and beyond. Most African GROs and MINGOs are in dire need of training in the fundamentals of development planning and financial management, leadership and community empowerment, creative problem solving, basic research techniques, human rights awareness and protection, and, above all, proposal preparation, network building, and advocacy. Appropriate training programs are vital to the success of promising innovative approaches to involving NGOs in development (such as the DFM). In some cases, tailored training programs and awareness-building might best be effectuated through north-south and south-south educational and cultural exchanges. In other cases, such as the Capacity and Infrastructure Building in Electronic Communications for Development of Africa project, the UN Economic Commission for Africa can provide valuable training. Basic training programs that focus on local government councilors and entire communities and incorporate field visits by training consultants also are of demonstrated utility in terms of sustainable development.[60] If given the opportunity, exiles and returnees with professional qualifications can be utilized to advantage in this training task and generally can play a critical role in development management on the continent. Finally, the importance of bureaucratic-reorientation programs that emphasize respect for and facilitation of community empowerment must not be overlooked.[61]

NOTES

1. James S. Wunsch, "Institutional Analysis and Decentralization: Developing an Analytical Framework for Effective Third World Administrative Reform," *Public Administration and Development* 11 (1991): 445.

2. Goran Hyden, "From Bargaining to Marketing: How to Reform Foreign Aid in the 1990s" (East Lansing: Michigan State University, MSU Working Papers on Political Reform in Africa, No. 6, 1993), p. 4; also see Sandip Sahota and Mark O. Lombardi, "Africa's Structural Adjustment Experiment: The Political Economy of Failure." Paper presented at the annual meeting of the African Studies Association, November 6, 1995, Orlando, pp. 7–9.

3. Douglas Hellinger, Fred O'Regan, Stephen Hellinger, and Blane Lewis, *Building Local Capacity for Sustainable Development* (Washington, D.C.: Development Group for Alternative Policies and Economic Development Programs, 1983), pp. 13–14; Peter Oakley, *Projects with People: The Practice of Participation in Rural Development* (Geneva: International Labor Organization, 1991), pp. 45–46.

4. Adebisi Adedayo, "The Implications of Community Leadership for Rural Development Planning in Nigeria," *Community Development Journal* 20 (1991): 25–27.

5. Thomas Callaghy, "Lost Between State and Market: The Politics of Economic Adjustment in Ghana, Zambia, and Nigeria," in *Economic Crisis and Policy Choice: The Politics of Economic Adjustment in the 3rd World*, ed. Joan Nelson (Princeton, N.J.: Princeton University Press, 1990), pp. 257–318; Norman Uphoff, "Grassroots Organizations and NGOs in Rural Development: Opportunities with Diminishing States and Expanding Markets," *World Development* 21 (1993): 607–22.

6. Alan Fowler, *Non-Governmental Organizations in Africa: Achieving Comparative Advantage in Relief and Microdevelopment* (Discussion Paper No. 249) (United Kingdom: Sussex Institute of Development Studies, 1988), p. 3; also see Eshetu Chole, "Linking Grassroots Organizations and Research Institutions in Africa," *African Journal of Public Administration and Management* 1 (July 1992): 57.

7. M. Esman and N. Uphoff, *Local Organizations: Intermediaries in Rural Development* (Ithaca, N.Y.: Cornell University Press, 1984), pp. 61–68.

8. Fowler, *Non-Governmental Organizations*, p. 3.

9. James Ransom, "The Akufo Akinyele Community Literacy and Health Project: A Model of Integrated Development," *Africa Today* 40 (1993): 74–78.

10. Judith Tendler, "Turning Private Voluntary Organizations into Development Agencies: Questions for Evaluation" (Program Evaluation Discussion Paper No. 2) (Washington, D.C.:USAID, 1982), pp. 3–7.

11. Fowler, *Non-Governmental Organizations*, pp. 8–9.

12. John Clark, *Democratizing Development: The Role of Voluntary Organizations* (West Hartford, Conn.: Kumarian Press, 1990), pp. 45–63.

13. Ibid., p. 10.

14. Fowler, *Non-Governmental Organizations*, p. 11.

15. Pierre Landell-Mills, "Governance, Cultural Change, and Empowerment," *Journal of Modern African Studies* 30 (1992): 543–67; Nicholas van de Walle, "Innovations in African Governance: Some Thoughts on Empowering

the Countryside," in *African Governance in the 1990s* (Atlanta, Ga.: Emory University, Carter Center, 1990), pp. 115–16; Norman Uphoff, *Local Institutional Development: An Analytical Source Book with Cases* (West Hartford, Conn.: Kumarian Press, 1986), pp. 206, 352–53.

16.   Joel D. Barkan, M. McNulty, and M.A.O Ayen, "Hometown Voluntary Associations, Local Development and the Emergence of Civil Society in Western Nigeria," *Journal of Modern African Studies* 29 (1991): 464–68.

17.   Peter Koehn, "Decentralization for Sustainable Development," in *Development Management in Africa*, eds. Sadig Rasheed and David F. Luke (Boulder, Colo.: Westview Press, 1995), pp. 77–79.

18.   "African Charter for Popular Participation in Development and Transformation" in *Africa's Problems . . . Africa's Initiatives*, ed. William Minter (Washington, D.C.: Africa Policy Information Center, 1992), pp. 28–29.

19.   U.S. Committee for Refugees. *World Refugee Survey* (Washington, D.C.: U.S. Committee for Refugees, 1994), p. 40.

20.   Michael M. Cernea, *Bridging the Research Divide: Studying Refugees and Development Oustees* (Washington, D.C.: The World Bank, Environment Department, 1994), p. 9.

21.   Ibid., p. 13.

22.   Robert F. Gorman, "Refugee Aid and Development in Africa: Research and Policy Needs from the Local Perspective," in *African Refugees: Development Aid and Repatriation*, eds. Howard Adelman and John Sorenson (Boulder, Colo.: Westview Press, 1994), p. 241.

23.   Cernea, *Bridging the Research Divide*, pp. 19, 32; Peter H. Koehn, *Refugees from Revolution: U.S. Policy and Third-World Migration* (Boulder, Colo.: Westview Press, 1991), p. 430; John Sorenson, "An Overview: Refugees and Development," in *African Refugees: Development Aid and Repatriation*, eds. Howard Adelman and John Sorenson (Boulder, Colo.: Westview Press, 1994), p. 185; Jan Sterkenburg, John Kirkby, and Phil O'Keefe, "Refugees and Rural Development: A Comparative Analysis of Project Aid in Sudan and Tanzania," in *African Refugees: Development Aid and Repatriation*, eds. Howard Adelman and John Sorenson (Boulder, Colo.: Westview Press, 1994), pp. 205–6; Gorman, "Refugee Aid," pp. 203, 236–37; Barry Stein, *Repatriation During Conflict* (Boulder, Colo.: Westview Press, 1993), p. 16.

24.   Sterkenburg, Kirkby, and O'Keefe, "Refugees," pp. 197–98, 206.

25.   John Sorenson, "Refugees, Relief and Rehabilitation in the Horn of Africa: The Eritrean Relief Association," in *African Refugees: Development Aid and Repatriation*, eds. Howard Adelman and John Sorenson (Boulder, Colo.: Westview Press, 1994), pp. 69–84.

26.   Koehn, *Refugees from Revolution*, pp. 431, 443; Sorenson, "Overview," pp. 186–87.

27.   Gorman, "Refugee Aid," p. 231.

28.   Koehn, *Refugees from Revolution*, p. 431.

29.   Stein, *Repatriation*, p. 16; also see the "Consortium Clearing House" approach described in Danish Refugee Council, "NGOs & UNHCR: New Challenge, New Vision," *Refugees* 3 (1994): 14–16.

30.   Articles 3.4 and 3.7 of the "Memorandum of Understanding on the Implementation of the Cross-Mandate Concept," p. 4.

31. Peter Koehn, ed., *Refugees and Development Assistance: Training for Voluntary Repatriation*. Final report and recommendations of an international symposium held at the University of Montana, Missoula, April 1994, pp. 6–9, 63–88.

32. Jacques Cuénod, "Refugees: Development or Relief?" in *Refugees and International Relations*, eds. Gil Loescher and Laila Monahan (Oxford: Oxford University Press), p. 237.

33. Koehn, *Refugees and Development Assistance*, pp. 76–77; Peter Koehn, "Refugee Settlement and Repatriation in Africa: Development Prospects and Constraints," in *African Refugees: Development Aid and Repatriation*, eds. Howard Adelman and John Sorenson (Boulder, Colo.: Westview Press, 1994), pp. 106–7.

34. Fowler, *Non-Governmental Organizations*, pp. 12–21.

35. Clark, *Democratizing Development*, p. 10.

36. Fowler, *Non-Governmental Organizations*, p. 21.

37. Namibia Development Trust, *Project Proposal for Organizational Workshop Programme* (Windhoek: Namibia Development Trust, Training Unit, 1991).

38. R. Apthorpe, "The Cooperative's Poor Harvest," *New Internationalist* 48 (1977): 4–6.

39. Esman and Uphoff, *Local Organizations*, p. 15.

40. See, for instance, Sakah Mahmud, "The Failed Transition to Civilian Rule in Nigeria: Its Implications for Democracy and Human Rights," *Africa Today* 40 (1993): 93.

41. Van de Walle, "Innovations," p. 117; Landell-Mills, "Governance," p. 564; Willard R. Johnson and Vivian R. Johnson, *West African Governments and Volunteer Development Organizations* (Lanham, Md.: University Press of America, 1990), p. 51. In addition, NGOs "sometimes work in isolation, and try to protect their own turf," Danish Refugee Council, "NGO's & UNHCR," p. 14.

42. Richard Jeffries, "The State, Structural Adjustment, and Good Governance in Africa," *Journal of Commonwealth and Comparative Politics* 311 (March 1993): 32–33.

43. Ethiopian Community Development Council, *African Refugees: Human Dimensions to a Global Crisis* (Arlington, Va.: Ethiopian Community Development Council, 1994), p. 35; Frederick W. Jjuuko, "The State, Democracy and Constitutionalism in Africa," *East African Journal of Peace and Human Rights* 2 (1995): 18.

44. Michael Bratton, "Enabling the Voluntary Sector in Africa: Policy Context," in *African Governance in the 1990s: Objectives, Resources, and Constraints*, ed. Carter Center (Atlanta, Ga.: Carter Center, 1990), p. 108.

45. Uphoff, *Local Institutional Development*, pp. 607–22; Bratton, "Enabling," pp. 104–14.

46. Clark, *Democratizing Development*, p. 43.

47. Ibid., pp. 39–42.

48. Fowler, *Non-Governmental Organizations*, p. 14.

49. Ebebe A. Ukpong, "Point of View: A North-South Divide?" *IFAD Update* (December 1993): 13; Frederick W. Jjuuko, dean of law at Makerere University, goes further. He contends that NONGOs are the "trail blazers for the new colonialism (of the Global State)." They aim to "freeze people in a conditioned local

setting incompatible with a national state" by "trying to depoliticize, localize, divide and rule." Jjuuko, "The State," pp. 23–27.

50. Johnson and Johnson, *West African Governments*, p. 7.

51. Clark, *Democratizing Development*, p. 36.

52. Johnson and Johnson, *West African Governments*, pp. 15–22.

53. Hyden, "From Bargaining," p. 9.

54. Ibid., pp. 10, 12–16.

55. Ibid., pp. 15–16.

56. Ibid., p. 14.

57. Ibid., p. 13.

58. Peter H. Koehn, *Public Policy and Administration in Africa: Lessons from Nigeria* (Boulder, Colo.: Westview Press, 1990), pp. 179–232; Peter H. Koehn, "Local Government Involvement in National Development Planning: Guidelines for Project Selection Based upon Nigeria's Fourth Plan Experience," *Public Administration and Development* 9 (1989): 417–36.

59. Hyden, "From Bargaining," p. 19.

60. Uphoff, *Local Institutional Development*, pp. 197, 199–200.

61. Ibid., pp. 212, 230.

8

"Managing" Development in Subsaharan Africa in the 1990s: States, Markets, and Civil Societies in Alternative Paradigms

Sandra Maclean

The development agenda in subsaharan Africa has been dominated in the 1990s by the philosophy and policies of structural adjustment and the pressures and expectations for democratization. This chapter examines the problem of "managing" development in this environment. It looks first at the concept of development management itself, briefly exploring its history and arguing that the dominant development agenda in subsaharan Africa is now (as it traditionally has been) determined by external actors and ideologies. The current agenda favors the market sector, with its main proponents being international financial institutions (IFIs) and with the prevailing ideology being neoliberalism. However, in spite (or, perhaps, because) of the dominance of the market, questions about the concomitant roles of state and civil society sectors have become increasingly salient. The chapter argues that, because it constrains the activities of these latter sectors, the externally constructed development agenda is not likely to promote economic growth or democracy in Africa, and, therefore, a new development agenda emerging from a rapprochement of African states and (re)vitalized civil societies is required. In addition, any such reconciliation requires radical changes in the assumptions and structures of the existing development agenda.

MANAGING DEVELOPMENT:
WHO MANAGES, WHO BENEFITS?

The idea that development is a problem to be "managed" was introduced by President Harry S Truman of the United States in his January 20, 1949, inaugural address, when he announced that the U.S. government would "embark on a bold new program for making the benefits of our (US) scientific advances and industrial progress available for the improvement and growth of underdeveloped areas."[1] Thus, "development" was launched as a new concern of Western foreign policy and the tone was set for north-south relations for the next 40 years. Most importantly, a new discourse was established — one that accepted unquestioningly certain observations and assumptions about relations between the industrialized West and the nonindustrialized areas of the world. One notion, implicit in Truman's speech, was that "underdeveloped" countries could reach the enviable status achieved by industrial nations if only they adopted "correct" (i.e., Western) policies and attitudes. It also was assumed that northern development theorists and foreign policy practitioners were appropriate actors to devise strategies for "improving" the south.

These assumptions have persisted throughout successive "development decades" even though various trends (and fads) have altered both the outward appearance of the policy agenda and the terminology of the discourse. These trends in direction and discourse coincide closely with shifts in the dominant production (and associated ideological) structures of the global political economy. Also, although the development agenda in the different countries of subsaharan Africa has assumed distinctive forms that have achieved varying degrees of success, general patterns reflecting global trends are discernable. Of particular salience is the recent shift in development ideology from the statism and nationalism of the early postcolonial years to the market-oriented internationalism of the present. Therefore, although Michael Bratton and Nicholas van de Walle argue correctly, in my view, that "diffusionist and structural interpretations only partly explain recent political events in Africa," they are less convincing when they state that, "in the course of transition, the *major* participants and the *dominant* influences in *every* case have been national" (emphasis added).[2] Even if, as Bratton and van de Walle claim, "elites and masses can (and do) engage in creative political behaviour,"[3] the universally applied, Western-dominated development agenda frequently defines the parameters of that behavior.

External agents exercise influence over African development through the diffusion of ideology as well as through the more obvious multilateral and bilateral loan and aid programs. One of the earliest of such influences in the postindependence period was associated with the dominant practice and philosophy of international and domestic political economy that John Ruggie has termed "embedded liberalism."[4] This emerged following World War II as a new hegemonic order characterized by the merger of interests between capital and labor within a Fordist production structure and the legitimization of the Keynesian welfare state.[5] The statist ideology associated with this order was extended from the industrialized world to developing countries partly through the theories and projects of "modernization." However, in the newly liberated former colonies of Africa, where the state's legitimacy was reinforced by recently aroused nationalist enthusiasms, there was ready acceptance for the global diffusion of the ideology of embedded liberalism. Therefore, in the early years of the development agenda, when the African state was enlisted as the principal agent for "delivering development" to its citizens, external (i.e., Western) and internal ideologies tended to converge.

The African state continued to be the predominant player in development throughout the 1960s and 1970s — from the initial "modernization" period, when emphasis was placed on creating efficient (i.e., Western-style) institutions and on adopting sound (i.e., capitalist) economic policies, through the "basic human needs" period, when the focus shifted to health, education, and other welfare needs of people.[6] However, although most African national policies demonstrated the influence of these externally created paradigms by initially adopting their liberal assumptions and objectives, later, in the case of many states, they did so by rejecting them. For example, dependency theory, which influenced political decisions in several African countries, emerged as a direct antithesis to Western liberalism.[7] Moreover, both the growth in African socialism and the increase in strength of the ideology of nonalignment can be explained in part as attempts to maintain some autonomy and gain some leverage in the competitive atmosphere of the Cold War.

In short, the development trajectories and strategies of postcolonial African states always have been either a reflection of or a reaction to the agendas set by the strongest international players. This dependence has become even more evident in the post–Cold War period; the collapse of the former Soviet Union has meant the loss of an alternative to the West either as a source of aid or as an ideological support. Moreover, the global shift, coinciding with the end of the Cold War, to post-Fordist production and the reemergence of neoliberal economics as the dominant theoretical and managerial paradigm produces pressure in Africa, as elsewhere, to open national economies to the global market and to reduce the level of state intervention in the economy. Africa became especially vulnerable to these pressures following the debt crisis of the early 1980s, which increased countries' reliance on the IFIs for new loans and assistance with debt reschedulings.

International organizations like the World Bank reflect and support the interests of their most influential members; in other words, they promote whatever orthodoxy prevails in the industrialized West. Therefore, although the World Bank in the 1960s advanced state-sponsored industrialization and in the 1970s promoted state-directed attention to basic needs, in the neoliberal period of the 1990s, it champions the market. According to the bank's current philosophy: "Governments sometimes intervene in the market to address political instability and other political constraints. But the result is that all too often, the combination of pervasive distortions and predatory states leads to development disasters. . . . (But) (i)mplementing the economic reforms considered in this Report is one way to confront the political constraints on development."[8]

The economic reforms referred to here are, of course, the controversial structural adjustment programs (SAPs), which include measures to liberalize and privatize economies.

Since SAPs were introduced in the early 1980s, a majority of subsaharan African countries have adopted either an IFI-sponsored or a homegrown version.[9] Within a decade of their introduction, however, it became clear that SAPs were not producing the beneficial results that their proponents initially anticipated.[10] According to World Bank officials, the disappointing results were due to lapses in the performance of African governments, and as a consequence they extended their concern from economics alone to include "governance."[11] In World Bank terminology, governance is "the manner in which power is exercised in the management of a country's economic and social forces for development."[12] Therefore, to promote better management, the bank advocates political restructuring measures that are intended to create well-functioning institutions, with those of Western liberal democracy serving as models.

According to some scholars, this unabashed espousal of Western liberalism really has less to do with democracy or development in subsaharan Africa than with promoting an agenda consistent with the needs of powerful forces in the north. For example, Gerald J. Schmitz argues that the bank's attention to governance is not directed to the remodeling of a developmentalist state nor does it have an empirical or moral basis for justification. Instead, its attempt to curtail the state's activity and power in order to release the market from the restraints of statism is an ideologically driven manifestation of the current hegemony of global neoliberalism.[13]

Although occasionally somewhat overstated, such views are consistent, as we have seen, with the historical pattern of development to date, and there is no new evidence to show that foreign policymakers in industrialized countries or officials of the IFIs have moved from their traditional philosophical position, which was premised on the notion that development is a process of unilinear growth and progress toward a universally agreed norm and the belief that international order (and well-being) is promoted by northern control of southern development. The two premises are related to the assumptions that the objective of development conforms universally to northern ideals and standards and, therefore, that northern experts have a clearer vision as to what processes and projects are most relevant.

The recent revisionism in official policy does not undermine these basic assumptions but, instead, reveals attempts by the dominant players to maintain the traditional structures of power in a changing global political economy. The World Bank's focus on governance and its increased attention to democracy and civil society are, to a large extent, merely a restatement in new terminology of the same philosophy that traditionally has been associated with the northern-dominated development agenda. Therefore, in concentrating exclusively on SAPs and governance as a new direction in development policy and discourse, there is a tendency to obscure that the current crisis of development rests, at least partly, in the patterns of continuity that attend the bank's persistent promotion of the existing global structures of power. As Schmitz remarks, "The emperor's new wardrobe camouflages what ought to be contested."[14]

(IN)COMPATABILITIES OF POLITICAL AND ECONOMIC LIBERALIZATION

What needs most to be contested is the current neoliberal faith in liberalization as a nostrum for unilinear and universal progress. Particularly questionable is the assumption that economic and political liberalization are complimentary processes. The World Bank's argument is that African governments have degenerated into systems of personal rule supported by patronage networks because these countries lack the strong civil societies necessary to hold states accountable. The regimes in these systems display rent-seeking, corrupt, and authoritarian behavior — creating an environment that, in the World Bank's summation, "cannot . . . support a dynamic economy."[15] In order to reverse this situation, the new World Bank policies rely on the liberal assumption that reducing the state will create political space to be filled by various associational forms, which will emerge to act as constraints on the state's activity.

Larry Diamond has argued that this process is already occurring in Africa: "African peoples have joined together in a breathtaking variety of voluntary associations. . . . As they proliferate and mature, such groups spin a web of social pluralism that makes the consolidation of authoritarian domination increasingly difficult. Although they are not explicitly political, they constitute a significant and often potent constitutency for responsive and accountable government."[16]

Diamond presents civil society as being oppositional to and separate from the state. In this liberal view, the state is essentially apolitical, merely a functional device that mediates among the various interests of society. However, in Diamond's view, there is a positive connection between structural adjustment and the proliferation of democratizing associational forms in African civil society. "Should these policies (SAPs) bear fruit, . . . they will not only rekindle economic growth, but will loosen the connection between state control and class formation. Both of these trends would bode well for democracy. . . . [Therefore] the continuation and deepening of economic liberalization is an important element in the construction of a viable democratic order in Africa."[17] Diamond's liberal view of the state and his assumptions about the value of reducing the latter's size follow earlier assumptions in comparative politics that economic and social development precede transitions to democracy.[18] Such theories on the sequence of economic growth and democratization have never been substantiated conclusively. Even less evidence exists to support the World Bank's present claims that economic development is not possible *without prior democratization.*

Furthermore, many African(ist) scholars question not only the issue of sequencing but also whether, at the present time, economic and political liberalization are compatible processes at all for most African countries.[19] Van de Walle, for instance, concludes that economic reform is extremely difficult for all African countries undergoing a transition to democracy and apparently impossible for most.[20] Bjorn Beckman discusses the opposite problem — that of instituting democracy in conditions of economic restraint; he worries that the governments of some countries are likely to respond with increased repression to the growing popular resistance to harsh economic policies.[21] Finally, even in those countries where democratization is proceeding or where its prospects are more propitious, the process may be halted or reversed if there is not concomitant sustained economic growth.

In general, what appears to trouble most critics is either that the World Bank's governance program has muddled objectives or that its objectives are unrealizable. On the first point, the prescriptions for reform in the governance program include "reducing the size of government, privatizing parastatal agencies, and improving the administration of aid funds," indicating that the bank's real concern is macroeconomic performance, rather than democratic development. In short, "the Bank has taken the technocratic approach, aiming the governance reforms at the encouragement of economic reforms, *rather than democratic politics*" (emphasis added).[22] Even if democracy were a primary concern, the prescriptions for its realization are problematic. As Adrian Leftwich states, the bank's "new orthodoxy assumes that there are no inherent tensions, conflicts or difficult trade-offs over time between the various goals of development — such as growth, democracy, stability, equity and autonomy."[23]

The essential economism of the bank's governance project places too much emphasis on the efficiency of state institutions while treating the fundamental problems of state legitimacy and popular participation as secondary or derivative issues.[24] It is not that the World Bank denies the importance of these factors; rather, it believes that they can be achieved simply by "rolling back" the state. However, as Manfred Bienefeld has argued, this rejection of the state and the renewed reliance on the market is based on an ideological, doctrinaire faith rather than on any empirical evidence that the policies can do what they are purported to be able to do.[25]

BRINGING THE STATE BACK IN

Still, one might argue that, despite apparent limitations in the World Bank's visionary zeal, the policies are, at least, a step in the right direction. Even if the processes of economic growth and democratization do not proceed in smooth, compatible, unilinear progression, as the liberal agencies proclaim, surely attention to even the institutional aspect of governance in Africa is welcome. The lengthy debate of recent years on the issue of state hardness or softness in developing countries seems to have been settled largely with respect to the African state; most analysts now appear to agree that the widespread authoritarianism on the continent is a sign of weakness rather than strength. The state in subsaharan Africa, with rare exceptions, does not appear to offer much in the way of developmentalist content or intent, having neither democratically structured polities nor efficiently run economies. Indeed, repression, the inability to enforce regulations, and a concentration of power at the center together constitute a crisis of the state that clearly is as serious as the economic crisis.

Nevertheless, there are several reasons why the state in Africa — weak, nondevelopmental, and undemocratic though it may be — should be reformed and not further reduced. First, the recent experiences of the newly industrialized countries of Southeast Asia suggest that states play a crucial role in economic growth. Second, on a moral basis, there is justification (and, arguably, responsibility) for the state to intervene in the economy to protect the welfare needs of its citizens. Third, strong states provide a necessary counterforce to economic globalization — a process that is contributing to an increasing welfare gap both between and within countries and regions.

A policy that calls for an abrupt liberalization of economies and a drastic reduction in the role of the state appears to ignore lessons of history. Specifically, the recent impressive economic growth records of the

Southeast Asian newly industrialized countries were, with the possible exception of Hong Kong, not achieved through laissez-faire economic policy but by intensive government intervention.[26] Moreover, aside from the economic efficiency of statist involvement, there is a political argument for a strong, rather than reduced, state. A central problem for African development (whether defined in democratic or economic terms) is the disjunction in state-societal relations. In conditions of severe economic constriction, SAPs reinforce this schism by curtailing the state's redistributive role. Such diminishing of the state's ability to provide collective goods is likely to generate hostile popular reactions, which may be contained by a repressive state or, alternatively, by an effective, authoritative (as opposed to authoritarian) one.

Although a "capable" reformist state might be either repressive or democratic, clearly, the democratic version seems preferable. At the very least, democracy means that all adult citizens have an equal say as to who governs and it means that there are institutional arrangements in place for the protection of human rights. Yet, beyond these basic principles, democracy is a contested concept, particularly as it is associated with variable views of the state and its relations to society. As defined in traditional liberal theory, democracy is based on the concept of negative freedom, connoting freedom *from* coercion by another or others (including the state) but not necessarily freedom *to* achieve one's objectives (especially if their achievement involves direct intervention by the state). Perhaps especially in the context of development, it appears that the issue of moral choice is more problematic than liberal theory allows; when the freedom to choose involves the satisfaction of basic needs, it is not merely a question of choosing among neutral objectives. Moreover, the international connections that define the development agenda make a problem of the notion that democratic institutions and cultures in every national situation are or can be decided by uncoerced rational choice.

The lack of democratic choice at the national level for people within poor countries traditionally has been explained away as the inevitable consequence of the anarchical international system. Now, as Bienefeld exclaims, with the Cold War restraints to unbridled capitalism removed, "there is less need [than ever] to sacrifice principles on the sleazy altar of *Realpolitik*" and, consequently, the globalization of production — both materialist and ideological — is able to proceed apace.[27] One notable feature of the globalization processes has been the "internationalization of the state," in which the state's concern has shifted away from domestic responsibilities toward the needs of international and transnational capital.[28] This shift in emphasis is reflected in various new forms and degrees of insecurity for the majority of the world's people. Although globalization creates "islands of privilege" for small groups of the world's people, it also is responsible for widening and deepening the gaps that exist among the majority of people in different countries and regions as well as among groups of people within countries.[29] One potential solution to the present globalization of insecurity would be the recapture of the state by popular forces.[30] However, the policies that presently dominate the development agenda militate against such a trend even as counterforces within civil societies continue to emerge.[31]

BRINGING IN CIVIL SOCIETY

Responses of civil societies to such pressures of insecurity have not been ignored by liberal scholars and agencies. However, just as their analyses of the state's role in development are flawed, so, too, is their assumption that the (re)vitalization of civil societies is a straightforward, unproblematic process. As the preceding quotes from Diamond suggest, liberals take for granted that democracy will result when individuals and groups in civil societies are permitted to choose their particular ends unrestrained by the state. Such an assertion presupposes the narrow view of democracy based on negative freedom, as already discussed. More importantly, it misses a fundamental point upon which even this narrow view of democracy is premised, namely, that democracy is constructed not only *for* the people but *by* the people. In other words, democratic practices are not likely to emerge from policies that are imposed from the outside.

Schmitz captures the essence of popular participation that top-down approaches such as the World Bank's inevitably miss: "Who participates, when, how, and to what effect, is enormously important to the depth and durability of democratization (and, one might add, development). . . . A participatory agenda ought to mean removing the obstacles [economic, gender, racial, cultural, etc.] to persons and communities developing the capacity for self-governance."[32]

Bank policies rely on institutional reform to provide "good governance" and thereby to establish the enabling environment, which will allow greater democratic participation. However, such policies do nothing to assist, encourage, or inform people who, until now, have had little or no experience with liberal democratic structures of governance. Ironically, as the current rhetoric celebrates "popular participation," these policies tend to avoid the people most affected. Moreover, the policies ignore an important stream of democratic theory, traceable from Aristotle through Jean Jacques Rousseau, J. S. Mill, and Alexis de Tocqueville, that teaches that participation involves "a continuing interrelationship between the working of institutions and the psychological qualities and attitudes of individuals interacting within them."[33] In short, participation involves "not just policies . . . but also the development of social and political capacities of each individual."[34]

CONCLUSIONS: TOWARD A
DEVELOPMENTALIST AGENDA

Ironically, the current development discourse is replete with references to the "democratic" objectives of popular participation, empowerment, social equity, sustainability, and so on, although the dominant international agencies continue to play major roles in maintaining an institutionalized structure of hierarchical control. Yet, more than ironic coincidence connects the present discourse and the unequal north-south relations. In fact, in many instances, it appears that the discourse of the dominant actors incorporates terms in order to defuse them of their radical content. By "deconstructing" such terms to expose the power relations that underly policies, it may be possible to propose an alternative strategy that is more authentically democratic. Schmitz's examination of the term "popular participation" is a good example of such a "de(re)construction" project:

Support for democratic participation therefore should mean empowering people to make their own decisions, not engineering the forms of "good governance" which other elites are expected to undertake. Taking strong actions against dictatorial regimes is one thing (and long overdue); prescribing the course of political and policy reform quite another. Donors, for all their invocation of politically correct language, have shown that they are not ready to surrender control over agenda setting to local democratic forces.[35]

Only by surrendering control to such forces can development management be brought into accord with the optimistic, but largely rhetorical, objectives of the current discourse. Neoliberals' narrow definition of democracy and overly economistic view of state-society relations are, by their nature, dismissive of the particularities and contradictions of the African situations. Consequently, they do little to facilitate processes that might help to establish some measure of state-societal accord, which, surely, is a precondition for sustainable development. Therefore, the project of providing increased opportunities for greater popular participation requires a reevaluation of the dominant players' ideologically based assumptions about national development and democracy. At the same time, however, any complete discussion of development management in subsaharan Africa cannot be divorced from its international and transnational connections. Not only has the history of African development been influenced by the diffusion of ideologies from outside, but also the marginal position in the global economy of subsaharan countries has reduced their ability to resist the pressures of dominant international financial actors.

In the final analysis, African development requires that the entire structure of the existing development agenda be reevaluated and reconstructed. A truly developmentalist agenda would, itself, be democratic. Democratizing this structure would involve, as a start, accepting that development is more than economic growth and institutional structures of governance, that it is "a process of realizing potential, maximizing choices and allowing people thereby to become more fully human."[36] Such a process would involve reevaluating traditional assumptions concerning the universality of values and unilinearity of progress, thereby questioning the overweening authority of northern viewpoints and voices. In addition, it would raise doubts about the legitimacy of a system that regulates the terms, definitions, and conditions of development solely on the basis of material dominance. Finally, a truly democratic agenda would recognize that northern issues — environmental degradation, urban violence, commodification, drug abuse, family and community disintegration, and so on — are also problems of development integrally related to those of the third world. It is only by understanding this issue of global connectedness that the management of development in subsaharan Africa will move toward more democratic and developmental conclusions.

NOTES

1. Harry S Truman, Inaugural Address, January 20, 1949, in *Documents on American Foreign Relations* (Princeton, N.J.: Princeton University Press, 1967).

2. Michael Bratton and Nicholas van de Walle, "Popular Protest and Political Reform in Africa," *Comparative Politics* 24 (1992): 420.

3. Ibid.

4. John Ruggie, "International Regimes, Transactions and Change — Embedded Liberalism in the Post-War Order," *International Organization* 36 (1982): 379–415.

5. Stephen Gill and David Law, *The Global Political Economy: Perspectives, Problems and Policies* (Baltimore, Md.: Johns Hopkins University Press, 1988), pp. 79–80; Alain Liepitz, *Towards a New Economic Order: Postfordism, Ecology and Democracy* (London: Polity Press, 1993).

6. See, for instance, Ankie M. M. Hoogvelt, *The Third World in Global Development* (London: Macmillan, 1982).

7. For a comprehensive discussion of the dependency experiment in Tanzania and the debate elsewhere in Africa, see Magnus Blomstrom and Bjorn Hettne, *Development Theory in Transition: The Dependency Debate and Beyond: Third World Responses* (London: Zed, 1984), pp. 138–62.

8. World Bank, *World Development Report 1991: The Challenge of Development* (Washington, D.C.: International Bank for Reconstruction and Development, 1991), p. 10.

9. Many bilateral donors require an International Monetary Fund "stamp of approval" before lending to an African country; therefore, even if the latter does not negotiate an official agreement with IFIs, it must abide by their guidelines.

10. Mamadou Dia, "Building and the Improvement of Governance: the Role of Indigenous Institutions." Paper presented at the African Studies Association Annual Meeting, December 1993, Boston; Trevor Parfitt, "Review Article: Which African Agenda for the 'Nineties? The ECA/World Bank Alternatives," *Journal of International Development* 5 (1993): 93–106.

11. Ibid.

12. World Bank, *Governance and Development* (Washington, D.C.: International Bank for Reconstruction and Development, 1992), p. 1.

13. Gerald J. Schmitz, "Democratization and Demystification: Deconstructing 'Governance' as Development Paradigm." Paper prepared for the Annual Meeting of the Canadian Association in International Development, June 7–9, 1993, Carleton University.

14. Ibid., p. 2.

15. Peter Gibbon, "Structural Adjustment and Pressures toward Multipartyism in Subsaharan Africa," in *Authoritarianism, Democracy, and Adjustment: The Politics of Economic Reform in Africa,* eds. Peter Gibbon et al. (Uppsala, Sweden: Nordiska Afrikainstitutet, 1992), p. 140.

16. Larry Diamond, "Introduction: Roots of Failure, Seeds of Hope," in *Democracy in Developing Countries, Volume 2: Africa,* eds. Larry Diamond et al. (Boulder, Colo.: Lynne Rienner, 1988), p. 26.

17. Ibid., p. 27.

18. Adrian Leftwich, "Governance, Democracy and Development in the Third World," *Third World Quarterly* 14 (1993): 605–24.

19. T. M. Callaghy, "Comments on Political Liberalization and Economic Reform in Africa and Political Liberalization and the Politics of Economic Reform," in *Economic Policy Reform in Africa's New Era of Political Liberalization.* Proceedings of a Workshop for SPA Donors (Washington, D.C.: U.S. Agency for International Development, 1993), pp. 103–7.

20. Nicholas van de Walle, "Political Liberalization and Economic Reform in Africa." Paper presented at U.S. Agency for International Development Workshop on Economic Reform, April 1993.

21. Bjorn Beckman, "Empowerment or Repression? The World Bank and the Politics of African Adjustment," in *Authoritarianism, Democracy, and Adjustment: The Politics of Economic Reform in Africa,* ed. Peter Gibbon et al. (Uppsala, Sweden: Nordiska Afrikainstitutet, 1992).

22. Michael Bratton and Donald Rothchild, "The Institutional Bases of Governance in Africa," in *Governance and Politics in Africa,* eds. Goran Hyden and Michael Bratton (Boulder, Colo.: Lynne Rienner, 1992), p. 265.

23. Leftwich, "Governance," p. 605.

24. Bratton and Rothchild, "Institutional Bases," p. 265.

25. Manfred Bienefeld, "The New World Order: Echoes of a New Imperialism," *Third World Quarterly* 15 (1994): 32.

26. Stephen Haggard, *Pathways from the Periphery: The Politics of Growth in the Newly Industrializing Countries* (Ithaca, N.Y.: Cornell University Press, 1990).

27. Bienefeld, "New World Order," p. 33.

28. Robert Cox, "The Global Political Economy and Social Choice," in *The New Era of Global Competition: State Policy and Market Power,* eds. Daniel Drache and Meric Gertler (Montreal: MacGill-Queens, 1991), p. 337.

29.   Stephen Gill, "'Globalization' and the Emerging World Order." Paper presented at workshop on Globalization: Opportunities and Challenges, March 1994, American University, Washington, D.C.

30.   Sandra   MacLean,   "Conceptualizing   Linkages: Development, Democratization and the Globalization of Insecurity." Paper presented at the annual meeting of the Canadian Association for Studies in International Development, June 12–14, 1994, University of Alberta.

31.   R.B.J. Walker, *One World, Many Worlds: Struggles for a Just World Peace* (Boulder, Colo.: Lynne Rienner, 1988), pp. 60–63.

32.   Gerald Schmitz, "Why Words Matter: Some Thoughts on the 'New' Development Agenda." Paper presented at the annual meeting of the Canadian Association for the Study of International Development, June 4, 1992, Charlottetown.

33.   Carole Pateman, *Participation and Democratic Theory* (Cambridge: Cambridge University Press, 1970), p. 22.

34.   Ibid., p. 43.

35.   Schmitz, "Why Words Matter."

36.   Tim Brodhead, "Applying Lessons from the South in the North," *Synergy* 5 (1993): 4.

IV

WOMEN AND EMPOWERMENT
IN AFRICA IN THE 1990s

9

Toward Equality for All?: International Human Rights and African Women

Lynn Berat

Beginning with the United Nations (UN) Charter of 1945, an ever increasing number of international instruments have enshrined an expanding corpus of international human rights norms. Although many theorists and practitioners take these norms to have universal applicability, some women's groups now are challenging this assumption with regard to the equality of women. As they point out, there are more than 20 separate treaties concerning women, but these are rarely enforced. The situation is particularly grievous in many subsaharan African countries, where women tend to comprise the poorest and least educated stratum of the population. As such states struggle to move from an authoritarian past to a more democratic future, the position of women is newly highlighted. This chapter explores the nature of international human rights for women and suggests ways that such rights, through the vehicle of the African Charter on Human And Peoples' Rights, can be employed by African women to secure economic and social gains. The first part examines the international status of women's rights, the second part discusses the nature of the African Charter and its place among international and regional human rights instruments, and the third part considers how African women may use the charter to advance their struggle for equality.

THE INTERNATIONAL POSITION

The UN Charter of 1945 committed UN member states to international cooperation in "promoting and encouraging respect for human rights and for fundamental freedoms for all without distinction as to race, sex, language or religion."[1] The Universal Declaration of Human Rights of 1948, which elaborated upon the rights in the UN Charter, recognized the inherent dignity and inalienable rights of all human beings as the foundation of freedom, justice, and peace.[2] Accordingly, it supported the rule of law as protector of human rights so that there need be no rebellion against tyranny and oppression.

Despite the formal recognition of women's equality found in these instruments, women continued to lag behind men in the political and economic spheres. Consequently, many women's groups, primarily in Western countries, sought specific human rights guarantees addressed to their concerns. Their efforts led to the promulgation of the UN Convention on the Political Rights of Women of 1953, the UN Convention on the Nationality of Married Women of 1957, and the UN Educational, Scientific, and Cultural Organization Convention on Discrimination in Education of 1960.[3]

Though not directed specifically toward women, the two 1966 UN covenants — the Covenant on Civil and Political Rights and the Covenant on Economic, Social, and Cultural Rights[4] — further expanded upon women's rights. Although the former made de jure equality possible, the latter dealt with issues of de facto equality that remain the most difficult to resolve. For example, article 2(1) of the Covenant on Civil and Political Rights requires state parties "to respect and to ensure to all individuals within its territory and subject to its jurisdiction the rights recognized in the present Covenant."[5] Moreover, "[all] persons are equal before the law and are entitled without any discrimination to the equal protection of the law. In this respect, the law shall prohibit any discrimination and guarantee to all persons equal and effective protection against discrimination on any ground such as . . . sex."[6]

The corresponding article of the Covenant on Economic, Social, and Cultural Rights is far less demanding. Hence, a party is asked only to "undertake to take steps. . . to the maximum of its available resources, with a view to achieving progressively the full realization of the rights recognized in the present covenant by all appropriate means including particularly the adoption of legislative measures."[7] Among the general rights acknowledged are the rights to work, fair wages, and conditions of service; to social security and insurance; an adequate standard of living and freedom from hunger; mental and physical health; and education and freedom from discrimination. Also recognized are the rights to establish and join trade unions and to strike.

The dichotomy between equality of opportunity (de jure equality) and equality of outcome (de facto equality) manifested by the two 1966 covenants was remedied in the UN Convention on the Elimination of All Forms of Discrimination Against Women (CEDAW) of 1979.[8] The convention, which originated during 1975, International Women's Year, entered into force on September 3, 1981. The convention establishes broad goals for eliminating discrimination based on sex or marital status. In article 2, state parties condemn all forms of discrimination against women and agree to follow immediately a policy aimed at eliminating such discrimination.[9] State parties also are obliged to submit reports to the UN secretary-general, charting their progress.[10] The reports are examined by the CEDAW committee that is charged with monitoring the progress of signatories in implementing the convention.[11] The committee meets annually to consider the reports and is empowered to make suggestions and general recommendations based on its examination of these reports. The committee also reports annually, through the UN Economic and Social Council, to the General Assembly.[12]

Although CEDAW has these reporting powers, the convention itself creates no machinery enabling states to complain of noncompliance by another state. It also does not accord individuals the right to lodge complaints about CEDAW violations. In this respect, it is different from and more limited than both UN covenants of 1966.[13]

Nevertheless, whether found in human rights instruments of general applicability or in instruments aimed specifically at women's concerns, by 1989, four years after the close of the UN Decade for Women, the prevailing international legal view was that freedom from discrimination on the basis of sex had become a substantive and independent human right with regard to international instruments. For example, the UN Human Rights Committee confirmed this conclusion and defined discrimination broadly to include "any distinction, exclusion, restriction or preference which is based on any ground such as race, color, sex, language, religion, political or other opinion, national or social origin, property, birth or other status, and which has the purpose or effect of nullifying or impairing the recognition, enjoyment or exercise by all persons, on an equal footing, of all rights and freedoms."[14]

It follows that the definition of discrimination has two key components: there must be a distinction that is not based on objective and reasonable justification and there must be no reasonable relationship of proportionality between the aim and the means employed to attain it. As applied to women, discrimination occurs if a distinction made on the basis of sex impairs or nullifies women's enjoyment, on an equal footing with men, of human rights and fundamental freedoms. Thus, by the beginning of the 1990s, few jurists doubted that women's freedom from sex discrimination had become a major international human right.

Indeed, the language of the UN instruments resonated in the text of many regional human rights instruments,[15] including the African Charter, drafted and ratified during the Decade for Women.

THE AFRICAN CHARTER

Adopted in 1981 under the auspices of the Organization of African Unity, the African Charter on Human and Peoples' Rights, also known as the Banjul Charter, came into force in 1986.[16] The Charter is a regional human rights instrument with counterparts elsewhere, namely Europe and Latin America.[17] According to the terms of the UN Charter, regional organizations for the protection of human rights may exist as long as they do not clash with the purposes and principles of the UN.[18] However, if there is a conflict between UN member states' obligations under the UN Charter and their duties under other international instruments, their charter obligations are deemed to be paramount.[19]

Hence, regional human rights instruments like the African Charter are not divorced from universal human rights jurisprudence emanating from the UN and its constituent bodies but form part of a larger global system of human rights. Indeed, regional human rights instruments, like those of general applicability, derive their strength from the human rights obligations of the UN Charter. Thus, the preamble to the African Charter affirms the promotion of international cooperation in light of the UN Charter and the Universal Declaration.[20]

Still, the link to universally applicable human rights instruments does not end there. With regard to the rights of women, the African Charter links itself to CEDAW and other instruments with the provision that: "The state shall ensure the elimination of every discrimination against women and also ensure the protection of the rights of the woman and child as stipulated in international declarations and Conventions."[21] This is an extremely broad provision, because it gives legal authority not only to international conventions but also to declarations that typically do not have the force of law.

In addition to requiring parties to create equality for women and to advance women's rights according to international legal standards, the charter also describes certain allegedly African values. For example, article 18(2) calls the family the custodian of morals and traditional values recognized by the community.[22] The problem with such a provision is that these moral and traditional values, often expressed in legal fora via the vehicle of customary law, frequently are antithetical to women's rights. Nevertheless, if one follows the interpretation that the African Charter must be read consistently with the international instruments, then the "morals and cultural values" mentioned in article 18(2) also must be consistent with the same international standards. Indeed, article 5 (1) of CEDAW, which the African Charter embraces, demands that signatories adopt measures to alter sexist prejudices so that any discriminatory practices based on gender or on sexual stereotypes may be eliminated.[23]

The African Charter goes beyond establishing that only the state has certain obligations to ensure women's equality; it also insists that individuals have certain duties. Articles 27–29 deal explicitly with individual duties.[24] Thus, there is a duty to respect other human beings and to treat them without discrimination. Also, there is a duty to engage in behavior that promotes and reinforces mutual respect and tolerance. With regard to women's rights, men are not to discriminate against women and must treat them with respect. Moreover, in article 29, the charter creates the duty for the individual to preserve and strengthen "positive" African cultural values in his or her relations with other members of the society, all in the spirit of tolerance, dialogue, and consultation.[25] The use of the word "positive" is, indeed, significant, because it recognizes that there may be certain aspects of culture and tradition that are not progressive. Following this logic, positive values would be those that foster women's equality.

Although, in theory at least, African women resident in countries that are signatories to the African Charter should enjoy full equality with men in the social and economic spheres, the reality is, as is well-known, far different. The African Charter demands that state parties "recognize [the right to freedom from discrimination]. . . and . . . undertake to adopt legislation or other measures to give effect to [it]."[26] Yet, African states have not enacted legislation giving effect to this requirement. Although most African constitutions do not prohibit discrimination on the basis of sex, the few — like those in Namibia, Zambia, and South Africa[27] — that do have not necessarily harmonized ordinary legislation with the constitutional ideal. Typically, the fact that their governments are signatories to the African Charter notwithstanding, women have no legal means — for myriad reasons, including lack of education, resources, and access to legal services — of securing equal rights within their home countries.

Although domestic avenues of redress usually are closed to women, the African Charter yet may prove useful in protecting women from discrimination. The success of efforts to rely upon the charter will depend largely upon the capacity of women's groups, perhaps allied with international human rights organizations, to use the African Charter to seek redress and, once that redress is sought, the effectiveness of the charter's institutional framework for dealing with abuses, namely, the African Commission on Human and Peoples' Rights.

ENFORCEMENT STRATEGIES

In their campaign to achieve equality, women cannot rely upon the men who dominate local and national governments to bring women's grievances forth.[28] Hence, any advancement of their cause must occur on both the national and international levels. First, women must overcome disunity and a lack of awareness of their rights. Second, once organized in local, national, and supranational bodies, they can proceed to bring pressure on the African Commission to push charter signatories to make their paper commitment to equality real. Such an approach faces myriad social, political, economic, and institutional obstacles, which, though daunting, perhaps are not insurmountable.

Women's Unity and National Efforts

As indicated, state parties to the African Charter agree, in article 1, to recognize the rights and freedoms guaranteed by the charter and to adopt legislation or other measures that give meaning to those guarantees.[29] Evaluated by this standard, most signatories have not fulfilled their charter obligations. However, beyond removing legal obstacles to equality, the nature of the other measures to be taken is not revealed in article 1. This lack of precision is not exceptional. For example, signatories of the International Covenant on Civil and Political Rights agree "to take the necessary steps. . . to adopt such legislation or other measures as may be necessary to give effect to the rights."[30] Similarly, the UN Committee on Economic, Social, and Cultural Rights stresses that, although the passage of appropriate legislation is desirable for the protection of the guaranteed rights, it does not exhaust state obligations under the treaty; thus, states must take all necessary steps.[31]

The African Charter goes beyond these other instruments in article 25, which provides that "state parties. . . shall have the duty to protect and ensure through teaching, education and publication, the respect of the rights and freedoms contained in the present Charter and to see to it that these freedoms and rights as well as corresponding obligations and duties are understood."[32] This provision extends state responsibility not only to governmental compliance but also to efforts to ensure that private citizens are made aware of the meaning of both the individual country's legislation and the international human rights norms those laws reflect.

It would appear that article 25 is central to crafting a strategy for women to employ the charter to their advantage. Women's groups can use the article to pressure their governments to treat them more equitably. Yet, such pressure cannot be brought against governments unless women are aware of the law and have the time and means to arrange meetings to discuss their legal position and plan a course of action. Given the overall low educational level of African women plus their often crushing workload, there generally has not been an overwhelmingly strong women's movement, particularly among rural women. Few women are acquainted with domestic law — often assuming, incorrectly, that discriminatory customs are sanctioned by national law — let alone the existence of international instruments like the African Charter.

However, increasingly, better educated women, usually in urban centers, are using their training and skills to militate in favor of greater equality for women. Indeed, such groups are even networking with their domestic counterparts in rural areas as well as with women across Africa and even beyond. These efforts have resulted in a growing discourse about human rights for women.[33] For example, in South Africa, likely because of that country's relatively high levels of education for African women and of urbanization, women from around the country have come together to fight to ensure that their new constitution's guarantees of equality are not ignored by predominantly male national and local legislatures.[34] Even so, the more educated women who often lead women's groups in Africa, especially lawyers, tend to remain unaware of the position of women in international law, particularly under the African Charter; therefore, the outreach and education programs of these groups generally do not focus on the broader universe of remedies available to women.

In order to help African women achieve their goals, it is appropriate that women's groups from around the world offer support to their African sisters and share their experiences in using international human rights law. The International Conference on Women held in Beijing in September 1995 eventually may prove to be the catalyst for the strengthening of African women's groups through greater international exposure, which may lead to greater international cooperation. The response of African governments to this kind of networking often has been to allege that African women are being misled and patronized by Western women; yet, a stronger argument can be made that women around the world share a commonality of interests and experiences regardless of their country of residence and that attempts by governments to discredit efforts at unity are based upon fear rather than deeply held political conviction.

Another avenue for creating greater awareness among women is for foreign donor organizations — both governmental and nongovernmental — not only to channel funding to women's groups but also to make equality for women and female empowerment conditions of grants for specific purposes (e.g., education and skills training) given to governments and other organizations. Indeed, increasingly, foreign donors are attaching such conditions to grants in the hopes that, for example, better education for African women will reduce the population growth rate and, thereby, lead to an overall improvement in a country's economic condition.

Although African governments again may object on the grounds that these kinds of conditions constitute impermissible interference in their domestic affairs, their desperate need for aid usually acts to overcome that objection, especially because African governments know all too well that, with the collapse of communism in the Soviet Union and eastern Europe and the suddenly rising economic fortunes of much of Asia and Latin America, the demands for aid are greater than ever.

Whatever the mechanisms that assist African women, as such women become more aware of their international human rights, particularly those that exist under the charter, they will be able to work to ensure that those rights are made concrete. Women can remind governments of their obligations under article 25 of the charter to eliminate discrimination and support the education of the populace about the illegality of discrimination. Having lobbied in this way, they also can bring suit in domestic courts, seeking enforcement of their rights. Such courts, of course, may be mere tools of the state, with little respect for the rule of law, a possibility that is enhanced by the fact that most African states are not functioning democracies. Having exhausted domestic remedies, African women then can proceed to bring their grievances directly before the African Commission on Human and Peoples' Rights, a path that likely will be as difficult as the domestic route, especially because the African Commission, the human rights arm of the charter, has ill-developed machinery and is institutionally weak because it is beholden to African governments for its funding.

Using the African Charter

The African Charter established the 11-member commission "to promote human and peoples' rights and ensure their protection in Africa."[35] However, financial constraints render the commission dysfunctional. Article 41 of the charter stipulates that the secretary-general of the Organization of African Unity (OAU) will provide the staff and services necessary for the commission to perform its duties effectively; the OAU is to cover the costs involved.[36]

In practice, the OAU has made available only limited funds, so that the commission meets but twice a year in eight-day sessions. This is inadequate if the commission is to examine the reports from states and human rights organizations on each country's progress in the human rights field.[37] Moreover, the brevity of the meetings leaves the commission no time to issue comments or formulate guidelines for reporting along the lines of the widely used directives and comments from the Human Rights Committee established under the International Covenant on Civil and Political Rights and the Committee on Economic, Social, and Cultural Rights created under the international covenant of the same name.

Inadequate funds also have meant that the commission is chronically understaffed, with only the semblance of a secretariat. Accordingly, it is not able to prepare documents for commission meetings, respond to correspondence from African nongovernmental organizations (NGOs), or conduct research.[38]

Even if these financial obstacles were to be overcome, the method of appointment of commissioners is politically charged. According to the charter, the commission's members are to be Africans of the greatest integrity and impartiality, known for their competence in matters of human and peoples' rights.[39] In practice, however, the method of appointment presents obstacles to finding such impartial individuals. The charter provides for the election of commissioners by the Assembly of Heads of State and Governments from persons nominated by state parties.[40] This has resulted in the selection of commissioners who often are ministers or other high government officials in their countries and who continue to hold those positions while they serve on the commission. Furthermore, states appear to make loyalty to the government a major consideration in the selection of nominees. This practice, therefore, calls into question the ability of the individuals so chosen to act impartially in situations in which their own government's — a government in which they continue to play a prominent role — human rights record is questioned. On a purely practical level, these full-time commitments have meant that the commission often has been unable to achieve a quorum.

That the commission is overwhelmingly male also does not serve to advance women's issues. To date, there has been only one woman commissioner.[41] A judge from Cape Verde, she was not sworn in until December 1993, the commission's fourteenth session. Her selection was the result of lobbying begun in 1991 by NGOs with observer status, who demanded that the commission adopt an affirmative action policy with regard to the appointment of female commissioners. The proposal encountered considerable hostility from some of the male commissioners, but eventually, a woman was chosen. One African journalist hailed the measure, noting, "It is only one woman alongside ten men, but a male bastion has been breached and the NGOs can only press on until the African Commission begins to reflect the African society in its composition."[42] It is not yet clear whether this appointment will make a difference in the commission's work.

The commission has the power to entertain matters raised by state parties and individuals. NGOs also may submit complaints if the person(s) directly affected by an alleged human rights violation cannot submit the complaint. The commission, however, has only advisory powers, limited to reporting its findings to the assembly, which decides whether and how to act.[43] Another constraint on the ability of women to get satisfactory results from the commission is that the charter requires the commission to keep all information — even the names of the parties — confidential until the assembly decides to the contrary.[44] This means that publicity, the most potent of all international human rights enforcement mechanisms, which serves both a preventive and an educational function, is, thus, eliminated in these instances. Still, there is nothing to prevent African women's groups and their international counterparts from disseminating these grievances to the media and relevant organizations.

In another approach to the use of publicity, women's groups also could endeavor to move the commission by calling upon it to interpret the charter to emphasize that women's equal rights are demanded by the equality provision in article 3. However, the charter provides only that state parties and African organizations recognized by the OAU may request the commission to interpret the charter.[45] It is uncertain as to whether an NGO granted observer status at the commission is thereby "recognized by the OAU."[46]

Nevertheless, women's groups can petition for observer status and then demand interpretations of the charter. The problem, of course, is that women's groups often are unaware that they can even apply for such status, because the commission, partly because of its lack of funding, has not published the procedures. If they are denied observer status, they can publicize that fact. If they are granted the status and then rebuffed on the ground that their status is not adequate to enable them to bring into play the charter's provisions, they publicize this as well. Even with Africa's often crushing infrastructural and communications inadequacies and frequently muzzled media,[47] it is still possible with phones, faxes, and even internet connections, which exist in some places, for women's groups to get far-reaching and almost instantaneous support for their cause, especially if they utilize established networks of women's groups around the globe. If women are able to get observer status, they then will be able to propose items for the agenda.[48]

The charter also empowers the commission to investigate human rights violations through its own initiative,[49] something unlikely to happen with regard to women given the current state of the commission's operations. Nevertheless, it also would be unfair to attribute antiwomen bias to the commission categorically. The same problems that afflict women's groups, that is, lack of knowledge about human rights, also are likely to beset male commission members, regardless of their educational backgrounds and political prominence. They, too, could benefit from human rights training programs funded by international donors. Similarly, their failure to communicate with women's NGOs is not unique to women but, rather, besets their approach to NGOs in general. There, too, relationships with NGOs need to be cultivated, a project that will require financial support.

One such initiative is already underway. For example, the International Commission of Jurists and the African Center for Democracy and Human Rights Studies have brought together African human rights organizations at a meeting parallel to the biannual commission meetings. There, the NGOs have been able to interact and formulate recommendations about how the commission can support their work and vice versa. These recommendations stress the creation of regular, efficient channels of communication, although this remains problematic, given the inadequacies of the secretariat.

Nevertheless, the commission, though severely handicapped by financial and other institutional constraints, still has the potential to be used by women's groups to achieve their goal of equality. The International Court of Justice Initiative is encouraging because it points the way for the commission to live out its promise of helping to advance the cause of women's rights in Africa; it would seem that donor funding and cooperation with reputable international human rights organizations may be the way forward. Although there may remain the temptation for African governments to castigate such an approach as impermissible interference in African affairs, it is conceivable that, in the current international climate, governments may not be willing to alienate donors whose goodwill is needed so desperately. Furthermore, governments may well bow to negative international publicity about their obstructive behavior. Overall, a functioning African commission would not only benefit women in Africa but also help African states to establish international credibility by showing their seriousness about improving the life of all their citizens. Also, it would allow African states to become full partners, rather than onlookers, in the creation and evolution of international human rights jurisprudence in our global village.

NOTES

1. 6 UN CIO docs. (1945), *Charter of the United Nations* (hereafter cited as UN Charter).
2. UN GAOR Res. 217 (III) (1948).
3. 193 UNT.S. 135; 309 UNT.S. 65; 429 UNT.S. 93 (1960).
4. 6 INT'L L.M. 368.
5. Covenant on Civil and Political Rights, 6 INT'L L.M. 368, article 2(1).
6. Ibid., article 26.
7. Covenant on Economic, Cultural, and Social Rights.
8. UN GAOR Res. 34/180 (1979) (hereafter cited as CEDAW).
9. Ibid., article 2.
10. Ibid., article 18.
11. Ibid., article 17.
12. Ibid., article 21.
13. See notes 6 and 7 and accompanying text.

14.   Proceedings of UN Human Rights Committee (1989); the committee made its comments in the context of the Covenant on Civil and Political Rights.

15.   Among these are the European Convention on Human Rights, 213 UNT.S. 221, and the American Convention on Human Rights, 9 INT'L L.M. 99 (1970).

16.   The Organization of African Unity was established by the Charter of the Organization of African Unity, concluded at Addis Ababa on May 25, 1963 (479 UNT.S. 39), and in force on September 16, 1963; 21 INT'L L.M. 1982 (hereafter cited as African Charter) (a detailed discussion of the charter is found in U. O. Umozurike, "The African Charter on Human and Peoples' Rights," *American Journal of International Law* 77 [1983]: 902).

17.   See note 15 and accompanying text.

18.   UN Charter, article 52.

19.   Ibid., article 103.

20.   African Charter, Preamble.

21.   Ibid., article 18(3).

22.   Ibid., article l 18(2).

23.   CEDAW, article 5(1).

24.   Ibid., articles 27–29.

25.   Ibid., article 29.

26.   Ibid., article 1.

27.   Republic of Namibia, Constitution, Act 1 (1990); Constitution of Zambia (1992) (women fought to include a provision barring discrimination on the basis of sex in Zambia's democratic constitution); Constitution of South Africa (1994).

28.   The numerical superiority of women in Africa and their potential voting power means that women have the possibility of influencing democratic constitutional change and ordinary lawmaking in such a way as to enshrine their rights. It would appear that adequate representation of women in government and public institutions is essential to achieving this goal.

29.   African Charter, article 1.

30.   International Covenant on Civil and Political Rights.

31.   Scott Leckie, "An Overview and Appraisal of the Fifth Session of the UN Committee on Economic, Social and Cultural Rights," *Human Rights Quarterly* 13 (1991): 545, 546.

32.   African Charter, article 25.

33.   See, for example, Clare Dalton, "Where We Stand: Observations on the Situation of Feminist Legal Thought," *Berkeley Women's Law Journal* 3 (1987–88); Bunch, "Women's Rights as Human Rights: Toward a Revision of Human Rights," *Human Rights Quarterly* 12 (1990): 485; Byrnes, "Women, Feminism, and International Human Rights Law: Methodological Myopia, Fundamental Flaws or Meaningful Marginalization?" *Australian Y.B. Int'l L*, 12 (1992).

34.   See, for example, National Conference of Women, Charter of Women's Rights (1994).

35.   African Charter, article 30.

36.   Ibid., article 41.

37.   As it happens, hardly any states submit the required reports. For example, only seven of the signatories met the deadline for the first report, and none did for the second. Isaac Nguema, "Legal and Infrastructural Constraints on the

Commission, in Fund for Peace." Report of the Conference on the African Commission, June 24–26, 1991, at 12 (hereafter cited as Conference Report). Subsequent compliance has been similarly low. Laurie Wiseberg, "The African Commission on Human and Peoples' Rights," *Issue: A Journal of Opinion* 22 (1994): 34, 36.

38. Makau wa Mutua, *African Human Rights NGOs and the African Commission: Strategies for Mutual Support*, Conference Report, at 24.

39. African Charter, article 31.

40. Ibid., article 3.

41. Wiseberg, "The African Commission," p. 35.

42. Ibid.

43. African Charter, article 53.

44. Ibid., article 59.

45. Ibid., article 45(3).

46. Ibid.

47. On press freedom in Africa, see Lynn Berat, "Democratization and Press Freedom in Southern Africa," *Africa Contemporary Record* (1992); Chris Ogbondah, "Press Freedom in West Africa: An Analysis of One Ramification of Human Rights,"*Issue: A Journal of Opinion* 22 (1994): 21.

48. Makau wa Mutua, *African Human Rights NGOs*, at 14.

49. African Charter, article 46. It also has the authority to investigate, at the request of the Assembly of Heads of the OAU, special cases that point to a series of grave violations. Ibid., article 58.

10

Barriers and Opportunities: The Role of Organizations in Nigerian Women's Quest for Empowerment

Mary J. Osirim

Despite the problematic nature of the state and the economy in postindependence Nigeria, women have made important contributions to the financial support of their families and to the development of their society and notable strides in their quest for empowerment as women. Their long history in income-generating activities has been traced at least as far back as the eighteenth century, when the participation of women in southwestern Nigeria as market traders has been well documented.[1] Accompanying these activities have been a myriad of businesses and village-based associations that facilitated the establishment and maintenance of women's enterprises over time.[2] During the past decade, however, the government's efforts to improve the economy through the creation of austerity and adjustment programs have jeopardized the position of women microentrepreneurs, such as market traders and seamstresses, in several ways. First, women already are concentrated in low-return ventures compared with men, who are more readily found in manufacturing and capital goods distribution, and women still experience severe limitations in their access to capital, training, and management development. Because of the persistence of patriarchy, women lack access to formal institutions that supply such support, and under difficult economic conditions, they encounter even greater competition from men who, as a result of displacement from formal sector employment, are seeking increased opportunities in small and microenterprises. Second, the economic crisis has made it less likely that women will obtain financial assistance from their relatives who, under such conditions, find it increasingly difficult to make ends meet. Acknowledging that women and the poor do, indeed, experience greater financial strains under adjustment programs, the Nigerian government has undertaken some efforts to improve the status of women with the establishment of some new organizations. Such groups as the Better Life Program and the People's Bank have been charged with the responsibilities of ameliorating the impact of the socioeconomic costs of adjustment on women and the poor.

This chapter seeks to explore the goals and potential impact of such programs on women, particularly those who work as microentrepreneurs in southern Nigeria. How do these initiatives compare with women's informal associations and nongovernmental organizations (NGOs) designed to meet their needs for capital and training, for example? In this regard, women's historical roles in the labor market and their empowerment efforts will be investigated. What theoretical perspectives best inform our understanding of the status of women and work in Nigeria and the prospects of improving their position in the future, especially as microentrepreneurs? These questions will be examined based on interviews conducted with the leaders of some governmental and nongovernmental organizations seeking to address women's economic and social concerns in 1992. Further reference will be made to fieldwork among microentrepreneurs in Lagos and Benin, Nigeria, in 1988. This study argues that poor and low-status women have benefited most often from their own efforts to create associations that directly address their class needs, as opposed to governmental and some nongovernmental organizations that, although voicing concern with the needs of the poor, mainly have served the interests of elite women. The creation of the People's Bank, however, appears to pose an interesting exception to this claim.

THEORY BUILDING: NIGERIAN WOMEN, DEVELOPMENT, AND THE INTERNATIONAL DIVISION OF LABOR

Although several theoretical perspectives within the sociology of development do shed light on the contemporary problems that Nigeria encounters as a third world nation, few have made any attempts to incorporate women into their analysis. Late dependency and world systems theory drew our attention largely to the external factors that retarded Nigerian development. Simply put, the division of the world first into core and periphery nations, based on their position in the global economy and the terms of trade, limited the potential of third world nations, whose trading patterns generally were limited to primary product exports by first world states. Women were regarded largely as absent or, at best, marginal to these activities, because primary product exports consisted of cash crops and, during colonialism and the immediate postcolonial period, women had limited access to this area of agricultural production. Women had been relegated to subsistence agriculture, and even when primary product exports shifted from farm produce to minerals, they were further absent from this process. Subsequent analysis of Nigeria's role in the international economy, particularly in the late 1970s by such theorists as Peter Evans,[3] established that, by virtue of her oil wealth, Nigeria could be considered a semiperipheral nation. In fact, Nigerian development, like Brazil's (according to Evans), was characterized by the existence of the triple alliance, in which the state, transnational corporations (TNCs), and private indigenous investors were partners in development. Of course, major investments and development initiatives were undertaken by the state in collaboration with TNCs, and those state actions to improve the participation of small- and medium-scale enterprises in national development largely focused on men's activities. State-sponsored institutions, such as the Center for Management Development, technical training institutes, and development banks, had little, if any, contact with women microentrepreneurs and, in fact, primarily assisted middle- and upper-middle-class men who had significant ties to formal institutions and were major participants in business associations and networks. Such formal institutions, associations, and networks generally remained outside the purview of women.[4]

More recently, scholars within the sociology of development have shifted their attention toward the comparative political economy paradigm in their study of third world development. This approach better addresses the contemporary problems in subsaharan African development because it combines an investigation of the external conditions with the internal dimensions advancing or retarding the process of change. Comparative political economy explores why different nation-states exhibit distinct patterns of accumulation and distribution over the course of their development. The autonomy of the state and the role of nonstate actors, such as social classes, also are viewed as important factors in the process of change. Further, subordinate classes also can influence historical outcomes through class action. Thus, this model begins to accord potential significance to the lower classes and subordinate actors in the state, such as lower status women, and recognizes their ability to affect the development process. There is no doubt that, historically, the actions of Nigerian women targeted against the atrocities of the state have affected policies and outcomes. Perhaps the best example of this is the Aba Women's War of 1929, waged against British colonial policies, but throughout the region (and in other areas of the continent), women also have rallied against other colonial legislation and the policies and politics of adjustment.[5]

Feminist contributions to the sociology of development have advanced and enriched the comparative political economy paradigm. Although acknowledging both the international dimensions of the division of labor, which are increasingly gender based, and the persistence of patriarchy at the level of the state and social relations, these theorists note that women are, indeed, subordinate actors whose contributions to development largely have been ignored. Women in the south are prime targets of TNCs in the search for cheap labor and nimble fingers to enhance TNCs' profitability. Feminist theorists have drawn our attention not only to how particular regions or nation-states are selected to become the producers of these goods and services but also to the differentiation in access to and returns from such activities, based on gender. Patriarchy has ensured that women remain concentrated in such population pools, because structural inequalities in the state and society assure that women historically have been restricted to attaining lower levels of education and must shoulder the responsibilities for biological and social reproduction.

Historically, although women in Nigeria have been disproportionately poor and relegated to lower-status positions and although for many, this continues to be the case, they have, through their income-earning activities, made significant contributions to their families and, through their associations, have empowered themselves. Through employing a feminist approach to the study of political economy, this chaper next explores the activities of women's groups to enhance their position and the impact and potential consequences of governmental organizations in their attempts to improve the situation for poor women.

WOMEN, WORK, AND EMPOWERMENT IN SOUTHERN NIGERIA: THE HISTORICAL BACKGROUND

During the precolonial period among the Yoruba in southwestern Nigeria, the African (or precapitalist) mode of production encouraged cooperation rather than competition among women and men in meeting the subsistence needs of the family.[6]

Although egalitarian relations did not exist between women and men, conditions between the genders were more equal than they were under colonialism, because both women and men participated in production. Subsistence agriculture and internal trade formed the basis of the economy, and women combined their responsibilities in these areas with their duties to raise the next generation to assume their productive roles in the future. Nigerian women did not view these roles as dichotomous; their roles as mothers, workers, and wives were interdependent.[7]

Children occupied a central place in the lives of these women — their participation in income-generating activities was a normal extension of their work, an expected part of life. Women worked primarily because they had children and viewed the fulfillment of such tasks as production and reproduction as a core element of their identities.

Among the Igbo in southeastern Nigeria, rural women also played a pivotal role in the production and marketing of food. Historically, a gender-based division of labor existed according to agricultural tasks and crops.[8] According to Bolanle Awe and Nkoli Ezumah: "Men had responsibility for land preparation, making mounds and planting yams. Women, in contrast, had responsibility for planting cassava, maize, sweet potatoes, cocoyams, vegetables, weeding the farm and transporting harvested crops."[9]

During the colonial period, agricultural production and market trade continued to provide the major opportunities for women's income earning. Greater inequality can be noted in women's and men's roles as the colonial government institutionalized a gender-based division of labor, in which opportunities in cash crop production were created for men.[10] "In Nigeria, the introduction of cocoa production provided men with a new source of wealth."[11] Under this system, women's work loads generally increased, because they were left tending the farmlands the men left behind.

Colonial practices and patriarchy combined to severely restrict women's access to formal institutions for education and employment during this period. Between 1859 and 1914, only two secondary schools were created for young women in Nigeria, compared with ten for young men during this period.[12] Within these girls' schools, the curriculum remained gender based and was focused on home economics, childcare, and nutrition.[13] Given these educational realities, very few opportunities existed for women in formal sector employment. In fact, women first were hired in the civil service in the 1940s because of the shortage of available male labor as a result of their participation in World War II. By 1945, only 550 women occupied positions in the civil service, and by the next decade, there were only 23 women employed as senior civil servants.[14] Needless to say, illiteracy rates remained high during this period and even exceeded 60 percent for women a decade after independence.

Women working as market traders, however, exhibited significant autonomy in their businesses. They made their own decisions involving their enterprises and controlled their financial resources. They frequently formed associations to protect their interests as traders, as noted by Peggy Sanday: "The women have organized trade guilds, which regulate the conditions and standards of the craft and protect the interests of their members. These are powerful organizations whose leaders play an important role in political activities."[15]

Some women's organizations existed for the purpose of providing credit to their members. The *esusu* rotating credit schemes were and remain important mechanisms for providing economic resources that enable women to establish and maintain their enterprises. The *esusu* has been described as: "An indigenous system through which people join hands to save money and help each other to meet credit needs. *Esusus* involve a group of people coming together and saving a mutually agreed upon amount of money on a predetermined day at regular intervals. The money realized after collection is given on a rotating basis to a member of the group and the process is repeated until everyone in the group has had a turn."[16]

The *esusu* has remained very advantageous for women's microenterprises for several reasons. First, in the absence of many banks in the rural areas, especially during the colonial period, and given the structural blockage that women experience, limiting their access to credit from banks, such as the need for collateral and titles to property in their own names, the *esusu* can provide them with needed capital. Second, the *esusu* imposes a savings discipline on traders, who otherwise might need to spend their earnings to meet demands in their household and among their extended family members. Third, their money is generally safe and easily accessible through the *esusu*, as opposed to the highly bureaucratized banking system. Further, unlike the case in banking, formal processes are kept to a minimum, although records of membership are held clearly.[17]

During the colonial era, market women in southwestern Nigeria further sought to protect their interests and promote women's rights through the creation of the first mass-based women's interest group, the Lagos Market Women's Association (LMWA).[18] This group ran one of the most profitable and efficient markets in Lagos in the 1920s and 1930s, the Ereko Market under the leadership of Madam Pelewura. The LMWA challenged the colonial government on many issues, including attempts to levy taxes on the women and the state's price controls on food during World War II. Beginning in 1932, the women waged many protests against the government to prevent the colonial authorities from taxing them and were victorious in their pursuits until 1940, when a tax was enacted on these market women. Even when this tax was finally imposed, Pelewura, the leader of the LMWA, vigorously challenged the officials by acknowledging the oppressive nature of colonialism. When she was informed that the British women paid the tax, she responded, "That England was where the money was made whereas Africans were poor owing to many factors over which they had no control."[19] Although the government would not abolish the tax completely, they did revise the law after these protests and Pelewura's anticolonial rhetoric. Later, the LMWA launched significant militant protests against the state for its scheme of price controls during World War II. This system of controls undermined the authority of Nigerian market women who controlled the distribution, marketing, and pricing of foodstuffs. After four years of intense activities by the LMWA, the government did remove the price controls. By this time, World War II had ended, and it is difficult to say to what extent this event, as opposed to the women's protests, was responsible for the change in policy.

Although many members of this association were illiterate, these women made weekly contributions to a fund to hire lawyers and translators to work with them in their interactions with the colonial officials.[20] Despite their lack of formal education, however, the LMWA remained a major vehicle for women's empowerment under colonialism, particularly through its attempts to address the concerns of poor market women at the bottom of the socioeconomic hierarchy.

Among the Igbo, market women's associations also existed that protected the interests of members and were involved in decision making about the prices of commodities. Kinship-based village associations, such as the *Inyemedi*, also existed and provided emotional support for members as well as promoted issues concerning women's welfare. Such issues included securing women's rights to particular land for farming and settling disputes involving men's claims for grazing lands.

In the Igbo town of Nnobi, the women's council, called *Inyom Nnobi*, was an especially significant group that wielded considerable power in the colonial period. The *Inyom Nnobi* consisted of five representatives from each ward of the town who were not chosen on the basis of age but were selected for their charisma, strong leadership abilities, and character. This organization was concerned directly with all aspects of women's lives, including their roles in the public sphere as market traders and their responsibilities and treatment as wives. Members of the *Inyom Nnobi* policed the markets and fined those who destroyed any goods or engaged in disrespectful behavior in these areas. This group also established a fund for its activities and the upkeep of the town, including the maintenance of public works. Perhaps the greatest demonstration of their empowerment was evidenced in the general strikes and demonstrations they waged against men, particularly for domestic offenses and threats to their livelihood. These women would refuse to perform sexual services and fulfill their household responsibilities, especially in response to any attempts to levy taxes on them without their consent or any actions that jeopardized their ability to support their children.[21]

Women who led the *Inyom Nnobi* likely were titled women who held the status of *Ekwe*. Acquiring this title was believed to lie beyond the control of any one living individual — the Nnobi goddess was supposed to give a woman the wealth to purchase this title. The reality, however, was that a strong association existed between the charisma, the diligent labor, and the economic success of a woman and the attainment of this status. Women who occupied this position usually achieved even greater success, because they were able to control the services of other women to create more wealth.[22]

Therefore, although social and political organizations among the Igbo (as well as many other groups) frequently were based on gender, women, through such associations as the *Inyom Nnobi*, were able to exert some authority over men, especially when men acted to limit their economic activities and the support of their children. Through this indigenous women's group and the process of acquiring status through titles, Nnobi women were able to control and expand their economic resources and contribute to the development of their households and communities, despite the vagaries of colonialism.

On the eve of independence in 1959, the National Council of Women's Societies was formed by elite women, with several branches throughout Nigeria. The early aims of this organization included establishing linkages with international organizations and providing scholarships for young women to attend secondary and tertiary institutions. Although this umbrella organization includes both elite and market women among its membership, it is argued here that its major goals have been and continue to focus on meeting the needs of elite women. The executive committees are comprised primarily of upper-middle-class and upper-class women. Although this is a voluntary association that proclaims that it is nonpartisan, it frequently has been recognized by the federal government as the major organization representing women.[23] Further, in addition to the collection of membership dues and other fund-raising efforts, the state provides this group with an annual grant, which amounted to N50,000 in 1992.[24] (Eighteen naira equaled approximately $1 in 1992.)

Thus, although women in southern Nigeria experienced significant limitations restricting their income earning and status enhancement during the precolonial and colonial periods, they did engage in the establishment of informal associations, networks, and formal organizations that did enable them to provide for their families, contribute to human capital formation, and oppose the state. The postindependence period brought with it new challenges; these, in many respects, particularly during the economic crisis of the 1980s and 1990s, have led to a deteriorating quality of life for lower-status women, especially those working in agriculture, market trade, and other microenterprises.

THE POSTINDEPENDENCE STATE, ECONOMIC CRISIS, AND WOMEN'S ORGANIZATIONS

Nigeria entered the postcolonial era as an agriculturally based economy that largely was able to provide for the nation's food needs. "By the late 1950s, between 75 and 80% of the country's foreign exchange earnings were derived from the export of cocoa, oil, palm products, cotton, rubber and groundnuts."[25] The late 1960s and the 1970s brought major developments in the oil industry, such that, by the end of the decade, Nigeria had clearly become a monoproduct-dependent economy in which oil accounted for more than 90 percent of all export earnings and agricultural production was allowed to deteriorate.

During this period, lower-class women remained concentrated in agricultural production and small and microenterprises, especially market vending. To promote rural development and to enhance their opportunities for income earning in these areas, women in southern Nigeria took the initiative in establishing cooperatives and new women's organizations to address their concerns. Despite the fact that women in Nigeria and subsaharan Africa generally produce more than 70 percent of all food on the continent, men and male farming activities continued to be favored by most governmental organizations and NGOs in the postindependence period. In the former Bendel state, for example, male extension workers passed on new farming techniques, gave seeds and fertilizers to men, and notoriously ignored women's productive activities in agriculture. Women lacked access to capital to purchase farm machinery and, yet, were accused of "being afraid" of such capital equipment. Kamene Okonjo explains: "Women were believed to be afraid of agricultural machinery and unable to follow instructions. The actual situation was they lacked access to credit for even simple, low-cost machinery, and yet, they didn't know how to run a tractor!"[26]

Beginning in 1969, women in Oyo state attempted to remedy this situation by organizing their own cooperatives in response to a development project, sponsored by the University of Ife (now Obafemi Awolowo University), that continued to marginalize their activities. The Isoya Rural Development Project introduced a new variety of yellow maize, which was to be grown and marketed as a cash crop by men and sold by their cooperatives. In this area, women had been raising white maize and benefiting from the sale of the surplus. Within two years, land that had produced the white corn was given over to the production of yellow maize, and women lost a critical source of income. These Yoruba women then became dependent on men and had to obtain capital from their husbands, a situation that these women described as "degrading and not very profitable."[27] This development project claimed that it had not ignored women, because it provided a home economics program focused on nutrition for the women (this was reminiscent of the educational policies of the colonial era). Women complained that what they needed was capital, and this was not addressed by this development project. With the assistance of some female extension workers, the women organized their own cooperatives. The Isoya Women's Cooperative Program purchased farm machinery for use by the women and fostered a strong sense of self-esteem and group solidarity. The men did resent women's ownership of farm machinery, which they believed should be under their control, and although they appeared pleased that "something progressive might reach their wives," this did not stop them from "giving the women of one group land from which the top soil had been scraped for road construction."[28] Despite the men's reactions, the women's cooperatives continued to expand and provided literacy and numeracy training for the women as well as instruction in agricultural methods.[29] These activities again demonstrated how women can empower themselves through their own organizations and improve their quality of life outside the auspices of official governmental or nongovernmental efforts.

In fact, internationally based NGOs generally had played a minimal role in efforts to improve the status of Nigerian women. With the oil boom of the 1970s, many agencies expected the state to assume the major responsibilities for development, including efforts to promote women and development.[30] Although this was not forthcoming during the boom period, it became even more difficult with the decline in the oil market, beginning in 1981.

Locally based NGOs for women attempted to meet some of their development needs in the early 1980s in the absence of major efforts by the government or international NGOs. The best known of these organizations is the Country Women's Association of Nigeria (COWAN), founded in 1982. In Lillian Trager and Clara Osinulu's description of this group, their goals appeared to be the most comprehensive for improving the position of rural women at that time. These included:

to increase the productivity and earning capacity of rural folks for a better living standard;

to promote programs for self-sustaining growth that could be replicated in various states;

to diversify economic opportunities in the rural areas through the promotion of rural crafts and the processing of farm products and by creating jobs for artisans in various fields;

to develop appropriate rural-based technologies for cottage industries and home-based production;

to train rural women in improved skills and management of small enterprises and to enhance self-reliant development; and

to associate itself with the government's plans to develop the rural areas, feed its population, and achieve self-sufficiency.[31]

According to Trager and Osinulu, COWAN has been an important vehicle for the empowerment of Nigerian women, particularly by improving their income-earning activities.[32] Some of the local groups that are members of COWAN have begun new systems for the marketing of fish as well as built their own infrastructure to facilitate the storage of products. Thus, this NGO formed by local women has demonstrated, as did several other associations that preceded it, that organizations created by indigenous women are more likely than many state or outside efforts to address the concerns of the poor, especially women.

STRUCTURAL ADJUSTMENT AND
THE STATE'S RESPONSE TO WOMEN

In an attempt to stem the tide of the economic crisis that began in late 1981, President Shagari began a series of negotiations with the International Monetary Fund (IMF) to gain a three-year extended facility loan.[33] These discussions continued over three regimes for more than two years. Debates between the government and the IMF raged over the fund's conditionality for the loan — over 17 conditions had been delineated for the government to meet, with the major disagreements surrounding three issues: trade liberalization, removal of the oil subsidy, and devaluation of the naira. Finally, after much public debate at the beginning of Babangida's administration in 1985, the Nigerian government rejected the loan.[34]

Although the IMF loan was formally rejected, Babangida introduced a structural adjustment program (SAP) in July 1986 that fit the standard IMF–World Bank model. Some of the major elements of the program included efforts to correct for overvaluation of the naira by setting up a viable second-tier foreign exchange market; attempts to overcome the observed public sector inefficiencies through improved public expenditure control programs and the rationalization of parastatals; and actions to relieve the debt burden and attract a net inflow of foreign capital while keeping a lid on foreign loans.[35]

Over the next few years, as had been the case in several other African nations, these measures resulted in the retrenchment of workers, the removal of government subsidies from many products and services, including oil, and a major devaluation of the naira. Such policies have had a particularly devastating impact on the poor, especially women, who are disproportionately plagued by escalating food, utility, health, education, and transportation costs.

Acknowledging that these policies had wrought many negative consequences for poor women, the state created some programs in the late 1980s to assist these women in bearing the social costs of adjustment. Some programs were targeted specifically at women; others were designed to alleviate the burden on the poor more generally. In this section, two of the major programs explored, the Better Life Program for Rural Women and the People's Bank, are state-created organizations.

Much of my information on these programs comes from interviews with some of their leaders, data presented at the international conference "Women in Africa and the African Diaspora: Bridges Across Activism and the Academy" in Nsukka in July 1992, and my observations from visits to Better Life Programs in southeastern Nigeria.

In 1987, the president's wife, Maryam Babangida, launched the Better Life Program for Rural Women to enhance the status of women during this period of economic crisis. The broad objectives of this program were to create awareness for mobilization to develop potential for national development and to raise the social consciousness of women, to stimulate and motivate women in rural areas to enhance their quality of life, to encourage the formal and informal education of women of all ages, to increase access to credit facilities, to encourage the formation of cooperatives, and to raise the quality of women's production and to create outlets outside Nigeria for export of these goods.

The governors' wives of the 30 states of the federation are the leaders of each state's Better Life Program. These programs are engaged in promoting women's ventures in both rural and urban areas. In 1991, the National Planning Committee of the Better Life Program boasted of many accomplishments, including establishing more than 9,000 cooperatives; supporting more than 1,400 cottage industries; and developing more than 400 women's centers, more than 130 livestock and fish farms, and 195 welfare projects. Each state develops and coordinates its own program, with an emphasis placed on providing assistance for income-generating activities. In Oyo state, for example, by 1992, 184 cottage industries had been established that produced yam flour, palm oil, and soap. These enterprises also devised a means of making simple machines to do this work, including the processing of *gari*. In addition, programs in adult literacy and health training were created, the latter of which enabled local women to treat simple ailments. The Oyo State Committee especially took pride in its role in helping to establish 62 registered cooperatives.[36] In other areas, such as in Borno state, these programs have begun to improve women's access to land.[37] Fifty acres of land were acquired in that state, which enabled women to begin wheat production.

Although these production efforts in Oyo and other states are noteworthy, my observations of *gari* processing activities in the city of Enugu revealed that much of the credit for establishing, operating, and supporting this business was given to the governor's wife and her entourage. From my conversations and observations at this and other sites in the area, such as sewing cooperatives, it appeared that few returns from these ventures were actually ending up in the hands of local, grass-roots women. Higher level returns, namely, in terms of status, seemed to accrue to the elite women closely associated with the governor's wife. In addition, problems of leadership have been noted in this and other governmental organizations designed to assist women in income-generating activities. Leaders chosen on the basis of political position in the state, such as being the wife of the governor, might not be committed to the same goals as poor women, to whom the organization's efforts are supposed to be targeted.[38] Much of the public criticism of the Better Life Program has resulted in its recent transfer to the National Commission for Women.[39] Thus, the gains derived from this program for poor, especially rural, women are likely to be insufficient to stem the tide of inflation under the SAP.

Perhaps the most potentially successful state-sponsored program created during this period was the People's Bank, established in 1989. This bank, which was started with a N30 million grant from the government, was based on the model of the Grameen Bank in Bangladesh. It was developed to address directly the credit needs of poor Nigerians, who often were "locked out" of the banking system because they were unable to meet the collateral requirements. Poor women have, thus far, been the major beneficiaries of these loans. To obtain a loan, women have to form cooperatives or informal associations and apply for a loan as a group, although they do not have to be in the same business. Each individual in the group can obtain a loan between N500 and N10,000. The application process involves a minimum of paperwork, with each form asking for name, address, age, and period of residence. Decisions about loans and repayment are made by residents, who are members of local organizations and well-known in their communities. Loans are made on the basis of knowledge about and trust in the recipients, and repayment can be enforced by members of the community via culturally sanctioned methods if necessary.

Over 200 branches and 500 satellite centers of these People's Banks are located throughout cities and villages in Nigeria. In rural areas where a bank has not been established, mobile banks arrive there on market days to provide financial services to the residents. The bank provides facilities for savings and loans but not checking accounts. Thus far, over N246,000,000 has been disbursed in about 550,000 loans, with 75–80 percent of these granted to women. Loan grantees have up to one year to repay their debts, and as of 1992, the repayment rate had been 92 percent. Women in small and microenterprises have been the major recipients of these loans. Their activities have included food preparation and catering, mat weaving, hairdressing, sewing, and soap making. In addition, the bank has established training schools providing free instruction in agricultural techniques, such as the use of fertilizers and farm machinery, as well as training in handicrafts for women.

In the future, the managing director hopes to privatize the bank so that it will "fully belong to the people." She also would like to provide opportunities for the poor to be able to go overseas for more specialized training and plans to mobilize community participants for the establishment of their own schools, hospitals, and day-care facilities. To accomplish these goals, the bank is seeking assistance from international donors.[40]

As compared with the Better Life Program and other government efforts in this period that were not discussed (such as the establishment of community banks), the People's Bank appears to have the greatest potential among state programs to actually improve the situation of lower-class women. One of the major reasons for this is the fact that there is a strong community base involved at all levels of the loan process — in order to obtain a loan, a group has to be "known" and "trusted" in their area. Although this bank began with a N30 million deposit from the government, in mid-1992, its assets had grown to N450 million, based on the support of many community residents throughout cities, towns, and villages in Nigeria. Efforts to remove any significant involvement of the government likely would be welcomed by the poor.

CONCLUSION

Although periods of economic crisis and political instability have plagued Nigeria throughout much of its history, women have launched many successful associations to enhance their income-earning activities and their contributions to their families. These efforts have included the development of rotating credit schemes, market associations that challenged colonial authority, village-based kinship groups, and rural development cooperatives to address their concerns as poor women. In the contemporary period, food producers, market traders, and small and microentrepreneurs are facing some of their greatest challenges to date, because economic crises combined with SAPs are worsening the conditions of their daily lives. Although this chapter argues that government-sponsored programs have, most often, not met the needs of women and, that, if they did, elite women were the most likely beneficiaries, the model of the People's Bank does appear to hold some promise for the future of these women. Hopefully, this example and other indigenous efforts can help women circumvent the structural blockage that they have experienced most often and empower them toward self-sustainable development in the twenty-first century.

NOTES

1. Peggy Sanday, "Female Status in the Public Domain," in *Women, Culture and Society*, eds. Michelle Rosaldo and Louise Lamphere (Stanford, Calif.: Stanford University Press, 1974); Brooke G. Schoepf, "Gender Relations and Development: Political Economy and Culture," in *Twenty-First Century Africa: Towards a Vision of*

Self-Sustainable Development, eds. Ann Seidman and Frederick Anang (Trenton, N.J.: Africa World Press, 1992).

2. Kameme Okonjo, "The Dual-Sex Political System in Operation: Igbo Women and Community Politics in Midwestern Nigeria," in *Women in Africa*, eds. Nancy Hafkin and Edna Bay (Stanford, Calif.: Stanford University Press, 1976); Cheryl Johnson, "Grass Roots Organizing: Women in Anticolonial Activity in Southwestern Nigeria," *African Studies Review* 25 (1982): 137–57.

3. Peter Evans, *Dependent Development* (Princeton, N.J.: Princeton University Press, 1987).

4. Mary J. Osirim, "Gender and Entrepreneurship: Issues of Capital and Technology in Nigerian Small Firms," in *Privatization and Investment in Sub-Saharan Africa*, eds. Rexford Ahene and Bernard S. Katz (New York: Praeger, 1992).

5. Judith Van Allen, "'Aba Riots' or Igbo 'Women's War'? Ideology, Stratification, and the Invisibility of Women," in *Women in Africa*, eds. Nancy Hafkin and Edna Bay (Stanford, Calif.: Stanford University Press, 1976); Cheryl Johnson, "Grass Roots Organizing," pp. 137–57; Gracia Clark and Takyiwaa Manuh, "Women Traders in Ghana and Structural Adjustment," in *Structural Adjustment and African Women Farmers*, ed. Christina Gladwin (Gainesville: University of Florida Press, 1991); Mary J. Osirim, "The Status of African Market Women: Trade, Economy and Family in Urban Zimbabwe," in *African Market Women and Economic Power*, eds. Bessie House-Midamba and Felix Ekechi (Westport, Conn.: Greenwood Press, 1995).

6. Simi Afonja, "Changing Modes of Production and the Sexual Division of Labor Among the Yoruba," *Signs: Journal of Women in Culture and Society* 7 (1981): 299–313.

7. Edna Bay, *Women and Work in Africa* (Boulder, Colo.: Westview Press, 1982); Barbara Lewis, "Fertility and Employment: An Assessment of Role Incompatibility Among African Women," in *Women and Work in Africa*, ed. Edna Bay (Boulder, Colo.: Westview Press, 1982).

8. Phoebe Ottenberg, "The Changing Economic Position of Women Among the Afkipo," in *Continuity and Change in African Culture*, eds. William Bascom and Melville Herskovits (Chicago, Ill.: University of Chicago Press, 1959); Victor Uchendu, *The Igbo of Southeastern Nigeria* (New York: Holt, Rinehart & Winston, 1965); Bolanle Awe and Nkoli Ezumah, "Women in West Africa: A Nigerian Case Study," in *The Women and International Development Annual*, eds. Ruth Gallin et al. (Boulder, Colo.: Westview Press, 1991), vol. 2, p. 189.

9. Awe and Ezumah, "Women in West Africa," p. 189.

10. Afonja, "Changing Modes"; Awe and Ezumah, "Women in West Africa."

11. Sara Berry, *Cocoa, Custom and Socio-Economic Change in Rural Western Nigeria* (Oxford: Clarendon Press, 1975); Emma Nina Mba, *Nigerian Women Mobilized: Women's Political Activity in Southern Nigeria, 1900–1965* (Berkeley: University of California, Institute of International Studies, 1982); Awe and Ezumah, "Women in West Africa," p. 179.

12. Babs A. Fafuna, *History of Education in Nigeria* (London: George Allen and Unwin, 1974); Awe and Ezumah, "Women in West Africa."

13. Awe and Ezumah, "Women in West Africa."

14.   La Ray Denzer, "Female Employment in the Government Service of Nigeria, 1885–1945." Paper presented at the Conference on Women's Studies: The State of the Art Now in Nigeria, 1987, Ibadan, University of Ibadan, The Institute of African Studies; Awe and Ezumah, "Women in West Africa."

15.   Sanday, "Female Status," p. 203.

16.   Sena A. Gabianu, "The Susu Credit System: An Indigenous Way of Financing Business Outside the Formal Banking System," in *The Long-Term Perspective Study of Sub-Saharan Africa: Economic and Sectoral Policy Issues,* ed. Agarwala Ramgopal (Washington, D.C.: World Bank, 1990), p. 123.

17.   Gabianu, "Susu Credit System."

18.   Johnson, "Grass Roots Organizing," pp. 137–57.

19.   Ibid.

20.   Ibid.

21.   Ifi Amadiume, *Male Daughters, Female Husbands: Gender and Sex in an African Society* (London, Zed Press, 1987).

22.   Ibid.

23.   A. R. Mustapha, "On Combatting Women's Exploitation and Oppression in Nigeria," in *Women in Nigeria Today,* ed. Women in Nigeria (London, Zed Press, 1985).

24.   Interview with the president, National Council of Women's Societies, Lagos, Nigeria, 1992.

25.   "The Economic Background of Balewa's Foreign Policy, 1960–1965," in *Nigeria and the International Capitalist System,* eds. Toyin Falola and Julius Ihonvbere (Boulder, Colo.: Lynne Rienner, 1988), p. 16.

26.   Kamene Okonjo, "The Role of Igbo Women in Rural Economy in Bendel State of Nigeria," in *Proceedings,* eds. F.I.A. Omu et al. vol. II, pp. 1027–28, cited in Renee Pittin, "Organizing for the Future," *Women in Nigeria Today,* ed. Women in Nigeria (London, Zed Press, 1985), p. 235.

27.   P. Ladipo, "Developing Women's Cooperatives: An Experiment in Rural Nigeria," in *African Women in the Development Process,* ed. Nici Nelson (London: Frank Cass and Co., Ltd., 1981), p. 124; Renee Pittin, "Organizing for the Future," p. 235.

28.   Ladipo, "Developing Women's Cooperatives," pp. 128–31, 236; Pittin, "Organizing for the Future," p. 235.

29.   Ibid.

30.   Lillian Trager and Clara Osinulu, "New Women's Organizations in Nigeria: One Response to Structural Adjustment," in *Structural Adjustment and African Women Farmers,* ed. Christina Gladwin (Gainesville, University of Florida Press, 1991).

31.   Ibid., pp. 347–48.

32.   Ibid.

33.   Thomas Biersteker, *Reaching Agreement with the IMF: The Nigerian Negotiations* (Pittsburgh, Pa.: University of Pittsburgh, Graduate School of Public and International Affairs, 1986); John Anyanwu, "President Babangida's Structural Adjustment Programme and Inflation in Nigeria," *Journal of Social Development in Africa* 7 (1992): 5–24.

34.   Biersteker, *Reaching Agreement with the IMF;* Anyanwu, "Babangida's Structural Adjustment Programme."

35.   Anyanwu, "Babangida's Structural Adjustment Programme."

36.   V.O. Ajayi, "Case Study of The Better Life Program in Oyo State." Paper presented at The First International Conference on Women in Africa and the African Diaspora, 1992, Nsukka, The University of Nigeria.

37.   Trager and Osinulu, "New Women's Organizations in Nigeria."

38.   Ibid.

39.   Anyanwu, "Babangida's Structural Adjustment Programme," pp. 5-24.

40.   Interview with the managing director of the People's Bank, Lagos, Nigeria, 1992.

V

TOWARD THE SUSTAINABLE DEVELOPMENT OF AFRICAN ECOLOGY AND ENVIRONMENT

11

Africa's Environmental Challenges: Deforestation and Development

Moses K. Tesi

This chapter focuses on the environmental challenge of deforestation. The analysis is done within the framework of the competition for socioeconomic development and the limited resources and economic alternatives available to cope with that competition.

African governments, like most others in the world, have, for years, paid very little attention to environmental issues. The relationship between the environment and economic development was a nonissue and was left outside the policy framework. However, the emergence of environmental issues in discourses on world affairs during the late 1980s and their rise to the top of the agendas on global issues in the early 1990s, which culminated in the Rio de Janeiro Earth Summit of the summer of 1992, has changed the dynamics of how the environment is viewed in Africa. African governments are required to strike a balance in their policies between the pursuit of socioeconomic development and environmental preservation and protection. How well this can be done is one of the major challenges that many governments on the continent face.

For most people in Africa, issues such as unemployment, low and falling earnings, and inflation form the basis of their concerns. Environmental issues that are viewed with alarm by Western officials are viewed without much interest. Still, the positions of Western officials on the issues cannot be ignored. The depth of Africa's economic dependence on Western countries makes most governments in the region vulnerable to Western pressure for stronger environmental regulations. They are inclined to listen, even if they will resist any demands that are made.

Deforestation, the loss of forest areas because of the cutting of trees, stands out among other equally important environmental problems because of the alarming manner in which it is taking place; its strong relationship with development; its strong overseas constituency; use of trees for the provision of building poles and energy; and the forests' value for biodiversity and medicinal and scientific uses. These forests also harbor the largest and most diverse species of animal, bird, and plant life in the world. For example, tropical forests are considered to shelter about two-thirds of the estimated 5 to 30 million species of plants, animals, and birds in existence. Also, various forms of forest products, such as wood, rubber, nuts, fruits, and resins, today serve as a source of income and food in many communities. Many more may be discovered in the future. The medicinal role of forest products goes back a long time for African traditional healers. For modern medicine, the scientific importance of tropical forests is growing as new discoveries are made. Noel Grove estimated that some 25 percent of "all prescription drugs with a market value of over 15 billion dollars per year in the United States, have plant extracts in them."[1] Approximately 70 percent of some 3,000 plants identified by the U.S. National Cancer Institute as containing cancer-fighting properties are found in tropical rain forests, including the Madagascar periwinkle, used in the treatment of leukemia, and extracts from wild yam plants that constitute the active ingredient in birth-control pills.[2] Other medical products of tropical origin include quinine, which, for a long time, was the major cure for malaria. The aesthetic value of forests in the attraction of tourists from all over the world has been very crucial for the economies of various countries. In recent years, forests are considered to play a crucial role in the control of global warming.

ENVIRONMENTAL DEGRADATION AND DEVELOPMENT

There are very few countries in the world that can claim to have spared their environments of human-caused damages. Human progress often has taken place at the expense of the environment. As human beings have progressed, they have done so by degrading the environment. Discoveries such as agriculture and the domestication of animals, which led to settled life, have, as a drawback, the systematic destruction of vegetation coverings and forests. Progress associated with industrialization has been accompanied by immeasurable environmental problems. Coal, which for a very long time was the energy backbone of industry, is known for the extensive environmental damages that accompany its exploitation. Manufacturing plants generate hazardous waste by-products, which, until the beginning of regulation, were disposed of in rivers or remote land areas without regard for their effects on animal, marine, or human lives. Consequently, some of the most highly developed and industrialized areas of the world, such as the northeast United States around the Great Lakes corridor or the Rhine River in Europe, are also among the most environmentally degraded areas in the world. Road, rail, air, and water transportation have brought about alterations of land and water forms at the same time that gas emissions from automobiles, ships, and factories generate newer pollution problems.

Africa's own experiences mirror the global trend of development-related environmental damages. The only exception is that, although the global trend has been one in which development has been achieved only at the very high cost of environmental degradation, for Africa, the relationship has been all negative. Countries in the region have had neither development nor environmental purity. In postcolonial Africa, within the span of more than 30 years into independence, hardly a country has attained a level of development considered to be exemplary, given the enormous efforts and resources that have been expended. This is true even for such countries as Botswana and Mauritius, which are considered to be Africa's success stories. Given their small size and enormous mineral resources, they could have done much better. The reasons for the development failures are multiple and familiar. They include corruption, mismanagement, wars, poorly thought out plans, dependence on agricultural and mineral exports, and the success of industrialized countries in thwarting Africa's secondary industries by way of protectionism. On the other hand, the level of environmental degradation generated by the failed attempts to develop is at a crisis-level high, without the development to show for it.

In effect, the West's own record of achieving development at the expense of the environment plus Africa's double-negative experiences on the two fronts only enhances the position that development and protection of the environment are two sides of the same coin. With careful planning, both can be achieved. The problem, however, is how to bring it about in practical policy terms.

THE DEFORESTATION PROBLEM

The problem of deforestation is global in nature, but it is more serious in the world's tropical forests. These are divided into tropical dry forests and tropical rain forests.

Tropical dry forests are forests identified by their open woodlands with thick undergrowth. Rain forests are distinguishable by their canopy of tree branches and leaves, underneath which vegetation is very scanty because of the lack of sunlight. Over 75 percent of the world's 1.6 billion hectares of tropical dry forests is found in Africa. Brazil harbors one-third of the world's rain forest, which measured around 3,575,000 square kilometers in 1980; of the remaining two-thirds, Indonesia and Zaire have 1,139,000 and 1,058,000 square kilometers, respectively. Beside Zaire, other African countries, including the Congo, Gabon, Cameroon, Madagascar, and the Central African Republic, have extensive rain forests. The four countries had a combined rain forest area of 686,000 square kilometers in 1980.

Deforestation has been taking place in Africa for centuries, but there has been nothing close to the present situation. Estimates of forest loss worldwide are considered to be around 15.4 million hectares annually, with Africa contributing 4.1 million hectares, or around 26 percent of the global total.[3] The distribution of the loss is continental, in that hardly a country in Africa has escaped it. However, immense disparities exist among countries, based on the extensiveness of their losses. Over half the losses have taken place in West Africa, where Côte d'Ivoire, Ghana, Togo, Benin, and Nigeria lead the way. There is very little left of forest areas in these countries. The World Bank estimates that 2 million hectares are lost each year in the subregion. Côte d'Ivoire, for example, was losing around 510,000 hectares and Nigeria, 400,000 hectares per year in the 1980s. In contrast, Gabon's annual loss was barely 15,000 hectares during the same period.[4] Outside West Africa, Madagascar's losses and those of Rwanda and Burundi have been equally staggering. Over 90 percent of Madagascar's rain forest has been lost during the past 50 years. Although Zaire's rain forest is still very massive, the fact that it was losing around 347,000 hectares per year in the 1980s leaves no room for comfort. It could well be that it is too late to save original rain forests in some of the countries. For example, in Burundi, only 41,000 hectares of rain forest are left. Even so, as Kevin Cleaver and Gotz Schreiber point out, countries such as Cameroon, Zaire, the Congo, Gabon, and the Central African Republic still have extensive rain forests, which, under proper policy guides, constitute the best hope for Africa in preserving some of its rain forests.[5]

Extensive forest losses are occurring in Africa's dry forests as well. During the 1980s, the Sudan was losing 104,000 hectares of its forests per year. Southward, Tanzania and Malawi have been experiencing losses at an accelerating rate. Figures obtained from the World Bank for 1989 showed Tanzania losing approximately 130,000 hectares and Malawi, 150,000 hectares of forests per year in the 1980s.[6] Significant losses also were registered in Niger and Mozambique.

EXPLAINING THE LOSSES: THE POLICY
CHALLENGES POSED TO THE BROAD PICTURE

Not less than three categories of human activities for social and economic survival are directly associated with the problem of deforestation: the human need for home and industrial energy; the human need for food, shelter, and comfort; the human need for work, a good income, and security. All are related and also reinforcing. When provisions are made for one, the burdens of the others are reduced. The exertion of industrial energy, for example, leads to the provision of jobs, an income, and security. The provision of jobs, an income, and security will generate food, shelter, and comfort, which will require the application of home energy to transform and prepare for human use. The specific aspects of the activities associated with deforestation in Africa, explained below, are rational manifestations of such human needs. Consequently, the deforestation problem is cast by many in Africa in a short-term economic and social context whose consequences in the long term may not be a priority.

THE SPECIFIC ISSUES

The provision of fuel wood, which is the principal source of energy used for cooking in most African homes, in the same way that gas or electricity is used in the Western world, is a principal cause of deforestation. It is estimated that over 90 percent of households in Africa use fuel wood for cooking. Industries such as fish smoking, pottery, brick making, and tobacco drying also depend on fuel wood energy for production. Drying cocoa beans and the heating of homes on cold nights and mornings in many parts of Africa also require much fuel wood energy. Like oil, fuel wood is a natural product, but unlike oil, fuel wood is replenishable. The felling of trees for the purpose of supplying fuel wood to households and industries will be less of a problem if efforts are undertaken to replenish the areas from which trees are cut. Such efforts have been slow in coming. Available data for 1984–86, for example, show that a total of 369,531 cubic meters of fuel wood was produced in subsaharan Africa alone.[7] This represented a significant increase for most countries from the 1974–76 level. Although some efforts have been made to replant exploited areas, the rate at which this is taking place is too sluggish and too low and has made very little difference. The record speaks for itself. Between 1984 and 1986, only 91,000 hectares were replanted in the entire continent. In contrast, Kenya experienced a 50 percent increase in deforestation, Mozambique, 54 percent, Ghana, 38 percent, Nigeria, 41 percent, and Côte D'Ivoire, 45 percent during the same period.[8]

As long as Africa's population continues to grow rapidly and as long as people rely on fuel wood for energy and others can earn a living by dealing in it, reduction of the supply will be quite a difficult thing to do. The way out is for people to be provided with the opportunity to access alternative energy forms. On the other hand, given the cost of alternative energy sources, income will have to rise significantly in order for most people to afford it. At the current rate of income and economic growth in the region, that is unlikely to happen anytime soon. This means that the option for most countries on which to embark immediately is design of a carefully thought out regulatory program for forests and fuel wood suppliers in which replanting is a key ingredient. When well-designed and managed responsibly, such a program will enable wood to remain the fuel of most people because of its affordability, without the threat to its source, while buying time for work on alternative cost-effective, forest-protective sources of energy.

Although it has been suggested that replanting does not guarantee regrowth of the same species and that it may take generations for the replanted forest to mature, these ought not be issues with regard to fuel wood exploitation. As a fuel wood strategy, the goal of replanting should be protection and preservation of unexploited forests rather than provision of a carbon copy of what has been destroyed. When replanting is combined with the protection of areas not yet exploited, people will not go into the interior of forests, because they can get their wood from the replanted areas much closer. Replanting will, thus, reduce the distance that people will have to travel in the search for fuel wood, and forests that are farther away will be better protected.

Industrial logging constitutes another major cause of deforestation in Africa. In terms of volume, this aspect of deforestation is only slightly higher than that caused by fuel wood supply. The amount exploited for timber purposes during the 1984–86 period was approximately 40,126 cubic meters.[9] For Cameroon, Gabon, Nigeria, Ghana, the Ivory Coast, and Zaire, timber exploitation is a very sure source of foreign exchange and resources. Four of the countries — Nigeria, the Ivory Coast, Cameroon, and Zaire — accounted for over 40 percent of the industrial wood produced in Africa in 1984–86. For these countries, the problem of deforestation needs to be weighed against the revenues that logging generates. Unfortunately, a significant proportion of the taxes and fees that the logging companies pay end up in private hands rather than in government treasuries. Only approximately 38 percent of taxes and royalties paid by logging concessions in Ghana went to the government.[10] Similar situations exist in Gabon, Cameroon, Liberia, and Côte d'Ivoire. The other side of this is the fact that the issue is not limited to the exploitation of logs. The *nature* of the exploitation is a primary contributor to deforestation because of the absence of selectivity in the process. For every one tree that is logged, many more go down with it. Also, the roads that are created by logging companies are used later by squatting farmers and fuel wood merchants to penetrate deep into forest interiors to create farms or fell trees for fuel wood.[11] Such individuals would not be able to penetrate deep into the interior of forests without such roads. However, this also means that forests that look untouched from the outskirts may be nothing more than empty skeletons.

Africa's rapidly declining forests also have resulted from public schemes, projects, and norms. Infrastructural facilities such as roads, rail lines, airports, and even resettlement schemes for victims of disasters are inevitable and necessary in today's world. Without them, people still will be living in the dark ages. At the same time, many public sector programs have been ill-advised, unnecessary, and wasteful when the costs in forest loss are compared with the benefits they were designed to achieve, for example, clearing forest areas as an indication of ownership and use, plantation development schemes, and resettlement schemes, such as the Volta scheme in Ghana, the Ujamaa village schemes in Tanzania, or the Bafang-Yabassi scheme in Cameroon.

Farming and the practices that accompany it are the other major cause of deforestation in Africa. The practice of shifting cultivation and the slash-and-burn method of preparing the way for cultivation are associated not only with deforestation but also with waste. The practice requires that new areas be brought under cultivation every so often and that areas under cultivation be left fallow for a certain period of time so that they can regain their fertility. When whole villages engage in the practice, it means the destruction of vast forest areas. Thus, the practice may be good for areas that have an abundance of land with few people interested in farming, but in Africa, where more than 70 percent of the people make their living through farming, there will not be enough land to go around or absorb new entrants into the occupation.

Notwithstanding the problem associated with shifting cultivation, agriculture is not very environmentally friendly. The more people that are engaged in farming, the more forest areas will have to be cleared to make way for the farms. This means that more habitat areas, biodiversity, and medicinal plants will have to be lost. It may appear contradictory because it challenges the conventional view that Africa has an abundance of land and because it runs contrary to the position of international organizations, such as the World Bank, that have steered African economies mainly in the direction of agriculture over the years. The reality is that not only is the amount of cropland limited but the process of bringing non-cropland areas with their poor soils under cultivation also is a very costly operation.

Improvements on current croplands and the conversion of non-croplands into croplands require the use of irrigation, fertilizers, and environmentally friendly pesticides, all of which cost substantial sums. In addition to immediate costs, irrigation requires the employment of energy to pump water into the fields; therefore, to the direct costs must be added the indirect cost of energy, which will fluctuate if oil is the type of energy used. Farmers actually may be able to afford the costs of such improvements if prices of their products are appropriate. On this issue, the story has been a disappointment. There are farmers in many countries who have made such improvements. For most, however, low prices for their products in the world market, the restrictions placed on certain products in some overseas markets, and the low and noncompetitive prices for which their products are purchased by their own governments leave them with very little to carry out any meaningful farm improvements.

Even if more cropland were to be available, from a development standpoint, excessive dependence on agriculture as a means to raise living standards is not very advisable. This can be seen even from the current situation in Africa. Even though an overwhelming number of people earn their living from farming, agriculture contributes only an average of 35 percent of the gross domestic products of the region. With improved methods, Africa can more than double its current agricultural production on the same cropland with far fewer people working the farms. In this sense, industrial development will better deal with the current ecological crisis.

Emphasis must be given to the fact that shifting cultivation has been practiced for decades in Africa without significant environmental dislocations. The reason for environmental degradation, as discussed above and as explained in a United Nations Environmental Program (UNEP) report, is not the practice of shifting cultivation but the increased number of individuals engaged in agriculture when there is a scarcity of cropland.[12] As new entrants have gotten into farming, the report points out, areas lying fallow are brought prematurely under cultivation, and previously uncultivated areas are brought under cultivation. The decreased lengths of fallow periods because of the upsurge of demand for cropland also is related to economic conditions — the absence of alternative economic activities to employ and provide an income to many people. Consequently, many countries, including Cameroon, Tanzania, Côte d'Ivoire, and Malawi, sought to deal with their economic problems by promoting a "back to the farm" ideology. During the 1980s through the 1990s, Ghana and Burkina Faso forcefully employed the strategy and have been quite successful in increasing farm production.

The limitation of arable land in comparison with the number of people seeking entry into farming raises yet another very sensitive issue on deforestation — the size of Africa's population. Because cropland is getting smaller and smaller, the belief is that Africa's population has become too large and, therefore, threatens the continent's carrying capacity. The annual rate of growth of Africa's population, which between 1980 and 1988 was 3.2 percent, as compared with 1.8 percent increase in annual food production during the same period, makes the argument very compelling, especially when approximately 100 million people faced serious food shortages.

Such a link between Africa's population size and deforestation is quite consistent with the association of its development problem with its population. What this argument suggests is that there is a need for not only an environmental policy but also a population reduction policy. Although the reasoning behind such a perspective is similar to the ecological balance argument, it also has been argued that, in pushing the population issue, proponents fail to take into consideration the idea that Africa is not overpopulated because it is underdeveloped but that, because Africa is underdeveloped, it is overpopulated.[13] Therefore, as standards of living rise, so, too, will the continent's population begin to decline. According to this view, African governments need to focus on poverty reduction schemes. With regard to deforestation, the provision of agricultural inputs to improve and increase yields from existing farms (without necessarily making a farmer allow a plot to lie fallow) and the diversification of the economy into industrial productions with access to overseas markets are seen as the remedy.

Given that a large and rising percentage of Africans are engaged in agriculture, a phenomenon contributing to deforestation in the region, that number could be reduced if people are able to find meaningful employment in industries. That would, in turn, lead to a reduction of the area under cultivation and the rate at which new areas are being brought under cultivation. The now larger nonagricultural sector with high incomes will provide a solid domestic market base for agricultural products to supplement overseas markets. This will raise agricultural earnings while making them less vulnerable. The high incomes in the agricultural sector will enable farmers to adopt improved farming techniques involving fertilizer use, mechanization, irrigation, and better breeds of seeds, which they can now afford. This again will lead to increased production to service the larger market. Also, higher returns in the nonagricultural sector will make the desire for more children for the purpose of providing additional help to families less attractive, because farmers will be able to afford paid help. Moreover, with higher incomes, Africans will be more able to afford non–fuel wood sources of energy for cooking and servicing the village industries. Therefore, the forests will be spared of tree exploitation to meet such needs. Equally important is the consideration that, with improved socioeconomic conditions, parents will be less prone to having many children simply because they seek to guard against the uncertainties of premature deaths resulting from poor public health conditions.

THE FUTURE OUTLOOK AND CONCLUSION

As this discussion shows, Africa has a serious deforestation problem. The reason for the problem is not that Africans do not care about their forests but that forest products and forest lands provide them with the basis for socioeconomic survival. However, if the forests are to be saved, Africans will need to use them in a sustainable manner. Sustainable use of forest areas and their products will require alterations in the pattern and direction of economic activities, the introduction of new institutional measures on forestry, and the generation of community activism and politicization of forest issues. This requires that a multiplicity of policies and regulations be generated and responsibly employed. Among programs that have been recommended for dealing with the current problem (most of which have already been discussed above) are replenishing forest areas after exploitation, outright ban on forest products, increasing the productivity of farm areas, protecting land and forest areas not being exploited, population reduction, strong regulatory institutions and laws, and bringing marginal areas under cultivation. What often is not mentioned but what is crucial is the need for a diversification of economic activities into industrial production, thus, steering economic growth and incomes. Also, the development of alternative cost-cutting home fuel sources will be critical in taking the pressure off forests.

Although, when jointly applied, these measures will contribute significantly toward saving forest areas in the region, the measures are expensive and require expertise and commitment, elements that are in relatively short supply. It should not be forgotten that the activities that have endangered forest areas are the result of economic problems. A proposal such as that made by Helmut Kohl of Germany for the establishment of a special fund to help Brazilian rain forest inhabitants find alternative sources of revenues or that by Ira Rubinuff of the Smithsonian Tropical Research Institute for the establishment of a World Bank to fund tropical forests and the Debt for Nature swaps for rain forest protection could reduce some of the financial burden. They will, nevertheless, be unlikely to resolve the root problem, even if some of them were realistic. The exchange of a country's debt for the promise to protect and preserve its forest fails to address the financing of the protection itself. Moreover, there is always the possibility of the country reneging on its promise after the debt relief. Besides, financing the protection of forests without dealing with the economic problems of the forest dwellers will not solve the problem — that of poverty. A final point about the future of deforestation in Africa is that, left in the hands of governments, very little will be left of Africa's forests. In countries with strong environmental regulations, such as the United States, the governments tend to act mainly when pushed by the people. In Africa's case, a principal setback is the absence of political

activism and politicization on such issues, on the part of both the governments and the people. Political activism by governments in most countries in the region has been lacking in generating strong, predictably
enforced environmental regulations. Recently, governments in various
countries have moved to establish environmental departments. Such
moves seem to indicate their seriousness on addressing the environmental issues. It is hoped, however, that these departments will have some
power and will be able to generate a solid institutional base for legislative,
regulatory, and enforcement programs to protect forest areas; for this, the
existence of strong environmental constituencies and advocacy groups is
indispensable, even in the presence of activist governments. Few African
countries have such constituencies. An exception worth emphasizing in
this case is the Green Belt Movement of Kenya, a mass environmental
movement that was founded in 1977 to mobilize people for tree planting.
Most other environmental organizations tend to be study oriented or
arms of international development or international environmental
groups. Also, there are only approximately 30 such groups in all of Africa,
excluding South Africa, which has 35 groups operating within its borders.
The experiences of the Green Belt Movement of Kenya also show that
activism for the environment may not be easy, because of constant harass-
ment from the government. As Wangari Maathai, the Green Belt leader,
points out, "African governments . . . do not want their people informed
or organized because organized groups threaten their position."[14]

The World Bank's recent initiatives seem designed to address this
issue. Its National Environmental Action Programs (NEAP) are meant to
enable governments to undertake environmental assessments in all their
plans and, so, bring certain environmental sensitivity to programs and
communities. The problem with this is that too much trust is placed in the
governments. The fact that a program is assessed and thought to be environmentally lacking does not mean that a government that wants it badly
will accept such an assessment. Without a group that feels so strongly
about it that it will challenge the state, very little may change. Even when
such a group exists, the judicial system must be independent enough to be
able to pass an independent judgment, even against the state. Current
democratic developments in some of the countries are too controlled to
generate an independent judiciary. Because the NEAPs have to work very
closely with governments, they will lack the independent corporate interests on environmental issues that ought to give them the type of intense
feelings that will make them want to challenge the government. Without
independent environmental advocacy groups, governments will continue
to be the advocates and the judges — two roles that do not go together.
Despite these shortcomings, the NEAPs will be able to make some contributions on research and education.

NOTES

1. Noel Grove, "Quietly Conserving Nature," *National Geographic* (December 1988): 818–44.

2. J. Vaughn Switzer, *Environmental Politics: Domestic and Global Dimensions* (New York: St. Martins Press, 1994), p. 284.

3. Ismail Serageldin, *Saving Africa's Rainforests* (Washington, D.C.: World Bank, 1993), p. 1.

4. Kevin Cleaver and Gotz Schreiber, "The Population, Environment and Agriculture Nexus in Sub-Saharan Africa," in *Africa Region Technical Paper* (Washington, D.C.: World Bank, 1991), tables 12, 13.

5. Ibid.

6. Serageldin, *Saving Africa's Rainforests*, p. 39.

7. Robert S. McNamara, "Africa's Development Crisis: Agricultural Stagnation, Population Explosion, and Environmental Degradation." Paper presented at the Institute on African Affairs' Conference on African Policy Issues, April 3, 1991, Washington, D.C., table 16.

8. Ibid.

9. Ibid.

10. Malcolm Gillis, "Tropical Deforestation: Economic, Ecological and Ethical Dimensions," *The South Atlantic Quarterly* 90 (1991): 7–38.

11. Cleaver and Schreiber, "The Population," p. 28.

12. United Nations Environmental Program, *The Disappearing Forest* (UNEP Environmental Brief No. 3) (Nairobi: United Nations Environmental Program, 1990).

13. Cf. Georges Nzongola-Ntalaja, "Africa's Development Crisis: A Response to Robert McNamara." Paper presented at the Institute on African Affairs Conference on African Policy Issues, April, 3, 1991, Washington, D.C.; Thomas Spear, "The Environment: White Man's Burden," *Christian Science Monitor*, November 30, 1990.

14. Daphne Topouzis, "Wangari Maathai: Empowering the Grassroots," *Africa Report* (November–December 1990): 30–31.

12

The Issues of Development and Environment in Africa: An Overview

E. Ike Udogu

This chapter briefly addresses some of the key elements that impact on development in Africa and their complexities. It also explores some environmental concerns that possibly could threaten the enhancement of ecological humanism in the continent.[1]

Developing nations have been defined euphemistically as regimes of delayed industrialization.[2] This is because these nations did not experience that great industrial revolution of the eighteenth century that spawned the process of modernization in western Europe and North America. Indeed, the emerging nations, especially in Africa, Asia, and the Middle East, began their industrialization process only after World War II, when many of these countries began to gain independence.

Because leaders of many of these developing countries assumed that modernization could bring them up to par with the developed nations, some enacted spurious policies to meet this goal and challenge, policies that did not always take into account the economic and ecological health of their respective polities. Possibly, the rationale for such policies issued from the pressure on the policymakers to address the problems of poverty, debt payment, and underdevelopment.

However, not only have Africa's social, economic, and political imbroglios continued to consolidate and formalize the continent's position and permanency in the periphery of the global economic system, they also have continued to marginalize its citizens. The relationship between ordinary Africans' ability to survive the daily pressures of life can, therefore, not be divorced from their quest to address or ignore environmental issues. Indeed, comprehending and tackling environmental phenomena in Africa becomes inconsequential when such concerns as food, healthcare, shelter, sending children to school, and so on preoccupy the daily agenda of most Africans. This is particularly frustrating and irksome given the intractability of the problem. For instance, a cursory examination of extant literature on development in Africa depicts a troublesome picture. This view is supported by such controversial indices as per capita gross national product (GNP), physical quality of life index (PQLI), and the more recent United Nations (UN) Human Development Index (HDI).

SUSTAINABLE DEVELOPMENT

Having taken cognizance of Africa's decline and the continued peripheralization of the continent economically, the UN in 1986 devoted the entire thirteenth special session to the strategy to safeguard the continent's economic survival.[3] The rationale for this action stemmed from the realization that Africa's economic quagmire had its roots in the continent's colonial history and that, unless solutions were provided, the negative effect could be of a global proportion — migration of Africans from their ancestral homes, brain drain, debt burden, and so on. Indeed, as to the historical antecedent of Africa's economic problems, Carl K. Eicher and Doyle C. Baker have contended that the colonial legacy of Africa contributed to agricultural underdevelopment after independence. They noted, *inter alia*, that Africans were excluded systematically from a number of colonial development schemes and from producing export crops and improved cattle; many peasant farmers were compelled to grow selected crops and maintain roads; colonialism often changed traditional land-tenure systems from communal to individual control, creating greater inequalities from new affluent farmers and ranchers and less secure tenants, sharecroppers, and landless workers; few attempts, if any, were made to train African agricultural scientists and managers; and research and development concentrated on export crops, plantations, and land settlement, neglecting food production by small-scale farmers and herders.[4]

Apropos of the issues of sustainable development, a concept popularized following the publication in 1987 of *Our Common Future*, was a challenge to the application of GNP per capita as the measurement of macroeconomic growth.[5] This was so, the report argued, because GNP failed to reflect the real physical capability of an economy to provide material wealth in the future or take into account the relative well-being of the society in general.[6] Definitionally, therefore, sustainable development is development that is "consistent with future as well as present needs."[7]

In the African context, the major concern was how to accelerate development so that economic deterioration would, at least, be put in abeyance while eschewing conditions that could lead to environmental disequilibria. One approach to this daunting question was provided in a World Bank report.[8] In their superb review of this report intended to lead to sustainable growth in Africa, Howard Stein and E. Wayne Nafziger chafed at the equivocation and contradictions of the World Bank position on sustainable growth in Africa. For example, the bank report suggests that "since most of the population is in agriculture, the best way to reduce poverty is to raise producer prices. . . . Further, the report emphasizes the importance of political legitimacy and consensus in policy, grass-roots participatory institutions, and models consistent with Africa's culture."[9] The former is problematic, because any attempt to raise producer prices invariably would result in higher prices for the commodities, because the cost of producing the goods would have to be passed on to the consumers. To begin with, the urban middle class is likely to resist such a policy (as in the gas hikes and riots in Nigeria). Moreover, the price of the commodities produced could be out of reach for the majority poor. The latter, on the other hand, contended Stein and Nafziger, "is the antithesis of the top-down dictatorial nature of adjustments implemented during the 1980s and presented in the report."[10]

Whereas the World Bank report was intended to provide a politicoeconomic anodyne to the developmental maladies that have afflicted the African continent, it was clear that its impact exacerbated and further marginalized the Africans. Indeed, prodigious writings in condemnation of the effect of this World Bank report and the structural adjustment program itself could fill many a shelf with weighty volumes. This was so because the implementation of some of the programs has resulted in political instability and economic dislocation, which has had the propensity for creating environmental degradation.[11] It led to rural-urban migration for jobs and the construction of bidonvilles in major cities, with deplorable sanitary conditions. To avoid possible political crises, regimes often ignore these squalid settlements.

POLITICAL CRISIS IN AFRICA

Although the present political crisis in Africa could be traced to the classical colonial policy of *divide et imperia*, the stringent conditions laid down by some lending nations, clubs, the International Monetary Fund, the World Bank, and other organizations have helped to augment the political imbroglios in Africa. These perennial problems, created by the defects of colonial policies in Africa and other external pressures for debt payment coupled with mismanagement and endogenous political and economic disarticulation, make environmental issues in Africa somewhat monumental. The wars, for example, in Mozambique, Angola, the Sudan, Somalia, Liberia, and elsewhere in the continent and the problems of displacement of thousands, perhaps millions, who live in unsanitary conditions and must scratch out a living in refugee camps create an abysmal environmental crisis. In addition, the defunct apartheid policy in South Africa, which balkanized the country into nonviable homelands or Bantustans (such as Transkei, Venda, and so on) creates environmental problems, because, in order to survive, the inhabitants will have to clear the surrounding bushes for homes, farmland, and firewood. Additionally, the policy of creating densely populated black townships (as, for example, Soweto) with minimal and lamentable sanitary facilities are environmental landmines capable of reducing life expectancy and increasing infant mortality rates. Attempts by the majority black population to reverse apartheid (or separate development), a policy responsible for these phenomena, led to political chaos, ethnonationalism, and clashes on a number of occasions, with disastrous consequences for some of the country's black population.

Robert H. Bates has contended that modernization, which African countries aspire to attain, "promotes potentially disintegrative forces in developing areas, and particularly, often gives rise to powerful ethnic groupings."[12] The rallying cry for ethnic solidarity in the struggle for the authoritative allocation of scarce resources tends to pit one ethnic group against another. This sometimes results in civil wars, for example, in Nigeria, Burundi, Kenya, the Sudan, South Africa, and elsewhere. The political dislocation that these wars create for the continent has been ominous in terms of poverty, development, and the environment.

In sum, because political crisis impedes development, the preceding analysis is a diagnosis that could have an impact on the perplexing issues of development, the environment, and the conditions of well-being in Africa. In a real sense, the foregoing analyses provide the "edifice" or superstructure for the succeeding brief discussion on development and the environment in the continent. Put another way, the issues examined so far, *inter alia*, determine the extent to which Africa could proceed with the process of development and also deal with environmental problems in order to improve the quality of life. To this end, they not only serve as the springboard from which to briefly assail these difficult questions but also shed some light on the central themes of this chapter.

DEVELOPMENT

The literature on development is extensive.[13] Luiz Bresser Pereira defined development as "a process of economic, political, and social transformation through which the rise in the population's standard of living tends to become automatic and autonomous. It is a total social process in which the economic, political, and social structures of a country undergo continual and profound transformation."[14] David E. Apter, while discussing the overlapping characteristics of development, modernization, and industrialization, defined development as resulting from "the proliferation and integration of functional roles in a community. . . . Industrialization, a special form of modernization, may be defined as the period in a society in which the strategic functional roles are related to manufacturing."[15] Development is an "historical process that occurs through stages and that eventually becomes self-sustaining."[16]

Perhaps Thorkil Kristenson best epitomized the complexity of this issue, given its transdisciplinary and fertilizational nature, when he noted that:

When a student of a certain discipline deals with development, he [or she] is bound to concentrate on those aspects of it in which his [or her] competence lies; this has often been done by the students of a number of disciplines. Not often, however, have the contributions of the various disciplines been combined in a really comprehensive study. We are therefore far from having what might be called a general theory of development of human societies. . . . A general theory of development would be much more than a theory of economic growth. It would deal with both economic, social, cultural, and political aspects of development, as well as with the relationship between man and the environment.[17]

This study does not deal with the theory of development per se; that is better left to the economists.[18] Rather, the issues are discussed here through the lens of political science. Given the contradictory analysis of the process of development in developing nations and elsewhere, that is, the often heated debates about the pros and cons of development, it might not be easy to deal with the subject completely satisfactorily.

For example, it is a generally accepted objective in many societies to endeavor to improve the standard of living and well-being (i.e., a condition of health, happiness, or prosperity) of its citizens. It, therefore, becomes important to identify development with raising the standard of living. Clifford Geertz takes umbrage at this issue and argues that "though it may be true, as an economic process, development is a dramatic revolutionary change, as a broadly social process it fairly clearly is not."[19] Apter notes that "included in this judgment is an emphasis on the importance of human capital or social capital, which seems to be more significant for modernity than resources."[20] Furthermore, Ken C. Kotecha and Roberts W. Adams have argued that, even though autarky is an impossible condition to realize today, no matter how well-endowed a nation might be with natural resources, many African states are on a wild-goose chase for a total economic independence. The determination to

pursue a policy of economic self-determination has led some governments to a policy of nationalization. This strategy sometimes impedes
national development.[21]

The argument has been that development (through industrialization)
would lead to an increased standard of living for African nations. This
view is explained by some social scientists within the context of conver-
gence theory.[22] This theory assumes that, as societies industrialize, they
would take on similar cultural (and political) characteristics.[23] Because
advocates of development, modernization, and industrialization in
African countries do not always take into account the socioeconomic and
behavior patterns of those whose lives they wish to alter through these
processes, conflicts are generated. These conflicts retard development and
augment environmental crisis, because fewer funds are allocated for these
needs during national crises.

Robert P. Clark has noted that "making the change from tradition to
modernity [among rural populations] requires unlearning or discarding
inappropriate values, behavioral tendencies, information, attitudes, and
personality structures and replacing them with modern counterparts."[24]
S. N. Eisenstadt argues that "disorganization and dislocation . . . constitute a basic part of modernization and that the process brings with it of
necessity the growth of social problems, cleavages and conflicts between
various groups, and movements of protest."[25] The causal factors are
urbanization, industrialization, political centralization, secularization,
and social mobilization, which are components of modernization.[26]

What C. E. Black wrote on modernization applies, *mutatis mutandis*, to
the above analysis. For instance, he alluded to the agony of modernization, which he claimed might, in the long run, hold out the hope for great
human progress but possibly at a high price in human dislocation and
suffering.[27]

Clearly, addressing the issues of development (or modernization)
would require a coordinated effort between the rural dwellers and policymakers if the disintegrative attributes and antinomy created during
attempts to improve the conditions of well-being for most Africans
through development are to be resolved.

ENVIRONMENTAL AND ECOLOGICAL CONCERNS

Environment has been defined as the surrounding conditions, or
forces, that influence or modify. It involves the aggregate of all the external conditions and influences affecting the life and development of an
organism. Ecology is the subdiscipline of biology that deals with the interactions between organisms and their environment and the population,
community, and ecosystem levels of organization. Human ecology

focuses on the relationship of human populations to the ecosystems of which they are a part.[28]

Humankind has, from time immemorial, endeavored to adapt to its environment. When the world's population was small and technology was less available, human beings were less of a threat to the environment. The advent of technology has made it possible for humans to reshape the environment in an attempt to take advantage of it, with little concern for possible ecological problems. Today, one of the pressing questions is an increase in the world's population — an issue that appears to be more poignant in Africa, which currently lacks adequate mechanisms for addressing this concern.

However, environmental problems in developing nations may be viewed from the economic and health perspectives. Thus, one hypothesis that may be constructed from the above is that African countries tend to be less concerned about the environment than developed countries — they are more concerned about daily survival. This view is borne out by the special report released by the UN concerning the debt crisis in this area — a report that is not reassuring.[29] It is noted that some 70 UN member states, especially developing nations, are about $1.3 trillion in debt. This debt, the UN General Assembly noted, has serious consequences for these countries, because it impedes the rates of growth and output in these areas.[30] Equally disturbing is the fact that economic and environmental crises exacerbate the already deteriorating conditions in Africa.[31] The inseparability of the problems of environment and poverty is one that hits home in the rural areas of the African continent. For example, in Africa, between 80 and 90 percent of the poor live outside the urban centers.[32] However, the problem afflicts both urban and rural dwellers, given the sociopolitical and cultural linkages between these two groups. Further, close to 280 million people in Africa grow food.[33] Also, 6 million people in many parts of the third world are shepherds. Together, they are involved, among other things, in the intricate web of sustaining these developing countries.[34] It is generally believed that any degradation of the environment in which these groups operate could lead to the overexploitation of the existing resources for their survival. Richard A. Carpenter and John A. Dixon contend that "rural poverty pollutes and despoils the environment because subsistence farmers have few alternative resources and usually cannot afford to conserve for the future."[35]

In Kenya, Ghana, and elsewhere in Africa, the clash between environmentalists and conservationists on the one hand and developers (i.e., leaders of developing nations, bilateral and multilateral donors, construction engineers, and consultants) on the other hand over environmental problems may be insurmountable because of conflicting interests. One area of major concern is the river basin project, which is intended to lead to sustainable development.[36] The assumption was that the construction of hydroelectric dams would provide energy while providing irrigation schemes that would increase agricultural output in the rural areas. The symbiotic relationship anticipated between the dams and crop production has not been fully realized. Indeed, Thayer Scudder has noted that "African nations have been developing the hydroelectric potentials of their rivers at the expense of the ecological resiliency, human populations, and agricultural potentials (i.e., live stock management, forestry, agroforestry, fisheries and crop culture). . . . On balance, the impacts of dam construction on down-stream riverine habitats have been negative."[37]

There is a paradox in the African continent in regard to the endeavor to provide cheap energy through hydroelectric power and its effect on rural population and the furtherance of ecological humanism. The construction of dams often has led to the resettlement of populations and the creation of ecological disequilibriums. Such resettlements have tended to be involuntary, because the majority of the people resist attempts to be uprooted from their ancestral and primordial homes. In addition, the relocation process is stressful, and the angst that follows such displacements tends to endure for a long time.[38] Also, the impacts on the politico-sociological factors, for example, the leadership structure, can be immense. Clashes between the "transplanted" population and the host are augmented by the competition for scarce resources, such as land, social services, and jobs.[39] For instance, in the 1960s, when the Aswan Dam was built in Egypt, less than 10 percent of the irrigated land intended for relocated Egyptians was ready for cultivation after the exodus of people to the area. In Ghana, inadequate farmland and sanitary conditions were provided for more than 700 communities that were settled into 52 new towns. Ironically, these settlements remain nonviable in the 1980s; in fact, the same scenario is played out in other parts of the continent.[40]

In Africa, the catastrophic effect of desertification and deforestation, forms of ecological degradation is ominous.[41] Desertification is taking place in the Sahel region of Africa, principally because of the loss of top soil, loss of forest cover, and insufficient fallow periods (because of population growth and civil wars). In addition, trees are cut down for firewood, and animals forage tree leaves. Such environmental degradation threatens that special plant and animal symbiosis (i.e., oxygen and carbon dioxide reciprocity). This view was given credence and articulated in *National Geographic* by William E. Ellis who lamented that, "Man has punished this barren realm, stripped it of trees and [bankrupted] the soil. Abetted, the desert advances and the region edges toward catastrophe."[42]

Another area of concern in Africa is conservationism, which may be construed as an ideology aimed at furthering ecological humanism. Policies formulated in this area have tended to be associated with the management and preservation of wildlife and wilderness for national economic reasons.[43] However, these milieus, which cover vast areas (endowed with natural resources, minerals, wildlife species, and so on), are inhabited fundamentally by the rural dwellers. Ironically, policies formulated to exploit the wealth of these areas often are made without consultation with the indigenous people. Such policy outcomes sometimes create conflicting and antagonistic relationships between the conservationist (as represented by the government) and rural interests.[44]

The situation is promising in some areas, though. For example, in East Africa and elsewhere on the continent, a number of environmental development programs have been implemented. The 1982 Parks and Wildlife Act of Zimbabwe is a good case in point. This Act, *inter alia*, created different zones of wildlife and land protection.[45] The same framework has been adopted at the Amoseli Park, Kenya; Simen Park, Ethiopia; and Pilanesberg, Bophuthatswana, to mention a few.[46] Notwithstanding those developments, it would not be wise to make the assumption that most countries are enthusiastic about addressing environmental problems. The conflicts that sometimes burgeon between developers (who tend to be profit motivated) and conservationists in the case of the African continent bear this out.

NOTES

1. The concept of "ecological humanism," as applied here, approximates what has been termed "ecological health" elsewhere. It represents "the relationship between people and their larger environment that is favorable to the biological existence of human beings and permits a superior quality of life. [It] means clean air, pure water, the prudent use of natural resources. It means respect for the planet, or partnership between people and resources." Neal Riemer and Douglas W. Simon, *The New World of Politics: An Introduction to Political Science* (San Diego, Calif.: Collegiate Press, 1991), p. 470. This concept is also used interchangeably with the term "sustainable development," a concept coined by the UN.

2. Mary Matossian, "Ideologies of Delayed Industrialization: Some Tensions and Ambiguities," *Economic Development and Cultural Change* 6 (1958): 217–28; also reprinted in Claude E. Welch, Jr., ed., *Political Modernization* (Belmont: Wadsworth, 1967), pp. 332–34.

3. Julius E. Nyang'oro, "Development, Democracy and NGOs in Africa," *Scandinavian Journal of Development Alternatives* 12 (June–September 1993): 281; Julius E. Nyang'oro, *The State and Capitalist Development in Africa: Declining Political Economies* (New York: Praeger, 1989), pp. 1–28; UN General Assembly, *Program of Action for African Economic Recovery and Development, 1986–1990* (New York: United Nations, 1986).

4. Carl K. Eicher and Doyle C. Baker, *Research on Agricultural Development in Sub-Saharan Africa: A Critical Survey* (East Lansing: University of Michigan Press, 1982), pp. 17–23; John Mukum Mbaku, "Political Democracy, Military Expenditures and Economic Growth in Africa," *The Scandinavian Journal of Development Alternatives* 12 (March 1993): 50.

5.   Gareth Porter and Janet W. Brown, *Global Environmental Politics* (Boulder, Colo.: Westview Press, 1991), pp. 5-51.

6.   Ibid., p. 50.

7.   Ibid.

8.   World Bank, *Sub-Saharan Africa: From Crisis to Sustainable Growth: A Long-Term Perspective Study* (Washington, D.C.: World Bank, 1989), pp. xiv–300; Ann Seidman, "Toward a New Vision of Sustainable Development in Africa: Presidential Address to 1990 Annual Meeting of the African Studies Association," *African Studies Review* 35 (April 1992): 1–15.

9.   Howard Stein and E. Wayne Nafziger, "Structural Adjustment, Human Needs, and the World Bank Agenda," *The Journal of Modern African Studies* 21 (1991): 177–87; Henry Bienen and John Waterbury, "The Political Economy of Privatization in Developing Countries," *World Development* 17 (May 1989): 619; Adebayo Adedeji, "Development and Economic Growth in Africa to the Year 2000: Alternative Projections and Policies," in *Alternative Futures for Africa*, ed. Timothy M. Shaw (Boulder, Colo.: Westview Press, 1982).

10.   Stein and Nafziger, "Structural Adjustment," p. 187.

11.   Akilagpa Sawyer, "The Politics of Adjustment Policy," in *Human Dimensions of Africa's Economic Crisis*, eds. Adebayo Adedeji, Sadig Rasheed, and Melody Morrison (New York: Hans Zell, 1990), pp. 212–36.

12.   Robert H. Bates, "Ethnic Competition and Modernization in Contemporary Africa," *Comparative Political Studies* 6 (January 1974): 457.

13.   For a concise bibliography on this subject, see Nyang'oro, *The State and Capitalist Development in Africa: Declining Political Economies*, pp. 159–69.

14.   Luiz Bresser Pereira, *Development and Crisis in Brazil 1930–1983* (Boulder, Colo.: Westview Press, 1984), p. 5.

15.   David E. Apter, *The Politics of Modernization* (Chicago, Ill.: University of Chicago Press, 1965), p. 67.

16.   Pereira, *Development*, p. 6.

17.   Thorkil Kristenson, *Development in Rich and Poor Counties: A General Theory with Statistical Analyses* (New York: Praeger, 1974), p. xii.

18.   Celso Furtado, *Development and Underdevelopment* (Berkeley: University of California Press, 1964), pp. 1–56.

19.   Clifford Geertz, *Peddlers and Princes* (Chicago, Ill.: University of Chicago Press, 1963), p. 2.

20.   Apter, *Politics of Modernization*, p. 69.

21.   Ken C. Kotecha and Roberts W. Adams, *The Corruption of Power: African Politics* (Lanham, Md.: University Press of America, 1981), p. 187.

22.   Robert P. Clark, *Power and Policy in the Third World* (New York: Macmillan Publishing Company, 1991), p. 69.

23.   Ibid.

24.   Ibid., p. 75.

25.   S. N. Eisenstadt, *Modernization: Protest and Change* (Englewood Cliffs, N.J.: Prentice Hall, 1966), chap. 2; Robert P. Clark, *Development and Instability: Political Change in the Non-Western World* (Hinsdale, Ill.: Dryden Press, 1974), p. 102.

26.   Clark, *Development and Instability*, p. 102.

27. C. E. Black, *The Dynamics of Modernization: A Study in Comparative History* (New York: Harper & Row, 1966), pp. 26–34.

28. Paul R. Ehrlich, Anne H. Ehrlich, and John P. Holdren, *Human Ecology: Problems and Solutions* (San Francisco, Calif.: W. H. Freeman, 1973), p. 6.

29. "Special Report on Debt Crisis," *UN Monthly Chronicle* 27 (March 1990): 89.

30. Ibid.; see also "Poverty," *UN Monthly Chronicle* 27 (September 1990): 45–50.

31. "Economic and Environmental Crisis Cause a Significant Deterioration in LDC economies," *UN Monthly Chronicle* 22 (November–December 1985): 92.

32. John W. Mellor, "The Intertwining of Environmental Problems and Poverty," *Environment* 30 (November 1988): 8.

33. "International Fund for Agricultural Development," in *Annual Report 1987* (Rome: International Fund for Agricultural Development, 1988), p. 18.

34. *World Commission on Environment and Development, Our Common Future* (Oxford: Oxford University Press, 1987), p. 13.

35. Richard A. Carpenter and John A. Dixon, "Ecology Meets Economics: A Guide to Sustainable Development," *Environment* 27 (June 1985): 9.

36. Thayer Scudder, "Conservation vs. Development: River Basin Projects in Africa," *Environment* 31 (March 1989): 4–9, 27–32.

37. Ibid., p. 28.

38. Ibid.

39. Ibid.

40. Ibid.

41. Penny Wakefield, "Is UNEP Still a Good Investment?" *Environment* 24 (May 1982): 10–11; George E. Moose, "US Environmental Policy and Africa: Challenges and Realities," *ASA News* 27 (January–March 1994): 22.

42. William E. Ellis, "Africa's Sahel: The Stricken Land," *National Geographic* 172 (August 1987): 140–79; M. Hulme, "Is Environmental Degradation Causing Drought in the Sahel?" *Geography* 74 (January 1989): 38–46.

43. Tobaias J. Lanz, "Environmentalism and Conservation in Africa: The Emerging Conflict in Development." Paper presented at the annual meeting of the South Carolina Political Science Association, March 14, 1992.

44. Ibid.

45. Ibid.

46. Ibid.

Bibliography

Abucar, M. H., and Patrick Molutsi. "Environmental Policy in Botswana: A Critique." *Africa Today* 40 (1993).

Adam, C., et al. *Adjusting Privatization*. London: James Currey, 1994.

Adedeji, Adebayo, Sadig Rasheed, and Melody Morrison, eds. *The Human Dimension of Africa's Persistent Economic Crisis*. New York: Hans Zell, 1990.

Adelman, Howard, and John Sorenson, eds. *African Refugees: Development Aid and Repatriation*. Boulder, Colo.: Westview Press, 1994.

Arntzen, Jap, and Elmar Veenendaal. *A Profile of Environment and Development in Botswana*. Gaborone: University of Botswana, 1986.

Berat, Lynn. *Courting Justice? South African Judiciary and the Protection of Human Rights*. New Haven, Conn.: Yale University Press, 1995.

____. "Democratization and Press Freedom in Southern Africa." *African Contemporary Record*, vols. 1990–92. New York: Holmes & Maier.

____. *Walvis Bay: Decolonization and International Law*. New Haven, Conn.: Yale University Press, 1991.

Bienefeld, Manfred. "The New World Order: Echoes of a New Imperialism." *Third World Quarterly* 15 (1994).

Black, David, and T. M. Shaw, eds. *Southern Africa after Apartheid*. Nova Scotia: CFPS Halifax, 1996.

Blomstrom, M., and M. Lundahl, eds. *Economic Crisis in Africa: Perspectives on Policy Responses*. London: Routledge, 1993.

Brown, Janet W., and Gareth Porter. *Global Environmental Politics*. Boulder, Colo.: Westview Press, 1991.

Cernea, Michael M. *Bridging the Research Divide: Studying Refugees and Development Oustees*. Washington, D.C.: World Bank, Environment Department, 1994.

Chazan, Naomi. "Africa's Democratic Challenge: Strengthening Civil Society and the State." *World Policy Journal* 9 (Spring 1992).

Chole, Eshetu. "Linking Grassroots Organizations and Research Institutions in Africa." *African Journal of Public Administration and Management* 1 (July 1992).

Clark, John. *Democratizing Development: The Role of Voluntary Organizations*. West Hartford, Conn.: Kumarian Press, 1990.

Dalton, Clare. "Where We Stand: Observations on the Situation of Feminist Legal Thought." *Berkeley Women's Law Journal* (1987–88).

Diamond, Larry. *Promoting Democracy in the 1990's: Actors and Instruments, Issues and Imperatives*. New York: Carnegie Corporation, 1995.

_____. *Class, Ethnicity and Democracy in Nigeria: The Failure of the First Republic*. Syracuse, N.Y.: Syracuse University Press, 1992.

_____, ed. *The Democratic Revolution: Struggles for Freedom and Pluralism in the Developing World*. New York: Freedom House, 1992.

Diamond, Larry, Juan Linz, and Seymour Martin Lipset. *Politics in Developing Countries: Comparing Experiences with Democracy*. Boulder, Colo.: Lynne Rienner, 1995.

Diamond, Larry, and Marc Plattner. *Political Culture in Developing Countries*. Boulder, Colo.: Lynne Rienner, 1994.

_____. *The Global Resurgence of Democracy*. Baltimore, Md.: Johns Hopkins University Press, 1993.

Fowler, Alan. *Non-Governmental Organizations in Africa: Achieving Comparative Advantage in Relief and Microdevelopment*. United Kingdom: Sussex Institute of Development Studies, 1988.

Garber, Larry, and Glenn Cowan. "The Virtues of Parallel Vote Tabulations." *Journal of Democracy* 4 (April 1993).

Gibbon, Peter, et al., eds. *Authoritarianism, Democracy, and Adjustment: The Politics of Economic Reform in Africa*. Uppsala: Nordiska Afrikainstitutet, 1992.

Gill, Stephen, and David Law. *The Global Political Economy: Perspectives, Problems and Policies*. Baltimore, Md.: Johns Hopkins University Press, 1988.

Good, Ken. "Interpreting the Exceptionality of Botswana." *Journal of Modern African Studies* 30 (1992).

Harvey, Charles, and Stephen Lewis. *Policy Choice and Development Performance in Botswana*. London: Macmillan, 1990.

Himmelstrand, U., et al. *African Perspectives on Development*. Aldershot: James Currey, 1994.

Huntington, Samuel P. *The Third Wave: Global Democratization in the Late Twentieth Century*. Norman: University of Oklahoma Press, 1991.

Hyden, Goran. *From Bargaining to Marketing: How to Reform Foreign Aid in the 1990s*. East Lansing: Michigan State University, 1993.

Hyden, Goran, and Michael Bratton, eds. *Governance and Politics in Africa*. Boulder, Colo.: Lynne Rienner, 1992.

Johnson, Willard R., and Vivian R. Johnson. *West African Governments and Volunteer Development Organizations*. Lanham, Md.: University Press of America, 1990.

Kalipeni, Ezekiel, ed. *Population Growth and Environmental Degradation in Southern Africa*. Boulder, Colo.: Lynne Rienner, 1994.

Koehn, Peter H. "Refugees and Development Assistance: Training for Voluntary Repatriation." Final report and recommendations of an international symposium, April 1994, University of Montana.

____. *Refugees from Revolution: U.S. Policy and Third-World Migration*. Boulder, Colo.: Westview Press, 1991.

____. *Public Policy and Administration in Africa: Lessons from Nigeria*. Boulder, Colo.: Westview Press, 1990.

____. "Local Government Involvement in National Development Planning: Guidelines for Project Selection Based upon Nigeria's Fourth Plan Experience." *Public Administration and Development* 9 (1989).

Konczacki, Z., J. Parpart, and T. M. Shaw, eds. *Studies in the Economic History of Southern Africa*, vol. 1, *The Frontline States*. London: Frank Cass, 1991.

Landell-Mills, Pierre. "Governance, Cultural Change, and Empowerment." *Journal of Modern African Studies* 30 (1992).

Lewis, Peter. "Political Transition and the Dilemma of Civil Society in Africa." *Journal of International Affairs* 27 (Summer 1992).

Liepitz, Alain. *Towards a New Economic Order: Postfordism, Ecology and Democracy*. London: Polity Press, 1993.

Manzetti, Luigi. "The Political Economy of Privatization through Divestiture in Less Developed Economies." *Comparative Politics* (July 1993).

Minter, William. *Apartheid's Contras: An Inquiry into the Roots of War in Angola and Mozambique*. London: Zed Books, 1994.

____. *Operation Timber: Pages from the Savimbi Dossier*. Trenton, N.J.: Africa World Press, 1988.

____. *King Solomon's Mines Revisited: Western Interests and the Burdened History of Southern Africa*. New York: Basic Books, 1986.

Molutsi, Patrick, and John Holm. "Developing Democracy When Civil Society Is Weak: The Case of Botswana." *African Affairs* 89 (July 1990).

Moose, George E. "US Environmental Policy and Africa: Challenges and Realities." *ASA News* 27 (January–March 1994).

Mosley, Paul, et al. *Aid & Power: The World Bank & Policy-Based Lending*, vol. 2, *Case Studies*. New York: Routledge, 1991.

Nelson, Joan, ed. *Economic Crisis and Policy Choice: The Politics of Economic Adjustment in the Third World*. Princeton, N.J.: Princeton University Press, 1990.

Nyang'oro, Julius E. "Development, Democracy and NGOs in Africa." *Scandinavian Journal of Development Alternatives* 12 (June–September 1993).

____. *The State and Capitalist Development in Africa: Declining Political Economies*. New York: Praeger, 1989.

Nyang'oro, Julius E., and T. M. Shaw, eds. *Beyond Structural Adjustment in Africa: The Political Economy of Sustainable and Democratic Government*. Westport, Conn.: Praeger, 1992.

Ogbondah, Chris. "Press Freedom in West Africa: An Analysis of One Ramification of Human Rights." *Issue: A Journal of Opinion* 21 (1994).

Ohlson, Thomas, and Stephen J. Stedman. *The New Is Not Yet Born: Conflict Resolution in Southern Africa*. Washington, D.C.: Brookings Institution, 1994.

Ojo, Olatunde. *Security in Contemporary Africa: Concepts, Issues and Problems*. Port Harcourt: Center for Advanced Social Science, 1996.

Osirim, Mary J. "The Status of African Market Women: Trade, Economy and Family in Urban Zimbabwe." In *African Market Women and Economic Power*, edited by B. House-Midamba and F. Ekechi. Westport, Conn.: Praeger, 1995.

____. "Gender and Entrepreneurship." In *Privatization and Investment in Subsaharan Africa*, edited by Rexford Ahene and B. S. Katz. Westport, Conn.: Praeger, 1992.

Rasheed, Sadig, and David F. Luke, eds. *Development Management in Africa*. Boulder, Colo.: Westview Press, 1995.

Serageldin, Ismail. *Saving Africa's Rainforests*. Washington, D.C.: World Bank, 1993.

Siddiqui, Rukhsana, A. "Privatization: A Comparative Study of Africa and Latin America." In *Review of African Political Economy* (in press).

____, ed. *Subsaharan Africa: A Subcontinent in Transition*. Aldershot: Gower-Avebury Press, 1993.

Stedman, Stephen John, ed. *Botswana: The Political Economy of Democratic Development*. Boulder, Colo.: Lynne Rienner, 1993.

Sulivan, John. "Business Interests, Institutions, and Democratic Development." *Journal of Democracy* 5 (October 1994).

Swatuk, Larry A., ed. *The South at the End of Twentieth Century*. London: Macmillan, 1994.

Udogu, E. Ike. *Nigeria: The Politics of Survival as a Nation State*. Lewiston, N.Y.: Edwin Mellen, 1997.

Uphoff, Norman. "Grassroots Organizations and NGOs in Rural Development: Opportunities with Diminishing States and Expanding Markets." *World Development* 21 (1993).

____. *Local Institutional Development: An Analytical Source Book with Cases*. West Hartford, Conn.: Kumarian Press, 1986.

Van de Walle, Nicholas. "Innovations in African Governance: Some Thoughts on Empowering the Countryside." In *African Governance in the 1990s*. Atlanta, Ga.: Emory University, Carter Center, 1993.

Waylen, Georgina. "Women and Democratization: Conceptualizing Gender Relations in Transition Politics." *World Politics* 46 (April 1994).

Weeks, J. *Development Strategy and the Economy of Sierra Leone*. London: Macmillan, 1992.

Weigle, Marica, and Jim Butterfield. "Civil Society in Reforming Communist Regimes: The Logic of Emergence." *Comparative Politics* 25 (October 1992).

Wiseberg, Laurie. "The African Commission on Human and Peoples' Rights." *Issue: A Journal of Opinion* 22 (1994).

World Bank. *Governance and Development*. Washington, D.C.: International Bank for Reconstruction and Development, 1992.

____. *Sub-Saharan Africa: From Crisis to Sustainable Growth: A Long-Term Perspective Study*. Washington, D.C.: World Bank, 1989.

Zack-Williams, Alfred B. *Tributors, Supporters and Merchant Capital in Sierra Leone: Mining and Underdevelopment in Sierra Leone*. Aldershot: Gower-Avebury Press, 1995.

Index

About the Contributors

Lynn Berat is the National Research Council Fellow at Yale Law School. A specialist in law and development, she is the author of *Walvis Bay: Decolonization and International Law* (1991), *Courting Justice? South African Judiciary and the Protection of Human Rights* (1995), and numerous articles. She was also a Visiting Fellow at the Center of Applied and Legal Studies of the University of Witwatersrand and University of Pretoria and has served as a consultant to both the MacArthur and Ford foundations.

Larry Diamond is Senior Research Fellow at the Hoover Institution, coeditor of the *Journal of Democracy*, and codirector of the International Forum for Democratic Studies of the National Endowment of Democracy. One of the most prolific writers on democracy, he has authored *Promoting Democracy in the 1990's: Actors and Instruments, Issues and Imperatives* (1995), *Class, Ethnicity and Democracy in Nigeria: The Failure of the First Republic* (1992), and *Developing Democracy: Towards Consolidation* (in press). Among his recent coedited books are *Politics in Developing Countries: Comparing Experiences With Democracy* (1995, with Juan Linz and Seymour Martin Lipset), *The Global Resurgence of Democracy* (1993, with Marc Plattner), and *Political Culture in Developing Countries* (1994, also with Marc Plattner). He has served as a consultant to the Asia

Foundation and the Agency for International Development and has been a Fulbright Visiting Lecturer at Bayero University, Kano, Nigeria.

Peter Koehn is Professor of Political Science and Director of International Programs at the University of Montana. His publications include *Refugees from Revolution: US Policy and Third World Migration* (1991), *Public Policy and Administration in Africa: Lessons from Nigeria* (1990), and numerous chapters and journal articles on African politics and development management. During 1995–96, he served as a leading consultant on decentralization for social planning projects for UNICEF in Eritrea.

Sandra Maclean is a fellow at the Center for Foreign Policy Studies at Dalhousie University. She works on nongovernmental organizations and the development of national and transnational civil societies. She has contributed to *Southern Africa after Apartheid* (1996) and the *Journal of Contemporary African Studies*.

Edward R. MacMahon is a Senior Program Officer and Director of West and Central African Programs at the National Democratic Institute for Internal Affairs. He was a codraftee of *Bangladesh Parliamentary Election, 1991* and *The New Democratic Frontier: A Country by Country Report on Central and Eastern Europe*. He has directed democratic development projects in west and central Africa as well as in eastern Europe, Pakistan, and Bangladesh. MacMahon served for a decade as Foreign Service Officer of the U.S. Department of State, Bureau of African Affairs.

William Minter is Senior Research Fellow at the African Policy Information Center, Washington, D.C. He was a member of the International Foundation for Electoral Systems Observer Mission to the Angolan elections. He is the author of *Apartheid's Contras: An Inquiry into the Roots of War in Angola and Mozambique* (1994), *King Solomon's Mines Revisited: Western Interests and the Burdened History of Southern Africa* (1986), and *Operation Timber: Pages from the Savimbi Dossier* (1988).

Olatunde Ojo is Visiting Professor of Political Science at the University of Montana. He has taught at several U.S. and Nigerian universities, including the University of Port Harcourt, Nigeria, where he was Dean of the Faculty of Social Sciences. His writings on African foreign relations and development problems have appeared in several books and journals, such as *International Organization, Comparative Politics Studies, Afrika Spectrum*, and *African Studies Review*. He is coauthor of *African International Relations* (1985) and author of *Security in Contemporary Africa: Concepts, Issues and Problems* (1996).

Mary J. Osirim is Associate Professor in the Department of Sociology, Bryn Mawr College. Her research is on gender, economic sociology, and the role of entrepreneurship in African development. She has conducted fieldwork in Nigeria and Zimbabwe for more than a decade. She is the recipient of the Rosalyn R. Schwartz award for teaching. Her writing has appeared in *African Market Women and Economic Power* (Greenwood, 1995), *Population Growth and Environmental Degradation in Southern Africa* (1994), *Privatization and Investment in Subsaharan Africa* (Praeger, 1992), and in several journals.

Rukhsana A. Siddiqui is Associate Professor and Chair of the Department of International Relations, Quaid-i-Azam University. She has held teaching and research positions at Yale University, University of Dar-es-Salaam, and Bilkent University. Her books include *Ideology and Socialist Transition in Tanzania* (1988) and *Subsaharan Africa: A Subcontinent in Transition* (1993). She has published on east and southern African political economy in *Annals of the American Academy of Political and Social Science, Review of African Political Economy*, and *Canadian Journal of Peace Research*.

Larry A. Swatuk is Senior Lecturer, Department of Political & Administrative Studies, University of Botswana. He was Post-Doctoral Fellow at the Center for International and Security Studies, York University and also a Visiting Lecturer at Rhodes University. He is author of *Between Choice in the Hard Place: Contending Theories of International Relations* (1991) and coeditor of *The South at the End of the Twentieth Century* (1994) and *Prospects for Peace and Development in Southern Africa in the 1990s* (1991).

Moses K. Tesi is Associate Professor at the Department of Political Science at Middle Tennessee State University and Executive Director of the Institute of African Affairs, Washington, D.C. He is the author of *Africa and the Changing Global Economy* (1996).

E. Ike Udogu is a National Endowment for Humanities Fellow and Associate Professor at the Department of Political Science and Geography, Francis Marion University. His publications include *Nigeria: The Politics of Survival as a Nation State* (1997) and *Democracy and Democratization in Africa: Toward the 21st Century* (1997).

Alfred B. Zack-Williams is Principal Lecturer in the Department of Sociology and Social Policy, University of Central Lancashire. He is the author of *Supporters, Tributors and Merchant Capital in Sierra Leone* (1995). He is a member of the editorial working group of the *Review of African Political Economy* and has authored several articles and reviews on the political economy of underdevelopment and survival in Africa.

ISBN 0-275-95142-1

90000>

HARDCOVER BAR CODE